Political S
in Latin America

V

Political Suicide
in Latin America

and Other Essays

JAMES DUNKERLEY

VERSO

London · New York

First published by Verso 1992
© James Dunkerley 1992
All rights reserved

Verso
UK: 6 Meard Street, London W1V 3HR
USA: 29 West 35th Street, New York, NY 10001-2291

Verso is the imprint of New Left Books

ISBN 0 86091 348 1
ISBN 0 86091 560 3 (Pbk)

British Library Cataloguing in Publication Data
A catalogue record for this book is available from the British Library

Library of Congress Cataloging-in-Publication Data
A catalogue record for this book is available from the Library of Congress

Typeset in Baskerville by Leaper & Gard Limited, Bristol
Printed in Great Britain by Biddles Ltd, Guildford and Kings Lynn

To Bill

Contents

Acknowledgements

'Reassessing Caudillismo in Bolivia, 1825–79' first appeared in the *Bulletin of Latin American Research*, Vol. 1, no. 1, October 1981; 'El Salvador, 1930–89' in Leslie Bethell (ed.), *The Cambridge History of Latin America*, Vol. VII, Cambridge 1990; 'Guatemala, 1944–54' in Leslie Bethell and Ian Roxborough (eds), *Latin America: From World War II to the Cold War*, Cambridge 1991; 'Political Transition and Economic Stabilization: Bolivia, 1982–89' as Research Paper no 22, Institute of Latin American Studies, University of London, August 1990; 'Mario Vargas Llosa: Parables and Deceits' in *New Left Review*, no. 162, March/April 1987; 'Reflections on the Nicaraguan Elections' in *New Left Review*, no. 182, August/September 1990. In some cases minor revisions have been made to the original version. A full chronology of Bolivia from 1982 to 1989 is provided in the initial version of the essay here. Thanks are due to the editors and publishers of these publications for permission to reuse the essays.

Preface

The essays in this collection were written between 1980 and 1990. Since most touch on developments during that decade there should be little need to elaborate upon the general context in which they were produced. However, these pieces do not directly address the 'big questions' raised about the political economy of Latin America during those ten years. There is here only an echo of the vibrant debates over dependency, bureaucratic authoritarianism, redemocratization and what we might call 'post-populism' – a relatively recent phenomenon that has yet to pass through that preliminary phase of academic discussion when the codes and conceits of iconoclasm are at their peak. The reason for my concentration is not that I think the broad comparative and thematic issues are unimportant – although they have often been treated in a manner conducive to irrelevance – but rather because there is still an acute need to deepen the empirical or historical work on which more overtly theoretical studies must depend. Even in the larger countries that possess a significant historiographical tradition there exists only a tenuous basis upon which to construct broad or 'strategic' interpretation. On the other hand, such a figurative division of intellectual labour is scarcely very healthy, and I hope that there are enough resonances of developments in the methodological and interpretative debates in these pieces to suggest that such issues may be considered just as fruitfully within the context of the 'specific' as within that of the 'general'.

It is a touch more difficult to avoid an apologetic tone with regard to the choice of countries treated here, if only because realpolitik joins academic fashion in stressing the importance of size and sophistication. Yet it should be clear why the last decade led to increased attention to Central America, which was almost totally ignored by the Anglo-Saxon academy prior to the Nicaraguan revolution. More important still, there are considerable dangers in discounting small and relatively obscure states and societies as either 'irrelevant' or 'unrepresentative'. Such an attitude has played no small part in impeding comprehension of those countries that manifest a disturbing capacity to upset the international 'pecking order'. I am convinced that one central reason for the destruction wrought by US policy in Central America and the Andean countries in recent years lies in Washington's profound misapprehension about the 'simplicity' of the affairs of its 'host nations'. This, of course, reflects an arrogance common to all imperialisms, adolescent and senile alike (no European can ignore this), but it is also sometimes evident in the attitude of those who abhor US interventionism yet persist in seeing those who suffer it simply as victims. There are many ways of being anti-imperialist, and it strikes me that not the least of these is to explore and celebrate the complexity, resilience and 'otherness' of societies that have long been oppressed and exploited but cannot be understood solely in these terms. Seen in this light, there is little difference between a study of the valleys of Oaxaca and one of the streets of São Paulo, no greater merit in that of thirty million Argentines than of three million Uruguayans.

Although I am aware that the challenge has not been met in the pages that follow, my aim has been to strike a balance between seriousness of purpose and excitement. This basic requirement of studying and writing history was first instilled in me by Gwyn Williams, an outstanding teacher who has never ducked the risks involved in trying to drive a salient between the careerist fetishisms of the academy and the careless certainties of the political world. It is a particularly necessary requirement in times like these when, lubricated with notions of 'the end of history' and the advent of 'postmodernity', both tendencies are firing on all cylinders, apparently heedless of the paradox that history herself has permitted such cannibalism. One might be tempted to be petulant about the hubris of the shrill heralds of the new-order-that-is-not or to await the simple, unforgiving passage of time, but it is altogether more rewarding to engage with the present in the conviction that this can never exhaust the possibilities of exploring the past.

Finally, it is worth registering that most of the pieces here relate to book-length studies where the interested reader will find rather more context, a fuller scholarly apparatus, and — on occasions — a somewhat less compacted style. The essay on *caudillismo* forms the introductory chapter of *Los Orígenes del Poder Militar: Historia del Ejército Boliviano, 1879–1935*. The chapter on Bolivia between 1982 and 1989 is effectively an update, in much less narrative style, to *Rebellion in the Veins, Political Struggle in Bolivia, 1952–82*. The essay on El Salvador provides a radical synthesis of *The Long War: Dictatorship and Revolution in El Salvador* as well as of the relevant sections of *Power in the Isthmus. A Political History of Modern Central America*, which also contains chapters on Nicaragua and Guatemala that cover those countries rather more extensively than is done here.

Oh, don't die, dear master ... Take my advice and live many years. For the maddest thing a man can do in this life is to let himself die just like that, without anybody killing him but just finished off by his own melancholy.

SANCHO PANZA TO DON QUIXOTE

When Nietzsche writes: 'It clearly seems that the chief thing in heaven and on earth is to *obey* at length and in a single direction: in the long run there results something for which it is worth the trouble of living on this earth as, for example, virtue, art, music, the dance, reason, the mind – something that transforms, something delicate, mad, or divine', he elucidates the rule of a really distinguished code of ethics. But he also points the way of the absurd man. Obeying the flame is both the easiest and the hardest thing to do.

CAMUS, *The Myth of Sisyphus*

It's been too hard living,
But I'm afraid to die.
I don't know what's up there
Behind the clouds.

SAM COOKE, 'A Change is Goin' to Come'

1

Political Suicide in
Latin America

I

The title of this loose essay is deliberately ambiguous.[1] 'Political suicide' is a phrase used freely and frequently in a number of languages. Very rarely, however, is it intended to mean the self-murder of a politician. In Japan perhaps, in China and Vietnam possibly, but almost everywhere else these days it is taken to mean self-destruction of a political career, policy or party rather than of a life. Of course, in its common, colloquial sense a 'political suicide' is seldom brought to conclusion without diligent abetting by others. It has the same finality and a comparable degree of determination to physical autoelimination, but we may question if it has the same awareness and thus willingness. Perhaps the borrowing of the noun to denote political self-destruction is a mark of the unpredictability and gravity that is attached to this. The practice of politics, whether as a vocation or in lesser forms, is so overtly and consciously tied up with survival that self-inflicted damage through fleeting rashness, professional ineptitude or irrational behaviour is naturally viewed as extraordinary. Yet even if we understand 'political survival' solely as the management of policy with sufficient efficiency as to ensure reproduction of power, it is so subject to contestation that an 'unforced error' is difficult to distinguish and worthy of the most radical appellation.[2]

One of the central characteristics of suicide is its difference from

1

homicide, although self-murder is held by some to be best understood as a subset of murder. Yet 'political suicide' has rarely been identified by analysts as having a pathology distinct from the conduct of politics as a whole. Perhaps I am here pushing an analogy provided by common parlance beyond tenable limits, but it is at least worth noting that over the last fifty years the study of politics has developed such an affinity for numerate notions of 'measurability' – as a brief glance at, say, *The American Political Science Review* will confirm – that it now upholds awe-inspiring pretensions to clinical precision.[3] One would not be surprised to stumble across an article that attempted to explain the incidence of 'political suicide', or indeed the suicide of politicians, on the basis of advanced mathematics, terminating a quadratic beating of the bounds with a prissy little QED. 'Political science' certainly possesses the methodological enterprise and disciplinary *amour propre* for it to compete with sociology, statistics or psychiatry, which have been centrally concerned with the understanding of suicide since at least the publication of Durkheim's magisterial study in 1897.[4]

It is probable that this lack of interest stems from the fact that in the modern period 'political suicide' has very rarely led to the real suicide of its author. Indeed, since Roman times the incidence of suicide amongst political figures has been so low in most countries that it is statistically far too insignificant to contribute to the broad morphologies constructed and debated by sociologists. To the best of my knowledge there are no outstanding examples in twentieth-century Britain, France or the United States.[5] Even among the leadership of the conquered Axis powers and the most prominent victims of Stalin's purges the numbers are relatively modest. As a result, the phenomenon is possibly best approached through the perspective of psychiatry, for which the suicide of a politician is at root no different to any other clinical case.

Biography, of course, is essential, but for the purposes of understanding politics it is insufficient; we cannot halt at the recognition of death and how we come to it as absolute manifestations of the universal and the unique. If the quotidian realities of even the most inspired and idealist political practice offer poor comparison with the philosophical and literary ruminations on this subject from Plato to Plath, it may be said that there is still some echo in that, like artists and thinkers, modern politicians confuse expressive form and personal identity; intersect the general and the particular; and manifestly combine elements of altruism, egoism and anomie – the three phenomena identified by Durkheim, before the emergence of psychoanalysis, as characteristic forms of suicide.

There is little point in being tyrannized by the definition when we are interested in exploration. I am sure that the deaths of Jan Palach and Adolf Hitler were both political suicides. Yet Palach's self-immolation in protest at the political repression imposed after the Soviet invasion of Czechoslovakia must be deemed distinct in key respects from Hitler's anticipation of an imminent fate at the hands of others. Whilst the hitherto anonymous young Czech's death served as much as a denial of shame as an expression of it, Hitler was clear that he was forced to escape it.[6] It is not the degree of choice that is determinant but the circumstances of compulsion. In a similar vein, it matters that it was Palach and not Alexander Dubček who killed himself, and that, unlike most of his peers, Goering forebore from suicide for both personal and political reasons until his trial had begun. Equally, one can discern different responses among the Bolsheviks persecuted so assiduously by Vyshinsky on Stalin's behalf. Tomsky ended his life upon knowing that he had been implicated at the trial of Zinoviev and Kamenev. Yet two years later Bukharin adhered to a different Stoic tradition in suffering the entire process of execration and the murder that he long knew awaited him at its end. Bukharin may perhaps be thought to have ensured his own death through his final refusal to respect the protocols of recantation, like Ridley (whose descendant committed a classic 'political suicide' in 1990), Latimer and Huss some four hundred years earlier. Yet Bukharin knew that his fate was sealed, and he chose to resist not death but the macabre pretext under which it would be delivered.[7] In my view he is more the antithesis of a political suicide than was Galileo, who simply put life above truth.

Bukharin's declaration that 'the confession of the accused is a mediaeval principle of justice' was a noble political statement made in a hopeless cause, but perhaps we should be mindful of its strictures for those cases where the 'accused' is assumed to have 'confessed' by committing suicide. This is an important feature in the insistence of the Chilean junta that Salvador Allende took his own life whilst, at the other end of the ideological spectrum, it even more clearly underpins the case made by the Sandinistas and the Salvadorean FMLN against their erstwhile comrade Salvador Cayetano Carpio. (Both cases will be considered in a little more detail below.) Such association is also evident in those cases where political murder is presented as suicide. In this respect the death of the leading Albanian politician Mehmet Shehu in 1981 would seem to be the most outstanding (unproven) modern example of a practice in which the disingenuousness of the assassins – almost always state forces – is as much a mark of arrogance as of convenience.[8] The relative frequency of this practice has engendered an equally common recourse to pre-emptive disavowal although, as in the case of Steve Biko, this provides very slight protection against those who are manifestly prepared to employ such methods.[9]

On the face of things, suicide through hunger strike could not be more different. Whether staged in conditions of incarceration or at liberty, this would seem to be the most deliberate and demonstrative method of martyrdom. Yet there are relatively few instances that reach the fatal conclusion embraced by Bobby Sands and his Republican comrades in Northern Ireland in 1981 (when, it should be recalled, the dying Sands was elected as an MP). This is surely because this method is almost always adopted as a two-edged challenge in which death will be averted upon concession of certain demands and yet if it occurs responsibility will at least be shared. Indeed, it is perhaps the most consciously political form of suicide, albeit far more often threatened than accomplished and in some political cultures – such as that of Bolivia – employed so frequently that it only acquires any significance when undertaken by a large number of people or maintained up to those physical limits at which irreversible brain damage is probable.[10]

Two other forms of suicide, or suicidal action, occur with some regularity in political systems, such as those of Latin America, where there is frequent repression and military conflict. The first is the taking of one's own life to avoid treatment by the enemy that may well fall short of death but certainly threatens indignity, pain and the coerced revelation of cultural or political secrets. The second is the 'constructive suicide' of deliberately placing oneself in a position that is virtually certain to lead to death. Again, in one sense the distinction matters not at all whilst in another it is of considerable consequence. The first type has a long lineage in Latin America, stretching from the mass and individual suicides of Indians at the time of the Conquest through the deaths of messianic followers of the Brazilian preacher Antonio Conselheiro at the end of the nineteenth century to the contemporary suicides by Salvadorean guerrillas faced with capture.[11] These could not readily be described as sacrificial deaths.

The second form is more commonly associated with both heroism and foolhardiness; it is also more directly military than political in nature. Although Latin American history is peppered with examples to match the Charge of the Light Brigade, one of the most outstanding recent instances is the assault by the British Colonel H.S. Jones on an Argentine position at Goose Green in the Falklands War. Jones may, of course, be thought a hero, a lunatic or just an unlucky man doing his job. It is highly unlikely, though, that anybody would see him as a political suicide despite the fact that a guerrilla of Sendero Luminoso engaged in a directly comparable act in the Peruvian sierra might easily be described thus because he or she was consciously fighting for an ideology against people of his or her own nationality. Here, however, there is less the intention than the preparedness to die. This may be objectively viewed as self-destructive but the subjective impulse is by no means necessarily directed to that end.

In fact, three modern examples of 'suicidal action' by Latin American guerrilla groups produced quite distinct political results, although in each case the immediate military operation was itself an unqualified disaster and produced many deaths. The assault on the Moncada barracks in Santiago de Cuba in 1953 by a group led by Fidel Castro proved to be a particularly potent 'heroic failure'. It ruptured the atmosphere of submission to Batista's recently imposed dictatorship and provided Castro not only with an invaluable strategic lesson for the future but also the opportunity to proclaim at his trial that 'History will Absolve Me' in an agile and passionate speech, whose prediction soon became reality. Castro turned defeat into victory – small wonder that the Bolivian army executed Ché Guevara within hours of capturing him in October 1967 – and he never lost a proclivity for taking sharp political risks.[12]

There were no guerrilla survivors from the occupation of the Colombian Palace of Justice by militants of the M-19 in November 1985. An organization dedicated to adventurous actions in a country with an exceptionally strong tradition of socio-political violence, the M-19 apparently staged the assault with the objective of opening negotiations, although these were never permitted by the military, which was prepared to raze the building despite the large number of hostages inside. What seems to have been designed as a daring 'propaganda action' – probably influenced by the Sandinistas' successful capture of the Nicaraguan Congress in August 1978 – ended in unbridled slaughter; the bluff was called. As a result, the M-19 began to consider offers of amnesty and reintegration into local politics. Yet, as it gradually embarked on this shift, its sympathizers became easy targets for the death-squads of the right. This provoked the not unreasonable complaint that by foreswearing the practice of killing, ex-guerrillas had effectively increased their chances of being killed. In parts of the country it was to all intents and purposes suicidal to conduct peaceable and traditional politics.

The most comprehensive case of recent political and physical suicide is also the most mysterious and controversial, raising questions as to its true authorship and reminding us — to sanitize an Anglo-Saxon vulgarism — that there are rarely plots without mistakes and vice versa. In all events, there is manifest evidence for the latter and some for the former in the attack by the previously obscure human-rights-oriented Movimiento Todos Para la Patria (MTP) on the military barracks of La Tablada in the outskirts of Buenos Aires in January 1989. This action was staged on the grounds that it would forestall an imminent coup attempt against the constitutional administration of Raúl Alfonsín, who had come to power in 1983 after an eight-year dictatorship itself largely provoked by guerrilla activity of the type now renewed out of the blue by the MTP. In the event, no coup was attempted and all but sixteen of the assailants were killed in an unequal exchange of fire that served greatly to boost military morale as well as the assertions of the high command that 'subversion' was once again stalking the land. Indeed, so unexpected, reckless and counter-productive was this initiative that many held the plausible conviction that the MTP leadership had been infiltrated and 'set up' by military intelligence.[13] If so, this was less a case of suicide than artful homicide, although a significant number of people were willing to put their lives in acute danger at the service of an extraordinary enterprise based upon a highly questionable assessment of the balance of forces.

So alien was this initiative not only to popular sentiment but also to the options for resistance current on the left, legitimately preoccupied with the threat of a coup, that the few survivors stood trial without any expectation of echoing Castro's performance of twenty-six years before, without claiming their fallen comrades as martyrs, and bereft of hope for an organization extinguished in one hopeless escapade. In contrast to the experience of the M-19, the MTP was the victim of both a wildly misconceived operation and popular repudiation because that action was so impervious to a very recent and bitter history. And in contrast to most proponents of armed struggle, habitually attacked for foisting upon others the sacrifices they themselves have accepted, the MTP risked all in a single act, of which it was the solitary victim. This appeared to be the foible of an isolated individual rather than of more than three score people. Yet in all three cases sacrifice was collective and thus effectively anonymous. It is the event, rather than the victims, that is remembered by all but their families and friends.

II

Early in his chronicle *Days and Nights of Love and War* Eduardo Galeano recounts in a few stark lines the case of the Peronist militant José Luis Nell, who, having been paralysed in the shoot-out at Ezeiza airport in 1973 upon Péron's return to Argentina after eighteen years of exile,

> decided to put an end to the impotence and the pity. He picked the date and place: an overpass at a train station where no trains passed. Someone took him there in his wheelchair and placed the loaded pistol in his hand. José Luis had been an iron-willed militant. He had survived bullets and jails and the years of hunger and clandestinity. But now he put the barrel in his mouth and pulled the trigger.[14]

We will never know if poor José Luis subtracted himself from humanity wholly because of his physical condition or if his death also owed something to that veritable case of political self-destruction that was Perón's return to Argentina. This had promised liberation in historical revindication but immediately collapsed in slaughter, corruption and chaos. Perhaps, after a generation of waiting, Nell, like many others, had grasped through the experience of a few days the reality which lay behind Perón's confession that, 'many Argentines come to this house to sell me on a different truth as if there were no other. What can I do? I believe them all.'[15] The cause of José Luis's infirmity had strong political links, but it would be extremely difficult to describe his death as a political suicide.

Likewise, if Lenin had been given the poison he requested of Stalin in February 1923 because of his acute illness and pain, it is probable that the world would have looked upon his death as the suicide of a politician rather than a political suicide.[16] On the other hand, had Trotsky acted upon his apparently serious consideration of this option at the end of his life, the fact that he had suffered so many setbacks and was subjected to constant Stalinist abuse and threats would, in all probability, have led to his death being seen as a political act although he was certainly unwell and still affected by the death of his children, particularly the suicide of his daughter Zina.[17]

A different difficulty is illustrated in the case of the Bolivian libertarian Arturo Borda, a prolific artist, writer and union organizer. In his encyclopaedic history of the Bolivian workers' movement Guillermo Lora recounts how Borda, at the age of seventy and still a hard-living bohemian, died in circumstances that raise questions less about politics than about where we might draw that tenuous line between fatal foolishness and deliberate decision which is often taken to distinguish the 'impetuous' from the 'serious' suicide:

> One Monday (when the sale of alcohol was prohibited) Borda had a terrible, urgent need for a drink; his guts demanded alcohol to keep on functioning. He went round all the bars of Chijini demanding a drink, and he was turned down flat everywhere. Eventually, he went into a tinsmith's workshop and pleaded for something to slake his tremendous thirst. He was told that the only thing they had was hydrochloric acid. Borda told them to give it to him and, taking a cup, poured its contents down his gullet. This draught of poison completely destroyed his oesophagus. In hospital the dying man uttered awful shrieks as his entrails were eaten away.[18]

Such a dreadful end would appear fully to justify the use of the English legal term for suicide 'while the balance of his mind was disturbed' – in this instance by a mortal need for alcohol. Yet the last words written by Borda before his fatal foray point to the inadequacy of this explanation:

> When one has spent a life tortured minute by minute, with one's most profound needs unsatisfied and highest ideals swept away by the insulting and outrageous waste of time, health and the fortune of vain fools, one is filled with such contempt that it is incomprehensible to anybody who has not experienced it.[19]

Borda died in June 1953, just over a year after the revolution that brought about many of the socio-economic conquests for which he had been struggling for most of his life. At the time of his death the unions exercised considerable power, the tin mines had been nationalized, and an agrarian reform was to be introduced within a matter of weeks. Although his individualist anarchism put him at odds with the ruling MNR, this was still a period of extraordinary social mobilization and exuberance, many of the quasi-feudal constraints against which he had railed for decades being ripped asunder. There had not yet occurred that decomposition and disillusionment that was already patent in Argentina when José Luis Nell killed himself. Perhaps, by contrast, it was the very realization of many of his aspirations, the necessary tattiness of the dream come true, that was unbearable. Borda, like Nell, was a man steeled by a life of commitment and adversity, possessed of exceptional energy, but, as in many other cases, this may have hindered rather than helped him when 'something snapped'.

It is not remarkable that periods of political crisis should produce suicides, but few have contested Durkheim's assertions, based on statistical analysis, that the overall rate is not significantly affected by the course of political life.[20] This, of course, is a particularly difficult corollation to demonstrate or rebut, not least because when public life is thrown into turmoil the reporting of deaths is likely to be less accurate than usual. We will move in a moment to the question of statistics, but it is here worth noting that the reported Latin American rate was quite constant during the 1970s and 1980s, even in those countries where the use of death-squads and 'disappearances' was extensive and cast the suspicion of suicide over victims of repression insofar as there remained a quotient of doubt over cause and responsibility.[21]

For some time after 1945 comment was made about the ostensibly low level of suicide in the Nazi concentration camps, even allowing for the fact that such arenas of death were unlikely to produce sharp discrimination over its precise cause. However, an abundance of exceptional literature from Bettelheim and Borowski through to Levi and Semprún has disturbed received beliefs in this respect.[22] There was certainly a limit to the 'political' character of that experience, which was so extreme as to resist comparison with what might be termed the 'normal' parameters of politics, even for a region like Latin America, but it must still raise doubts about Durkheim's observations. Equally, some attention must be paid to the fact that until quite recently historians have tended to focus on periods of public crisis. As a consequence, our enhanced knowledge of these may have engendered an exaggerated perception of private trauma compared to that experienced in more stable times. Such an emphasis upon exceptional circumstances and calling is upheld by Camus, who relegates the suicides of the Chinese revolution to a footnote on the grounds of their 'honourable' motivations, and it is strongly inferred by Alvarez, who, despite the fact that he was writing at the start of the 1970s, makes no mention of Vietnam and only touches on political suicide through a brief note on Palach.[23]

The case of the deposed Guatemalan president Jacobo Arbenz illustrates two more specific, but still related, problems. First, unlike that of Nell and, to some degree, Borda, his death was reported as accidental. Yet we may legitimately harbour some doubt about this when, having been overthrown by a CIA invasion in 1954, Arbenz spent the rest of his life in peripatetic exile, manifesting progressive depression as he failed to find political solace in Czechoslovakia, the Soviet Union, Uruguay, Cuba or Mexico. Equally, the suicide of his most beloved daughter and difficulties in his marriage so compounded political failure that six years before his death he confessed that his future was 'to vegetate, to do nothing, to ruminate.'[24] In January 1971, aged fifty-eight, he was found drowned in the bath of his Mexican home.

Arbenz had led a valiant political enterprise of autonomy from Washington in the early 1950s, but when the US finally moved to crush it he had not put up the resistance that might have been expected of a young army officer. Although the struggle had been pathetically unequal and his regime was no less celebrated by anti-imperialists than it was denigrated by the US government, there was enough of a sense of shame about its rapid collapse to taint its leader with dishonour. In all events, Arbenz's state of mind was such that accidental death in a bath-tub seems most unlikely. At the very least this example should put us on our guard against the under-reporting of suicide that the experts stress so frequently.

The second point is equally simple: Arbenz died seventeen years after the most crucial event in his life. Here we might also recall that Bettelheim, Levi and Borowski killed themselves at some temporal distance from the terrors of the concentration camp. In each case psychoanalysis would surely place that experience at or near the core of the decision to die, but there is no ready means within the type of statistical appraisal undertaken by Durkheim to allow for such a 'delay mechanism' that might – or, equally, might not – produce some correspondence between political life and the incidence of suicide.

III

In his study of suicide directed at a popular audience Alvarez attempts to debunk a number of fallacies in much the same way as did Durkheim eighty years before.[25] Most of his points are well made, but the effort to destroy the myth of 'national tendencies' towards suicide is rather inept because it jumps between disregarding statistics as unreliable and depending on these selfsame numbers to show that countries broadly believed to have high rates – for instance, Britain and Sweden – in fact have lower rates than some other nations.[26] In this respect Alvarez wants to have his cake and eat it, especially since he is far less concerned with history than with psychiatry and literature. He would have been well advised to skip rapidly round a longstanding methodological minefield, and it seems probable that he was making a good point badly; if faced with undependable data that you cannot improve either use them consistently with qualification or drop them entirely. Since the objective here is not exactitude but suggestive observation, it seems reasonable to employ the figures given for cause of death in the United Nations Demographic Yearbooks in order to sketch a broad context within which Latin American political suicides have taken place. Needless to say, since regional statistics are very questionable, we should register all the usual caveats and a couple more besides.[27]

One of Durkheim's central theses was that suicide was more common in Protestant countries than in those dominated by the Catholic faith, where the role of the family is stronger and the sanction of the Church much more acute than in the more industrialized and individualized societies conducive to his 'anomic suicide'.[28] Although these are broad and disputable criteria, on the basis of reported figures Latin America would appear to fit the general pattern. First, *as a region* Latin America had a significantly lower rate than most 'northern' countries from the late 1960s to the mid 1980s – a period for which there is some semblance of continuity in the figures. The average rate of ten Latin American countries for the first half of the 1970s and the first half of the 1980s was 5.3 per 100,000 people.[29] This can be compared with that of some other countries calculated on the same basis: Spain 4.2; Canada 13.4; USA 12.1; UK 8.2; Belgium 19.0; Sweden 19.9. The proximity of the Spanish and Latin American figures is unsurprising given cultural and socio-economic similarities, and it is worth noting that if the very high incidence in El Salvador in the early 1980s, during a period of civil war, is excluded from the calculation of the Latin American figure, this would be 4.6. However, it is also noteworthy that whilst Belgium is a highly industrialized society, it also has a nominal Catholic majority, complicating an easy corollation between religious beliefs and the incidence of suicide.

Second, there are discernible differences within Latin America, the more secular, industrialized and 'modern' countries registering the higher rates: Uruguay 11.0; Argentina 7.4; Venezuela 5.0. Third, in Latin America the suicide rates are much lower than those for homicide (except for Costa Rica – a relatively 'non-violent' society) whilst in the 'northern' states the suicide rates are higher than those for homicide (less markedly so in the USA, a notably 'violent' society). Comparable figures are only available for the early 1980s – a period of considerable political violence in Central America but relative quiescence in South America – the Latin American average rate for suicides being 4.4 per 100,000 people against 22.0 for homicides.[30] (The average for the 'northern' countries listed was 12.3 for suicide and 2.0 for homicide although there is far greater coincidence between the UK homicide rate and those of Chile and Costa Rica than that of the USA.) Despite some marked internal variations, then, there is a perceptible 'regional' pattern for both types of death and the relation between them. Even if we allow a healthy margin of error for these figures, accepting both administrative shortcomings and religious prejudice as the cause of probable under-reporting for Latin America, it would still be hard to argue that this closes the formal gap to an insignificant distance.

Of course, these figures provide us with an exceptionally slim basis upon which to make any sense of those cases of political suicide that have occurred, since these are far too few to permit any corollation with the relatively large numbers that comprise the general rate. It is certainly worthy of remark that whilst there are a number of instances of political suicide in Latin America the general rate there is quite modest. Nevertheless, it is to the culture of public comportment and political practice that we have to look in order to tease out more telling factors.

One necessarily runs the risks of caricature in suggesting some possible answers in this connection. First, and least contentious, is the fact that the relative violence – open or suppressed – of Latin American public life places its conduct at times of crisis close enough to the military sphere that those elements of the military outlook that suspend survivalist logic permeate into political culture. Second, the Hispanic traditions bequeathed by a colonialism established when feudal notions of honour were still strong – although it was largely undertaken by a less than seigneurial class – have endured with remarkable strength beyond the extinction of the duel elsewhere in the world and despite a formidable history of dishonourable conduct by powerful soldiers and civilians alike.[31] The space between what is done and what is seen to be done may be considerable but the importance given to appearances is no less so. Third, the stress given by Catholicism to martyrdom and sacrifice combined with a much stronger social and religious culture of death than exists in Protestant countries upholds a correspondingly more acute notion of heroism and margin against which it is judged.[32] Whilst suicide is more strongly deemed sinful, it simultaneously embraces the ultimate consequences of heroic conduct and the sacrifice entailed by defiance of religion. When all is lost – or believed to be lost – the sanction of the Church blocks the only means by which to grasp victory from the jaws of defeat and irreversibly to enshrine adhesion to an earthly code of honour. For the faithful, political suicide constitutes a final terrestrial act of vindication of both person and cause, but it also embodies a courageous decision to meet God voluntarily devoid of grace. On the other hand, we should not ignore those subterranean but remarkably persistent currents of secular spiritualism that discourage fear of death by investing it with a more pronounced transience in the process of reincarnation.[33] If all suicides both celebrate and deny the sting of death by effectively inverting the Jesuit maxim that 'the end justifies the means', belief in the transmigration of souls gives this a very particular resonance.[34]

IV

Such eminently contestable observations will always be inadequate for the comprehension of individual experience, which, at a certain point, defies any external explanation. All the same, there is some value in looking briefly at a number of cases if only to gain a sense of the differing contexts of and responses to this extraordinary phenomenon. In choosing these I have limited myself to (sometimes disputed) cases of suicide by political figures which, as should now be clear, does not cover all the possibilities of political suicide.

Allende

Salvador Allende died at between 1.50 and 2.20 p.m. on 11 September 1973, shot at least twice in the head and possibly more times in the body. Although the uncertainty about his wounds and who inflicted them is the subject of sharp controversy, it is also a natural consequence of the fact that the president of Chile died in the midst of a battle in and around the Moneda palace which had been partly destroyed by aerial bombing and was the scene of confused fighting between several dozen bodyguards and rebel troops who had broken into the building after attacking it for over four hours. Moreover, the testimony of one plausible witness to Allende's last moments has not been fully consistent in the various forms in which it has been presented by himself and others over the last seventeen years.[35] No doubt some of the several versions of Allende's death would be disproved were his body to be examined by an independent forensic team to check the post-mortem report produced by pathologists working under military direction on the day of his death just hours before he was interred in a sealed coffin. This, though, is not the place to make detailed conjecture on such matters, nor to engage in the fierce debate that has already generated an extensive literature. For our limited purposes it is sufficient to register that the military junta which deposed the president declared him a suicide whilst most of his supporters on the left subscribe to the view that he was shot down by his assailants. As a result, what might otherwise be thought a matter of strictly secondary importance has acquired acute political connotations.

Allende died when he was sixty-five years old, having served as president for nearly three years at the head of the Unidad Popular (UP) left-wing alliance, which was dedicated to the 'peaceful road to socialism' and respect for constitutional limits and procedure at a time when the strategy of armed revolutionary struggle still exercised considerable influence over the Latin American left. Although Allende by no means repudiated armed struggle *tout court* and maintained close links with Cuba and North Vietnam, he was adamant that such a strategy was not applicable to Chile, and it is clear that he harboured a profound aversion to violence and greatly feared the prospect of civil war.[36] He was subsequently criticized by some for choosing to defend his government from the palace with a small group rather than attempting to organize mass opposition to the coup from the workers' quarter of Santiago.[37] His final messages to the population on 11 September are notable for their warnings against hopeless resistance. As he once said to Régis Debray, then the leading theorist of guerrilla warfare in Latin America, 'how many masses are needed to stop a tank?'[38] This dislike of political violence was the personal conviction of a now elderly man who, although a veteran member of what was a quite radical Socialist Party, was also a respected member of the national elite, a bourgeois in all but his political beliefs.

However, it is of vital importance that the conviction of the in-dividual was also at the heart of government policy, firmly upheld by the Communist Party and broadly supported by the Socialist Party, the two largest components of UP. On the other hand, the radical left both at home and abroad viewed UP's observance of constitutional norms and attempts to introduce social change within the context of the capitalist state as at best a reformist capitulation and at worst a treason-able deliverance of the masses into the hands of a traditional army that, sooner or later, would end their illusions in a bloodbath. Notwith-standing the country's forty years of elected civilian governments, the revolutionary left (and, indeed, a good part of the right) held that, ultimately, class interests could and would only be assured through violence, and that by failing to comprehend this UP was embarked on a course that was in partisan terms suicidal but in a wider sense a betrayal of socialism and its supporters. Such a view was naturally fortified by the military coup, its bloody aftermath, and the experience of nigh on two decades of repressive autocratic rule under General Pinochet. Whilst the radical left excoriated the UP experience as a

15

'farce' and its leaders as comprehensively culpable, the UP parties themselves gradually engaged in self-criticism, albeit rarely in terms that rejected their enterprise as entirely misconceived.[39] This process, and the doleful experience of the populace under an oppressive regime that continuously justified its actions in terms of the disorder and provocations of the UP, sharpened the sense in which Allende's heroism was associated with failure – a failure not just to obtain his objectives but also to avoid their very opposite. In the light of this irrefutable fact it was of transcendent importance that the traditional *politico* devoted to compromise and pragmatism should uphold the honourable cause to which they had been directed by making a sacrifice that was their absolute antithesis.

Salvador Allende was described as 'the first dreamer of the republic', but he was well aware of the threats to his government, and long before its existence was threatened he declared that he would only be taken from the Moneda in a coffin.[40] This resolve is fully evident in the several radio broadcasts he made on the morning of 11 September as the palace came under attack and it became increasingly obvious that the rebel forces would prevail. At 8.30 a.m. he declared,

> I shall not leave the Moneda. I shall not resign. I call on the workers to remain at their stations in factory or plant. I am at this moment anticipating expressions of support from soldiers determined to defend their government. I renew my determination to continue to defend Chile and the authority the Chilean people have placed in me. I shall pay with my life to defend the rights of Chileans . . .[41]

An hour later, when the balance of forces had become more clear, Allende made his last public speech:

> Surely this will be my last opportunity to address you. . . . My words are not spoken in bitterness, but in disappointment. They will be a moral judgement on those who betrayed the oath they took as soldiers of Chile. . . . I shall pay with my life for the loyalty of the people. . . . The seed we have planted in the worthy consciousness of thousands upon thousands of Chileans cannot remain forever unharvested. . . . They have the might and they can enslave us, but they cannot halt the world's social processes, not with crimes nor with guns. . . . The people should defend themselves but not sacrifice themselves. The people should not let themselves be riddled with bullets nor cut down, but they should not let themselves be

humiliated either.... Other men will overcome this dark and bitter moment, when treason strains to conquer.... These are my last words, and I am sure that my sacrifice will not be in vain. I am sure that this sacrifice will constitute a moral lesson which will punish cowardice, perfidy and treason.[42]

These frequently quoted words were broadcast as the army began its assault on the palace and some four hours before the president died. They combine defence of political principle with a poignant expression of personal commitment in such a way as to convince that Allende had already decided to die. Nonetheless, it is notable that before he did so he interrupted the organization of the palace's defence to negotiate with his enemies, who throughout the morning offered him and his family safe conduct out of the country. On at least three occasions Allende discussed terms of surrender with the generals attacking him, and if his conditions for leaving the palace proved unacceptable to them, he still talked with them about his resignation.[43] At the same time, he was at great pains to secure the safety of those around him, insisting that there be no personal martyrdom. Even two hours after the palace had been bombed the attackers offered its defenders the chance to surrender, and although Allende had no reason to trust the word of his enemies, there is little evidence to suggest either that they meant to kill him or that he believed that they would.[44] It is implausible to claim that he killed himself simply in anticipation of execution at their hands.

Two further points deserve mention. First, Allende was a great admirer of President José Manuel Balmaceda, who had committed suicide in 1891 after defeat in a civil war fought against the bulk of the army and interests popularly associated with foreign nitrate companies. As noted by Pablo Neruda three days after Allende's death and nine before his own, Balmaceda was the only Chilean president respected by the left because of his nationalist beliefs and sacrifice on their behalf. Neruda, very ill and consumed by the tragedy of the moment, links the two martyrs and mentions that Allende's death was called suicide by the generals but rejects this: 'They couldn't pass up such a beautiful occasion. He had to be machine-gunned because he would never have resigned from office.'[45] Yet if Allende undoubtedly refused resignation and surrender, he could still have followed the heroic example of Balmaceda, and would perhaps have been revered for doing so had the junta not declared that he had died by his own hand. Second, at about 1.30 p.m., once it became clear that the end was near, the president's trusted adviser Augusto Olivares quietly left Allende's presence and shot himself. The ultimate defence of honour was not only enshrined in history and already proclaimed to the world, it had now been undertaken by a close friend. Allende, a freemason and man recognized even by his fiercest foes to have a deep sense of loyalty, could not, even as the fighting closed in on him, have failed to see this act as an example to be followed. It is not certain that he took this course, but neither is it unlikely. Why, then, is the image of the assassinated man so important even to those who would accept his suicide to be no less a sacrifice?

In approaching this question we should recognize that the issue of Allende's death still arouses deep passions both because it occurred quite recently and because under Pinochet's dictatorship public debate over it and the other victims of the military was effectively frozen, only to be resumed after the return to constitutional government in 1990. Sentiment has been sharpened by expression and certain features of popular memory have been compressed by enforced 'forgetfulness'. If the prolonged autocracy has made the UP government appear to be from a different epoch – nearly half the population was born after 1973 – the end of the dictatorship also makes it seem as if it happened only yesterday. In one sense this proximity has meant that Allende has not become myth: the person is still distinguishable from the symbol even though the symbol itself has much to do with a benign avuncular figure ill prepared but resolved to make a stand against the forces of barbarism. This image is nowhere caught more vividly than in the final photo of the president standing in the portals of the Moneda dressed in casual clothes, with a helmet askew on his head, a rifle in his hand, and bespectacled eyes to the sky as if, disbelieving, he needed to see for himself the approaching machines of destruction.

Of course, there are many who recall the man *en carne y hueso*, with all his vices, and the UP government was sufficiently fractious, ill organized and embattled for Allende to generate as much exasperation amongst its friends as he did hatred and denigration amongst its opponents.[46] Yet for many – including those on the left who were implacable critics of UP – to call Allende a suicide would be both to traduce his memory and to present a propaganda gift to the military. Now that they have left office things may be expected to change somewhat, but it is still hard to imagine that Gabriel García Márquez, accused of iconoclasm for his brilliant but less than heroic depiction of Bolívar in his dying days, might undertake a similar project for Allende, whose killing he denounced in terms that were so vigorously engaged and political.[47] The paradox is that the late president has become as depersonalized as any distant hero whose individual character was long since subsumed by sacrifice.

Perhaps the key to this lies in the place occupied by Allende's death in the opposition to Pinochet and his junta. The declaration of the deposed president's suicide was one of the military's very first acts upon seizing power. Neruda's reaction was widely shared; why should their already gross perfidy not extend to a self-serving lie of the type evidently peddled during the months of conspiracy? To believe that the declaration was true not only precluded the assignation of unalloyed responsibility by introducing a miniscule but critical space between suicide and 'constructive homicide', it also required some suspension of the necessary conviction that such terrorists lacked the slightest vestige of credibility. The months after the coup were not a time for complications, and if some people predictably depicted Allende's death in politically instrumentalist terms, many more were clearly disposed to accept these since they confirmed the military's original sin. Equally, one should recognize that as the regime consolidated its grip through more structural repression Allende's death, which nobody could deny, in a way came to represent those of the thousands of 'disappeared', whose fate was concealed by a wall of silence and disinformation. As these lies about the military's victims became systematic the conviction that, out of shame and malice, they had similarly distorted the real circumstances of their most infamous act became justified in itself and as a source of solace in confronting that purgatorial space between the belief and knowledge of death which precludes true grief and instils the most insidious transference of guilt. While such doubts remained Allende could not be permitted to enter history.

Salvador Allende's death can be seen as a 'classic' political suicide. It embodies all those elements – failure, embattlement, despair and the choice of heroic sacrifice – associated with Greek or Roman tradition. Yet it is more than this, for the experience of defeat is responded to in a manner that is both unambiguously modern and strongly resonant of the Christian tradition. In his final words Allende projects an image of

19

resurrection that has clear echoes of Christ's example in revindication through rebirth. However, this is patently secular and modern in its stress upon 'social processes' based on collectivities rather than the individual. Allende himself will be replaced by 'new men', the crimes of the military will not withstand the broad movement of history. The president, an elected representative, dies alone but for a cause that is greater than himself. This is altruism, but it is also an institutionalized altruism driven to an extreme by circumstance. The tragedy can readily be justified because the understanding that there was 'nothing left' extends well beyond the individual affected. Indeed, it is possibly because he took a decision that many others would also have taken under the same conditions that there exists such ambiguity about his death. In all events, it is an exceptionally rare case of 'necessity'.

Carpio

The death in April 1983 of the Salvadorean guerrilla leader Salvador Cayetano Carpio ('Marcial') shares a number of characteristics with that of Allende. Both men were in their mid-sixties, having greater prestige and experience as radical militants than their comrades. Both were confronted by a traumatic shock that had resulted in unexpected death and destroyed their political dreams. And neither – in my judgement – was faced with certain death at the hands of others. Yet, apart perhaps from their age, which may be interpreted equally well as making them more or less vulnerable to the demands of the moment, these similarities are not extraordinary, and there are many differences.

Carpio was a worker, accustomed to repression and violence at first hand. A tough and intransigent Marxist–Leninist, he was above all suspicion of innocence with respect to the lowest common denominator of political struggle in his country. After many years as general secretary of its Communist Party he had fought for a decade as the leader of the Fuerzas Populares de Liberación (FPL), a politico-military group of rigorous doctrinal and organizational discipline dedicated to winning a revolutionary civil war of the type that Allende had endeavoured at all costs to avoid. Carpio's death, like that of Allende, remains shrouded in mystery and controversy. But these do not relate to the final responsibility for his killing – nobody disputes that he shot himself in the heart at 9.30 p.m. on 12 April in the

Managua house he occupied with his wife and a few close comrades who informed the Sandinista security police immediately and never came under suspicion of foul play. However, the critical difference from the case of Allende lies in the fact that Carpio was driven to suicide not by the enemy against whom he had fought all his adult life but by a bloody dispute within his own organization. The betrayal that he faced and of which he was accused was of an entirely different order to that confronted by the Chilean president. It was one of intimates, people conjoined by many years of shared adversity and whose policies were defended in public with a unity and conviction no less fierce than the internal debates whence they emanated. The conditions of prolonged clandestinity and the waging of a brutal civil war appeared to have forged an optimal personal and collective resilience through discipline. When this collapsed the failure and disgrace could not simply be of an individual; the insufficiency of the individual was necessarily a reflection of their political community. A bonding which in many respects paralleled that of a family was effected by more than the love bestowed by shared blood, and only with inordinate difficulty could it be sundered without bloodletting.

Of course, such phenomena have long been prey to an antiseptic sociology. Yet this has yielded very little of worth for understanding the complex actions of individuals within an organizational context that successively requires of them the initiative and disputation associated with 'ordinary' political parties and the abstinence from discussion of a type ordained by military hierarchy. The historical failures and victims of such systems of 'democratic centralism' are legion; perhaps the most emphatic recent example of fatal implosion was in Grenada, several months after Carpio's death and a few weeks before its cause was made public.[48] However, it is worth registering that the Salvadorean left had already experienced in the execution of the celebrated radical writer Roque Dalton in 1975 the dreadful consequences of penalizing dissidence with death. For some this confirmed the pathological nature of a local radicalism as divided as it was strong.[49] Yet by mid 1980 the several contending factions of the left had combined in the Frente Farabundo Martí para la Liberación Nacional (FMLN), which established a joint command but within which the FPL's slogan of 'Revolución o Muerte' was but one of five. This was an essential step towards operational unity in the civil war against the US-backed regime, but if Carpio was prepared to make major concessions towards former

21

opponents and serve on the high command, he was not willing to treat this as an alliance that, however great its strategic importance, presaged dissolution of the FPL or the abandonment of its core programmatic positions.

When, late in 1982, the course of the war posed this possibility he therefore found himself under pressure not just within the FMLN, where it was to be expected and was part of 'external' politics, but also within the FPL itself, where Carpio was faced with opposition from those who had previously shared his criticisms of the rest of the left and thus could be seen as deserting the cause. The protocols of democratic centralism demanded that Carpio contest the moves towards negotiations with the government and unification of the constituent organizations of the FMLN first and foremost inside the FPL. In some respects this was unremarkable, but Carpio's last speeches and declarations strongly imply that he believed he was fighting not so much over tactical positions as for the very survival of his party.[50] Moreover, he was doing so against the opposition of the FPL's second-in-command, Mélida Anaya Montes ('Ana María'), who easily won the debate over strategy held in January 1983. Carpio formally accepted this defeat; but over the next two months he continued to voice opposition to the formation of a united party of the left and argued that negotiations with the government were an absolutely subordinate feature of revolutionary strategy. Although not expressed in polemical fashion, this was certainly pushing the freedoms allowed by democratic centralism to, if not beyond, their limits, especially since the FPL was both at war and in an exceptionally delicate position with regard to its allies in the FMLN. Carpio was faced with a dilemma. Either he could submit to the FPL's rules and watch it move towards what he feared was dissolution, or he could attempt to salvage the party from what he considered a disastrous course by breaking the very rules that he had long argued distinguished it from the rest of the left. This dilemma was very possibly more troubling to him than the accusations that he was too old, intransigent and out of touch, although it must have been difficult to dissociate such charges, which were not without some foundation, from the arguments over policy and programme. Whatever the case, the impending crisis was brought to a head in a completely unexpected and violent fashion that entirely altered the terms of the conflict.

The agreed facts concerning the débâcle of April 1983 are as follows. On 1 April Carpio travelled from Nicaragua to El Salvador to present his position to FPL militants. Two days later he travelled to Libya. On the 6th, while Carpio was still in Tripoli, Ana María was found horribly murdered in her Managua house. On the 9th the Sandinista police arrested Rogelio Bazzaglia ('Marcelo'), the head of the FPL's security apparatus and a close ally of Carpio's, together with two accomplices, both militants of the FPL and supposedly aligned with Ana María. On the same day Carpio returned to Managua from his Libyan trip and attended Ana María's funeral in the company of the Sandinista leaders Tomás Borge and Daniel Ortega. His appearance was that of a sick and depressed man. On the 11th an official Sandinista communique stated that Bazzaglia had confessed to the crime, saying that he had been generally directed ('orientado') by Carpio. The FPL leader made no public response to what was, from any viewpoint, an act of betrayal. A declaration by the FPL issued at the same time attributed the murder to the CIA. On the 12th three further members of the FPL were arrested, Carpio having been placed under house arrest and directed to resign all his posts. He killed himself that night. On the 21st the FMLN issued a statement which called for a full investigation of the facts but made no charges against Carpio. The results of any investigation were never subsequently published, and neither was any evidence of Carpio's complicity in the crime made public beyond Bazzaglia's confession, which was obtained under interrogation. The leadership of the FPL passed into the hands of Leonel González, a supporter of Ana María who had been fighting in El Salvador at the time of her death.

Despite the absence of a public accusation, Carpio's detention made it quite evident that he was under direct suspicion, and, in fact, the charge seems to have been laid against him immediately. It is this question that occupies almost all of his farewell note to the FPL:

> I have been attacked, persecuted, goaded and calumnied a thousand times by the bestial enemies of the people and I have withstood and overcome all this, fortified by the cause of the workers, peasants and the people.... But it is one thing to struggle against the intrigues of imperialism and quite another to be subjected to injustice, calumny and infamy by my own brothers. A black plot to stain my revolutionary life and inflict severe damage on the FPL is under way and coming to its conclusion ... that which saddens me, and which I cannot endure, is that revolutionary comrades are tricked and accept as true the calumny, the perfidious invention and the besmirching of a revolutionary proven a thousand times

in the popular struggle. Acceptance means not only the destruction of my established revolutionary record but also an attack on the ranks of my beloved organization, as if its members were infiltrated by the enemy.... I cannot support the abuse of my person, the infamous effort to implicate my name, even indirectly and by sly insinuation, in the terrible loss of our companion Ana María.... I am uplifted by the idea that my modest contribution, maintained firmly in every act of my life until the very end, to the interests of the proletariat and people in some way helps and will help the genuine interests of the people in its happy future. Revolución o Muerte! El Pueblo Armado Vencerá![51]

The contents of this note were not widely known until December 1983, when the new FPL leadership issued a declaration that openly accused Carpio of ordering Ana María's death, of cowardly committing suicide 'to evade his responsibility and save his reputation', and of engineering the factionalism that created the crisis in the first place.[52] This statement opened a polemic over both the details of the affair itself and the wider question of political morality.[53] Since the facts that exist in the public domain provide no basis upon which to make a firm and impartial judgement on responsibility for the murder, there is little value in pursuing that issue further in this context. If Carpio did indeed instruct Bazzaglia, either directly or perhaps in the manner that Henry II secured the removal of Thomas à Becket, this would be tantamount to an act of 'political suicide' since there was no chance that the Sandinistas, or for that matter Cuban intelligence, would fail to investigate it vigorously. Equally, there was no sense in which an act of this nature could be justified on grounds of 'revolutionary justice', as distinct from that of the Nicaraguan state or popular tradition. It was manifestly indefensible in every respect. In light of this, one should not completely discount the possibility that, whether responsible or not, Carpio perceived that Bazzaglia's confession made it likely that he would be subjected to a court martial and shot. He may, then, have been escaping what he sensed to be an inevitable fate.

Nevertheless, the sense of failure remains unaltered, and according to the conventions of the FPL Carpio, as its commander, could not avoid a significant quota of blame for the disaster that had befallen it. Although the insistence on self is prominent in his last words, it is also qualified by subordination to the collective, the shame of betrayal being made intolerable by the very fact that it affected both the individual and the group. Carpio's depression is tangible; the written challenge he offers his accusers is less forthright than one might expect and it was not given a posthumous response. Perhaps he felt compelled less to die than to follow Ana María, a comrade of many years with whom he had enjoyed amicable relations before this crisis, even though it was already clear that her death would be treated as one of a martyr in a way that his could not be. It is, though, one thing to note that he was denied martyrdom and another to suggest that he sought it. This does not appear to me to be the case simply because the knowledge that his death could not expunge the taint of dishonour did not deter him from ending his life.

Vargas

All political analysis is confronted with the critical gap between the categorization of the general and the characterization of the specific. For our present purposes it is as well to make a clean breast of the already palpable fact that this space cannot be closed. Yet, whilst it is useless to seek a systematic explanation for political suicide, we cannot entirely ignore the fact that Latin American politics has long been depicted by both academic typologies and popular 'common sense' as possessing a strongly personalist nature. Moreover, this view has progressed well beyond the comfortable limits of Whig history in its embracing of the concepts of the authoritarian personality and charisma as well as in its sensitivity to the material and cultural origins of *caciquismo, caudillismo* and *coronelismo*.[54] Such a perspective is far from wholly incompatible with the complexities of contemporary political economy despite its constant vulnerability to the temptations of a simple individualist determinism. Even if the modern epoch has produced an emphatic institutionalization of the broad liberal, authoritarian, radical and populist strains of political practice, it certainly has not fully eradicated the culture of leadership-in-itself and person-as-ideology. This may be increasingly parochial, accepted as mystification, recycled through the veneration of martyr figures or drenched in disavowal, yet it persists in a particular form that is insufficiently explained by organization theory or the incidence of dictatorship.

The case of Fidel Castro may be considered an anomaly on a number of grounds, but it remains an exceptionally potent one. Similarly, it is easy to dismiss as a complete anachronism the personalist dictatorship of Alfredo Stroessner, who was ousted in 1989, having ruled Paraguay for thirty-four years. Yet Stroessner's person provided the vital bond for a system of clientelism and machine-politics, based on the Colorado Party, that was a good deal more modern than suggested by its expressive condensation in the Caudillo. Neither regime can be understood without significant attention to human prowess and frailty. However, if the decrepit Stroessner was, like his peer Somoza before him, too wedded to the worldly rewards of power to do anything more than savour their remnants once it was taken from him, one could readily envisage Castro taking his own life in the wake of defeat. In all events, his example illustrates a coincidence between individual and regime that is distinct from both the general logic of political leadership and the necessity imposed by crisis, exemplified in different ways by Allende and Carpio.

This attribute is frequently identified with that much disputed term 'populism', more easily presented through personification than its notoriously fluid amalgamation of the mechanics and discourses of nationalism, mass politics, people-before-class and poor-above-rich.[55] The fact that such personification was as much lived as imputed makes it notable that only two national leaders closely identified with such a politics were driven to take their own lives: Getúlio Vargas of Brazil (1954) and Germán Busch of Bolivia (1939). It is also worth remarking that neither man's name was subsequently adopted by a significant political movement, although their influence was as strong in life and death as that of other figures who became 'institutionalized' through an appropriation that in itself confers heroic status (Cardenismo in Mexico; Velasquismo in Peru and Ecuador; Peronismo in Argentina; Sandinismo in Nicaragua, and so on). One may debate whether this 'isolation in history' stems directly from suicide, but it does free us at least from some of the dangers of confusing the enigmatic qualities of the individual with those of the movement.

Getúlio Vargas occupies a prominent place in the pantheon of Latin American populists despite the fact that it was only in the final years of a long political life that his policies justify such inclusion. Indeed, even after Vargas recognized that World War II had rendered redundant his corporatist Estado Novo and required the reformulation of its suppressed popular voice as a more vibrant *trabalhismo* he remained the diligent opportunist, cautious and dependent until the end upon clientelist deals. Yet this shift, like those which had previously enabled him to establish the Estado Novo in 1937 and dominate the overthrow of the Old Republic in 1930, sharpened the personalist and paternalist character of his politics, which had been tempered in the provincial power struggles of Rio Grande do Sul. Vargas formed political parties but existed apart from them. He presided over regimes but survived their collapse. He may be associated equally strongly with the pseudo-democratic arbitration of regional oligarchic interests (1930–37), the authoritarian corporatism of the Estado Novo (1937–45) or the re-distributionist rhetoric of his final, and only elected, term (1951–54).

Vargas, then, was not just a survivor but a champion survivalist. At the time of his death, at the age of seventy-one, he had been president of Latin America's largest country for nigh on twenty years (1930–45; 1951–54), governor of one of its richest states for two years, and had occupied state and federal offices for over forty years.[56] The management of political power had filled the bulk of his adult life. Of all the cases of suicide discussed here his is the one for which it is most plausible to advance the explanation that it was motivated by the loss of power in itself. There is, though, a problem with this insofar as Getúlio had been removed from office late in 1945, reluctantly accepting the intervention of the military shortly prior to the elections that would be won by his chosen successor General Eurico Dutra. By that stage Vargas's manipulation of the official unions, his overtures to the Communist Party that he had repressed only a few years earlier, and his adoption of a buoyant – but scarcely fiery – populist rhetoric had stoked up a campaign for his candidacy known as *Queremismo* after the slogan 'Queremos Getúlio' ('We want Getúlio'). It may be pressing a point to suggest that the use of such a term encapsulated Vargas's personalism, but it is undoubtedly the case that by this stage support for and opposition to Getúlio had exceeded in both scope and passion the limits justified by his record and promises. Indeed, the demoniza-tion undertaken by his opponents – in large part erstwhile allies jettisoned over his erratic trajectory during the previous fifteen years – played a vital part in consolidating his image as saviour. In 1945 he accepted this role precisely by leaving office and effectively entering opposition. Despite his precipitate removal by the officers who had long, and not so subtly, refereed the rules of the political game, Vargas was in an optimum position to assume the mantle of the prophet outcast, and he could justifiably expect to be recalled to power on a popular mandate. In one sense, then, one can discount the experience of 1945 as one of defeat. It should also be noted that, aside from blatantly fraudulent *continuismo*, there is a quite extensive tradition in the region of presidents returning to office after a period 'out in the cold'. Although some examples of this suggest variations on Marx's dictum of tragedy repeated as farce, not all cases are so emphatic in their disappointments, despite an inevitable imbalance between expectation and gratification.[57] To be sure, this pattern had barely been established when Vargas returned to office in January 1951, but it was clear that he now had to meet the expectations nurtured over five years on the sidelines, and although he scrupulously sought to modulate these during his campaign, the vindication provided by victory was matched by the challenge. Moreover, it was apparent that there would be no further chances.

The record of the Vargas administration of 1951–54 is not so desultory for it to be deemed an abject failure except, crucially, in the sense that it did not, and probably could not, equal the ambitions held by Getúlio himself, let alone his constituency amongst the poor. Now unable – by virtue of the Cold War and economic stagnation as well as his more focused political discourse and patronage network – readily to ring the changes between nationalism, order and redistribution, Vargas responded to increased worker discontent by introducing an inflationary minimum wage policy and tacking a course that was insufficiently accommodationist to placate the masses but threatening enough to generate right-wing attacks and military disquiet. In the 1930s and 1940s Getúlio had proved able to overcome this familiar scenario, but by April 1954 he was confronted by a rapidly closing pincer movement from which escape looked highly unlikely because his alignment was unprecedentedly clear and his promise was exhausted. The scenario was of a veteran politician trumped by both a burgeoning crisis and the very fact that he was a veteran politician.

The last weeks of Vargas's presidency and life were not, however, dominated by the repudiation of the 'father of the poor' by his 'children'. Although they no longer rallied to him as required, matters were brought to a head by a scandal not entirely dissimilar to that which afflicted Carpio and a refusal to surrender office that bears some parallels with that of Salvador Allende. The scandal, about which very little doubt remains, was the attempted assassination of the virulent opposition journalist Carlos Lacerda by a gunman hired by Gregorio Fortunato, chief of the presidential palace guard. Lacerda, aware that the violence of the attacks against Vargas in his *Tribuna da Imprensa* had put his life in some danger, was guarded by disaffected members of the airforce, and in the attack a major was killed although the journalist himself escaped with a minor wound. This naturally drew considerable attention to his renewed offensive, now conducted as much on the radio as on paper, whilst an already deeply discontented military rounded on the government and were obviously moving towards a coup. The capture of the gunman and revelation of the source of his orders brought matters to a head, although Vargas himself was not directly implicated and, expressing shock at the utterly unexpected ambush, declared, 'I have the feeling that I am drowning in a sea of mud.'[58]

On 21 August Vice-President Café Filho responded to the opposition and military offensive by proposing to Vargas that they both resign, permitting congress to elect successors to serve out the term. Getúlio responded by declaring that he would only leave the palace dead. Two days later Café Filho made his suggestion to congress itself, thereby breaking with Vargas and leaving him isolated against demands for his resignation. Yet even the day before this 'betrayal' he had responded to the request that he go from the respected officer Marshal Mascarenhas de Morais with the words, 'I will only leave here dead.... I am too old to be intimidated and I have no reason to fear death.'[59] So it proved to be, although in the early hours of 24 August Vargas had agreed at a cabinet meeting that he would only take leave of absence, not resign. Perhaps such a diplomatic formulation might have assuaged Getúlio's sense of honour and pride, but it was not allowed to stand by the military, and, hearing of their rejection of this option, Vargas shot himself just after 8 a.m.

The suicide letter left by Getúlio Vargas has been described as 'the strongest nationalist appeal he had ever made'.[60] And, indeed, there is some question as to its authenticity, but it seems unlikely that it was completely concocted by others, and it cannot sensibly be treated in the same manner as his other declarations.[61] In all events, it stands as a remarkable example of self-justification, defiance and exhortation:

Once more the forces and interests which work against the people have organized themselves afresh and break out against me.

They do not accuse me, they insult me; they do not fight me, they vilify and do not allow me the right to defend myself. They must silence my voice and impede my actions so that I shall not continue to defend, as I have always defended, the people and especially the humble. I follow my destiny. After decades of domination and plunder on the part of inter-national economic and financial groups, I placed myself at the head of a revolution and won. I began the work of liberation and I installed a regime of social freedom. I had to resign. I returned to the government on the arms of the people. The underground campaign of international groups joined that of national groups which were working against the regime's efforts to ensure employment.... They do not want the worker to be free. They do not want the people to be independent....

I have fought month after month, day after day, hour after hour, resisting constant, incessant pressure, suffering everything in silence, forgetting everything, giving myself in order to defend the people who are now deserted. There is nothing more I can give you except my blood. If they want to go on draining the Brazilian people, I offer my life as a holocaust. I choose this means of being always with you. When they humiliate you, you will feel my soul suffering at your side. When hunger knocks at your door you will feel in your breast the energy to struggle for yourselves and your children. When you are scorned my memory will give you the strength to respond. My sacrifice will keep you united and my name will be your standard....

... to those who think that they defeated me, I reply with my victory. I was a slave of the people, and today I am freeing myself for eternal life.... Hatred, infamy and slander have not conquered my spirit. I have given you my life. Now I offer my death. I fear nothing. Serenely I take my first step towards eternity and leave life to enter history.[62]

There can be little doubt that Vargas meant not the general history of the past but the particular history of the great; the only future he provides for is one under his shadow. Evidently designed to provoke a popular backlash, such unrestrained rhetoric suggests a strong streak of megalomania. In the event, the mass protests were short lived, the rioting and attacks against Getúlio's enemies falling away once his body had been returned to his home town. The man certainly became a folk hero, and his death was the subject of much popular lamenta-tion, but if he was a martyr to a cause beyond himself, this was too diffuse to permit political momentum to be galvanized by sentiment. The heirs and associates of Vargas continued to dominate Brazilian politics for a further decade yet they did so primarily on the basis of their own reputations, through party deals, and under the vigilance of the military, which, in 1964, finally took power itself. Its policies were in many respects not dissimilar to those of the Estado Novo except that the twenty-one-year regime remained throughout 'institutional' and resistant to all personalist infections. If nothing else, Getúlio Vargas appeared to have exhausted the personalist potential of Brazilian politics for the rest of the century – a monopolization which in itself may be compared to that achieved through a very different route by Perón in Argentina.

Busch

The suicide of Germán Busch in August 1939 is different in most respects from those we have already described. Although at the time of his death Busch had been president of Bolivia for two years, having previously served as army chief of staff for two years, he was only thirty-five years old. His death bears the hallmarks of youthful impetuosity driven on by an inebriated melancholy as well as the fury of a determined military mind thwarted by manoeuvre and hidden interests. The man of action brought to office by decisive deeds and identification with a resolutely anti-political code of honour could not endure the intrigue integral to political power, let alone the fact that this had rapidly transformed the omnipotence associated with the presidency into a most public form of impotence. A brilliant soldier who had already suffered three years of brutal war against Paraguay in the deserts of the Chaco (1932–35) and witnessed the sacrifice of thousands of his compatriots for a nationalist ideal they saw as betrayed by the senior commanders and *políticos*, Busch took office through a coup (1937) with the impossible mandate of translating an idealism born in the terrible experience of the trenches into a new political order. Already a hero, he found himself trapped in a world that denied him at the same time as it venerated him. In this sense there is some logic to a death that in its immediate circumstances seems absolutely needless and futile.

Busch not only lacked any sensitivity for political life, like many an army officer he also had no programmatic bearings or coherent ideology around which to construct a viable team or to consolidate the fervent support of the Chaco veterans. Highly prone to depend upon his instincts and appreciation of character in the manner that had served him so well as a daring commander, his policies careered across

31

the ideological spectrum. This was not uncommon in the Latin America of the 1930s, when the collapse of oligarchic liberalism spawned a wave of corporatist experiments that embraced sharply contradictory permutations of populism and authoritarianism. Yet rarely were such enterprises so condensed and confused as that in Bolivia, where an exceptionally small and powerful group of tin mineowners (the Rosca) continued to control the commanding heights of the economy whilst the experience of the Chaco had politicized the lower orders and produced a form of schizophrenia in an officer corps divided between, on the one hand, vindicating the sacrifice of its men and salvaging honour from defeat, and, on the other, controlling radical discontent and the spectre of a materialist collectivism.[63] It was in this context that Busch, whilst still chief of staff, backed the quasi-fascist proposal of his predecessor Colonel David Toro to introduce obligatory trade-union membership as well as enforced conscription of the unemployed into the army. However, once he had removed Toro for succumbing to the influence of the Rosca, the young colonel convoked a constituent convention that had a very broad representation, was the scene of fierce ideological dispute, and produced a charter of unmistakably progressive character. Once again, though, Busch changed tack, the faction-fighting and continual realignments provoked by the post-war upsurge perplexing and irritating him. Without any warning or clear cause, besides the fact that the convention's social reforms were bearing little fruit in the face of the Rosca's deft non-compliance, he declared a dictatorship on 24 April 1939. The manifesto he issued in making this move is typical of military declarations in its language and style, but Busch, unlike most authors of such proclamations, not only subscribed to the letter of his pronouncement, he also felt bound by its spirit:

> With the same faith, with the same spirit of sacrifice with which I defended Bolivia in times of battle, offering my life at each and every moment, I want to undertake a new campaign which will save this decaying nation. Beginning today, I am initiating an energetic and disciplined government, convinced that this is the only road which will permit the invigoration of the Republic, in the international and internal arenas. The country needs order, work and morale to fulfil its destiny.[64]

Unremarkably, given the fascist undertones of this declaration, the constitution was suspended and scheduled elections cancelled.

However, there was no significant repression of the popular movement, and early in June Busch completely ambushed the Rosca, which was confident that it now had the young soldier in its pocket, by introducing a proposal made by the left wing in the convention requiring the mining companies to deposit all their gold and foreign exchange in the central bank. This measure effectively threatened full fiscal control of the country's most powerful entrepreneurs, who had long resisted far less radical initiatives on the part of governments trying to secure for the state some claim on the fabulous profits of the tin companies.

Aware of the pervasive influence of the mineowners and determined to slice through what he perceived as the Gordian knot restraining the progress of mainland America's poorest country, Busch declared that those who attempted to evade the stipulations of the decree, either directly or by reducing production, would face full confiscation of their property and the death sentence.[65] When, within hours, he was informed that the prominent mineowner Mauricio Hochschild was preparing to take just such action, Busch had the magnate arrested and was only prevented from executing him by an extremely stormy cabinet meeting, in which his ministers, keenly aware of the severe beating the president had personally given the elderly and renowned conservative writer Alcides Arguedas, managed to convince him of the illegality and counter-productive consequences of such a move. Busch eventually acquiesced, but he had been dissuaded from the only type of action he understood. Over the following weeks his government lost its direction and authority and he, perhaps aware that the key moment had passed, lost himself in bitter, romantic speeches.

Germán Busch shot himself early in the morning of 23 August 1939, having spent the night at his home drinking and dancing with his wife and brothers-in-law, both officers. As the night wore on he became increasingly drunk and depressed, and his brother-in-law Colonel Carmona had already restrained him once from shooting himself when, according to the colonel, who was later predictably suspected of murder, Busch suddenly drew his Colt revolver and blew out his brains.[66] Under the circumstances it is unsurprising that Busch, alone of our cases, died without explaining or justifying his decision in a public declaration. In retrospect it is possible to discern the furious exasperation that drove him to it in his speeches and precipitate actions. The accusations against Carmona lacked any tangible evidence or plausible motive, and, although deeply suspicious, the dead

33

president's considerable public following found greater solace in the slogan 'Only Busch could kill Busch', which revived the reputation for almost superhuman powers that he had won in the Chaco.[67] At the same time, the very impotence that had so angered him was underlined by the lack of any concern on the part of the generals and Rosca placemen to attend his corpse or guard against popular protest as they scrambled to divide up the spoils held back by the disturbing maverick. Within hours the Rosca was firmly back in control, the defunct dictator's decrees being either annulled or left to collect dust on the statute books.

Busch became a hero for the nationalist movement that was to lead the 1952 revolution, and his example of fearless Bonapartism exercised an influence over elements of the military for much longer. However, this example is often overshadowed by that of another young Chaco veteran, Major Gualberto Villarroel, who died as president in July 1946, lynched by a mob organized by the same interests confronted by Busch.[68] Villarroel's death also possessed suicidal qualities in that although it was plain that his regime was defeated, he refused to leave the presidential palace, facing his end as a matter of honour. The fact that he died at the hands of others and in such terrible fashion – copied from the example of Mussolini – ensured Villarroel's status as a martyr more readily than was possible in the case of Busch. Aside from its more obvious features, this hierarchy of heroism may have something to do with the fact that Busch was a *Camba*, a native of the sparsely populated lowlands, as well as being of German descent. Raised in the provincial tropical city of Trinidad and lionized for his valour in the more distant wastelands of the Chaco, he was an 'outsider' not only in that he did not come from the Andean heartland of Bolivia but also in the claustrophobia that one senses overtook him in the narrow confines of La Paz. Perhaps, on that freezing night as the pianist Luna struck up a *bolero de caballería* – a magisterial air of profound emotion – Germán Busch entered a loneliness beyond that instilled by draughts of pisco and the failure to fulfil a transcendent mission. He was not just far from home; he was also separated from the dead of the Chaco plains, where, as he continually stressed, he had been ready to lay down his life in a struggle he understood. Now, confronted by a more insidious and cowardly enemy that maimed him in silence and without valour, he chose to return to the certainties and community that had made his life.

Chibás

On 5 August 1951 Eduardo Chibás declared to the listeners of Havana's CMQ radio station, 'People of Cuba keep awake. This is my last knock at your door.' Chibás then shot himself. The bullet entered his stomach, and he took ten days to die. Nobody outside the studio heard the shot because the microphone had been turned off before Chibás fired, although it would appear that he had intended both that the discharge be broadcast and that he only wound himself. The pathetic qualities of the event are heightened further still by the fact that a week earlier another radio station had put out a spoof of Chibás's histrionic broadcasts in which he had committed suicide on the air.[69] Such an imitation of comedy by tragedy was not, in fact, so unexpected in the case of Chibás, who had established a reputation for eccentric behaviour, fighting duels and public emotionalism.[70] Our last example, his suicide is probably the one most clearly explicable in terms of personality rather than politics. Nonetheless, if at the age of forty-four Chibás might be said to have carried the turbulence of adolescence into his middle age, he was still a political figure of consequence.

Chibás was a child of what passed for oligarchy in newly republican Cuba, his father owning sugar mills, coffee plantations and a railway. He had travelled to the US and Europe as part of a privileged upbringing, but on returning to Cuba during the dictatorship of General Machado in the 1920s Chibás threw himself into radical student politics and participated in a number of plots that preceded the overthrow of the autocrat in 1933. Although jailed and exiled under the dictatorship, Chibás remained a fierce opponent of both political terrorism, which was rife in Cuba through most of his adult years, and corruption, which was, if anything, more extensive. Thus, his two primary convictions gave him a platform guaranteed to attract friends and enemies aplenty in the turbulent post-war years between Batista's first, constitutional regime and the imposition of his dictatorship in 1952. Chibás was a supporter of Grau San Martín's Auténtico party, founded on the basis of the 1933 revolution but soon riven by factionalism and corruption once Grau came to office. The fact that Chibás himself never entered government may have something to do with the fact that he was a man of independent means and did not need to receive or dispense patronage. Whatever the case, he excelled at revelation, criticism and denunciation, using the radio – well established in an advanced, US-dominated economy – to finger those responsible for for malfeasance and *gangsterismo*. These ills were habitually bemoaned and decried by politicians but very rarely by directly naming names, which in the violent climate of the late 1940s was a decidedly risky undertaking. It is probably in this light that one can best understand the suicide in May 1947 of the Mayor of Havana, Fernández Supervielle, who found himself unable to control a city that ran on graft as a result of having become what in today's euphemism would be known as a leisure centre, servicing increasingly affluent North Americans with brothels, casinos and seaside holidays. Chibás railed against this and soon became what in later years would be termed a 'whistle blower'. Although he held wider beliefs – a pronounced nationalism, hostility towards the Communist Party – the core of his politics was a pugnacious moralism which readily merged into character assassination.

It was this trait that lay behind his decision to break from the Auténticos and form the Ortodoxos (Cuban People's Party) in 1947, not least in order to oppose the candidacy of Carlos Prio Socorras, whom Chibás considered the embodiment of corruption and whom he had wounded in a duel shortly after the split. Prio won the elections of 1948 by a clear margin, securing three times as many votes as Chibás, who trailed badly and was increasingly viewed not only as a 'single-issue' figure but also as unstable. Still, the issue was at the forefront of political life and Chibás's image as a firebrand assured him significant support. He could not be ignored or easily rubbed out. The real question was whether he could retain the impetus of his crusade and inflict damage on the Prio administration, which from the turn of the decade had come under increasing pressure from right and left alike.

It was perhaps predictable that Chibás should eventually overplay his hand. However, it was an artful turning of the tables by one of his victims that lured him into an unsustainable position; this was no straight case of 'political suicide'. Late in June 1951 the minister of education, Aureliano Sánchez, accused Chibás of speculating in coffee, harbouring dictatorial ambitions, and being an 'apostle of untruth'. Chibás, in return, charged Sánchez, a former comrade on the student directorate of 1927 with whom he had not previously quarrelled, of speculating in lumber. Sánchez rapidly produced evidence to rebut this charge and challenged Chibás to an extensive debate on radio – hitherto Chibás's preferred forum. Clearly wrong-footed, Chibás declared that he would bring decisive incriminating evidence to Sánchez's ministry on 21 July, but he was not allowed to enter, increasing tension and anticipation further. As a result, when Chibás finally revealed his material on television the following week its inconclusive nature damaged him much more severely than it did Sánchez. It was this that prompted the radio spoof which in turn provoked the embarrassed – but scarcely disgraced – Chibás to stage the wildly misconceived gesture that ended in his death.

It is undoubtedly the case that the exchange with Sánchez had damaged Chibás's political standing although the charges against him were as poorly substantiated as those he himself had made. Chibás had more to lose than did Sánchez in making questionable imputations of dishonour. His own credibility and honour were placed in question, and however disproportionate his response may seem – even if it had not ended so tragically – one can discern a deeper failure behind a mistake of the type that all politicians commit with some regularity. Chibás had not only been bested at his own game, his moral crusade had been reduced to self-serving muck-raking. If, compared to the other examples, the issue at stake was distinctly trifling and well within the managerial capacity of an averagely hard-nosed politician, it still raised the question of virtue, common to all these cases. Recognition of this should qualify any judgement of what by all reasonable standards appears to be an absurd act of advertisement, replete with all the melodramatic devices of a radio *novela*, which, given Chibás's proclivity for the medium, does not cause great surprise. The medium, however, is not the message. Allende's last resort was Chibás's first choice, and the differences between them far outstrip the similarities.

V

The central importance of how death will be seen and acted on – how it will be given meaning – distinguishes all these suicides, notwithstanding their own differences, from the less comprehensive forms of resignation that would meet comparable public and private needs in many other parts of the world. Clearly, the high incidence of violence is a significant factor in this response to the experience of defeat, but it would be a mistake to view it as more a cause than an effect of a

37

political culture where morality and conviction occupy a different space to that in the professionalized politics of 'post-industrial' societies. In these public policy and management have increasingly taken the bicephalic form of science and theatre, translating cynicism from a character trait to a way of life.[71]

There is assuredly much to decry in the Manichaean qualities of Latin American politics that give such unhampered expression to perversity and brutality in the name of virtue. Yet it is only from the standpoint of vacuous indifference that the pursuit of virtue in itself can be viewed as an exotic and primitive vanity. As we have seen, the form this pursuit takes can be exaggerated beyond the point of comprehension, and its price is often excessively high, but if these possibilities are removed the properties of conviction are reduced to those of opinion, which is no more a mark of civilization than is belief one of barbarism.

Notes

1. Since I have no professional expertise in this subject, which is rarely discussed by those who do not, it is perhaps worth explaining that my interest was aroused in the spring of 1990 by the rare suicide of a British MP, John Heddle, the otherwise undistinguished Tory member for Mid-Staffordshire, that of a much admired historian, Tim Mason, and inquiries by the biographer of Benjamin Britten about my uncle, Piers, who was a close friend of Britten's and had killed himself thirty years earlier. Because I believe Piers's suicide had a lot to do with his experience as a soldier and POW in World War II, I dedicated this piece to him my book *Orígenes del Poder Militar en Bolivia*, enabling me to dedicate this piece to the memory of Javier Monje, who died in 1986. For suggestions and help I am most grateful to Trevor Smith, Bill Schwarz, Eilis Rafferty, Alex Wilde, Bob Archer, Neil Belton, Penny Woolcock, Ana María Aguilar, Alessandra Guerzoni and Barbara Dunkerley, none of whom could possibly agree with more than a small part of what I have written.

2. Barry Ames, *Political Survival. Politicians and Public Policy in Latin America*, Berkeley 1987, adopts the minimalist, or functionalist, perspective depicted here and explicitly disowns any pretension to understanding the phenomenon beyond the parameters given by public expenditure.

3. See, for example, Douglas Madsen, 'A Biochemical Property Relating to Power Seeking in Humans', *American Political Science Review*, vol. 79, 1988, pp. 448–57. The abstract for this piece reads as follows: 'The disposition to seek power in a social arena is tied in this research to a biochemical marker, whole blood Serotonin. This finding constitutes the first systematic evidence of any biochemical property in humans which differentiates power seekers from others.'

4. Emile Durkheim, *Suicide. A Study in Sociology*, London 1952. The best introduction to Durkheim is Steven Lukes, *Emile Durkheim. His Life and Work: A Historical and Critical Study*, London 1973. The literature on suicide is immense, covers several

disciplines, and remains exceptionally controversial. As will be obvious, I have read very little of it and could harbour no ambition to contribute towards it. The concern here is primarily with politics, albeit the experience of politics in what one might term the 'end-zone'.

5. In Britain, aside from the case of Heddle and another Midlands Tory MP, Jocelyn Cadbury, we should note the faked suicide in the 1970s of the Labour minister John Stonehouse, who was undergoing a personal crisis, and the mysterious disappearance in the 1920s of the radical figure Victor Grayson, whose political career had become exceptionally erratic and suffered major reverses as well as being associated with the shady world of espionage. However, the possibility of a homosexual connection would, at that time much more than now, have provided just as strong an incentive to 'disappear' by one means or another (Reg Groves, *The Strange Case of Victor Grayson*, London 1975). The most celebrated – or infamous – case of a British political suicide is that in 1822 of the Anglo-Irish aristocrat Robert Stewart, Viscount Castlereagh, a bitterly reactionary individual whose disposition for repression in both countries underpinned such popular hatred that the man himself declared that between popularity and unpopularity, 'unpopularity is the more convenient and gentlemanlike'. Shelley's furious *The Masque of Anarchy* contains the memorable lines, 'I met murder on the way –/He had a mask like Castlereagh', and Byron was little less vituperative. If Castlereagh was true to his time in fighting a duel – in 1809 against Canning on Putney Heath – Edward Thompson is justified in identifying in him pronounced psychopathic tendencies. *The Making of the English Working Class*, London 1968, p. 770, n. 1; H.M. Hyde, *The Strange Death of Lord Castlereagh*, London 1959. It is also worth noting that Wolfe Tone, leader of the United Irishmen and a man of political views absolutely counterposed to those of Castlereagh, also committed suicide, but this was on the night before his execution. The incidence of suicide in the families, and particularly amongst the sons, of politicians is quite common, and there have been several recent examples in the United Kingdom.

6. In his personal will, dictated a day before his death, Hitler stated, 'My wife and I choose to die in order to escape the shame of overthrow or capitulation.' H.R. Trevor-Roper, *The Last Days of Hitler*, London 1947, p. 183.

7. Technically, Bukharin confessed, but this was only after Stalin threatened to kill his family, and to the end he treated Vyshinsky and his theatre with open contempt. Harold Denny, who covered the trial for the *New York Times*, wrote, 'Mr Bukharin alone, who all too obviously in his last words expected to die, was manly, proud and almost defiant. He is the first of the fifty-four men who have faced the court in the last three public treason trials who has not abased himself in the last hours of the trial.' Quoted in Stephen F. Cohen, *Bukharin and the Bolshevik Revolution. A Political Biography, 1888–1938*, New York 1980, p. 380. The same cannot be said of Arnaldo Ochoa, the distinguished Cuban general who was tried in July 1989 for corruption and drug trafficking. Although the charge of trafficking was unsupported by evidence given in court, and despite the plausible suspicion that Ochoa had construed some of his activities to be at the service of the state as well as to his personal benefit, he pleaded guilty from the start and, towards the end of his evidence, declared, 'When a human being is discredited he's a nobody. And, well, I believe no further words are needed. The facts are many and I'd prefer that action be taken on those facts.' Having accepted death, he told the court, 'My last thought will be of Fidel and the great revolution he has given our people.' *Case 1/1989. The End of the Cuban Connection*, Havana 1989, p. 100; Julia Preston, 'The Trial that Shook Cuba', *New York Review of Books*, 7 December 1989.

8. *The Artful Albanian. The Memoirs of Enver Hoxha*, ed. Jon Halliday, London 1986, pp. 327–30. It will be recalled that a few years later the same suspicion surrounded the mysterious death of the solitary prisoner of the Allied Powers in Spandau prison – a man known as Rudolf Hess, then under US supervision, extremely old and a highly unlikely victim of murder except, perhaps, insofar as this may have taken the form of 'assisted suicide'. The *Falange Socialista Boliviana* long claimed that the death of its leader, Oscar Unzaga de la Vega, in a failed coup attempt in April 1959 was at the hands of the government, which in turn insisted upon his suicide and went to the extreme of calling in a Pan-American Commission to investigate the case, which was eventually (and persuasively) declared a suicide.

9. Biko carefully instructed his friend Donald Woods that any presentation of his death as by self-hanging, suffocation, internal bleeding or starvation would be a cover for murder. Woods, *Biko*, London 1987, p. 213. It is also worth noting with regard to the Moncada barracks attack discussed below that all but three of the assailants who died were executed after capture and that Fidel Castro narrowly escaped death twice (once by poisoning) whilst in custody – a fact that was most effectively denounced at his trial. Peter Bourne, *Castro*, London 1986, p. 92; Castro, *On Trial*, London 1968, p. 12. Dario Fo's tragi-comedy *Accidental Death of an Anarchist* provides a sharp political as well as dramatic depiction of this practice in modern Italy.

10. To the best of my knowledge there has been no fatality directly attributable to a hunger strike in Bolivia despite the fact that thousands of people, mostly on the left but sometimes from the right, have made recourse to it over the last forty years. Nevertheless, both the tangible suffering and symbolic power of this form of protest has produced a number of signal victories although President Hernán Siles's habitual exploitation of the device in the 1950s and 1980s when thwarted in office became increasingly theatrical and tantrum-led.

11. For the period of the conquest, see Nathan Wachtel, *The Vision of the Vanquished. The Spanish Conquest of Peru through Indian Eyes, 1530–1570*, London 1977, p. 155, and 'The Indian and the Spanish Conquest', *The Cambridge History of Latin America*, ed. Leslie Bethell, Cambridge 1984, Vol. 1. For the 'Canudos campaign' of the 1890s in Brazil, see Euclides da Cunha, *Os Sertões*, Rio de Janeiro 1902 (translated as *Revolt in the Backlands*, London 1947, and complemented by a literary depiction of the same episode in Mario Vargas Llosa, *War of the End of the World*, London 1984). Note should also be taken of the mass suicide of a North American religious sect in Guyana in 1979, as well as the high incidence of suicide amongst members of Brazilian tribes that were clearly threatened by ethnocide from the mid 1980s in the Amazon region. For the FPL and FMLN, see Fermán Cienfuegos, *Veredas de Audacia. Historia del FMLN*, San Salvador 1989; Charles Clements, *Witness to War*, New York 1984. My thanks to José Gutiérrez for his information and reflections on the Salvadorean case, which will be taken up more fully below.

12. Bourne quotes Castro as warning his group, 'this is a suicide action' in *Castro*, p. 79. Yet only three rebels were killed in the attack itself, and in his defence speech Castro declared, 'When I became convinced that all efforts to take the barracks had become quite futile, I began to withdraw our men ...' *On Trial*, p. 20. Although he is a psychiatrist, Bourne does not explore Castro's character in great depth. Of course, all major politicians must take risks, but Castro has an especially long list to his name from the rupture with Washington in 1960 and the missile crisis of 1962 through the 'Ten Million Ton Harvest' campaign of 1970 to the Mariel expulsions of 1980 and the repudiation of perestroika in 1989. The defence of Cuba has always been projected as an enterprise to be taken unto death. For a more detailed biography, see Tad Szulc,

Fidel: A Critical Portrait, London 1986. For a full account of the Moncada attack, see Hugh Thomas, *Cuba: The Pursuit of Freedom*, London 1971, pp. 824–44. Ché's guerrilla campaign in Bolivia very rapidly became a lost cause, and when he was finally captured by the army his captor, Gary Prado, hesitated to give him a canteen of water because he might poison himself. However, despite a severe asthma attack, exhaustion and a bullet wound, Guevara showed no sign of doing so, calmly observed that he probably would not be shot immediately and, by all accounts, faced his execution with impressive dignity. Our detailed knowledge of this campaign derived from the diaries of Ché and other combatants makes it plain that while it was disastrously conceived and executed, it was never intended to be a sacrificial undertaking. General Gary Prado, *La Guerrilla Inmolada*, Santa Cruz 1987; *The Complete Bolivian Diaries of Ché Guevara and Other Captured Documents*, ed. Daniel James, London 1968. By contrast, the US Black Panther leader Huey P. Newton positively celebrated the notion of 'revolutionary suicide', but as in so much of Newton's political discourse, this idea was projected with such melodrama that even its metaphysical qualities were grossly diminished. *Revolutionary Suicide*, New York 1973.

13. For a synoptic account that considers the possibility of a 'black operation' by the military, see Joe Schneider, 'The Enigma of La Tablada', NACLA, *Report on the Americas*, vol. XXIII, no. 3, September 1989.

14. Eduardo Galeano, *Days and Nights of Love and War*, London 1983, p. 24.

15. Tomás Eloy Martínez, *La Novela de Perón*, Buenos Aires 1985, frontispiece.

16. This incident acquired an especially controversial character because, late in his life, Trotsky used it to infer that Stalin might well have killed Lenin. *Stalin*, New York 1946, pp. 372, 376, 381. For commentary, see Baruch Knei-Paz, *The Social and Political Thought of Leon Trotsky*, Oxford 1978, p. 528; Isaac Deutscher, *The Prophet Outcast. Trotsky, 1929–1940*, Oxford 1963, pp. 453–4. Significantly, Trotsky omits the entire incident from his autobiography, written in 1929, *My Life*, London 1975, where the coverage of Lenin's illness skips from November 1922 to March 1923, pp. 500–2. In this regard, it may be of some relevance that when the leading left oppositionist Adolf Joffe committed suicide in November 1927 (for reasons that must be linked as much to his illness and marital problems – unmentioned by Trotsky – as to politics) the section of his final letter addressed to Trotsky criticized him for excessive expediency. Ibid., p. 560. Although no serious authority doubts that Lenin made the request to Stalin, not even those accounts sympathetic to Trotsky give credence to his later suggestion.

17. For the impact of Zina's suicide, see Deutscher, *Prophet Outcast*, pp. 195–8. This event is brilliantly captured in Ken McMullen's film *Zina*, 1985. Exhausted, believing himself to be suffering from arteriosclerosis despite his doctors' diagnoses, and clearly mindful of Lenin's agonizing end, Trotsky openly referred to suicide – 'cut short ... the too slow process of dying' -- in his will of 27 February 1940. Deutscher, *Prophet Outcast*, pp. 477–8. There may be a lingering suspicion of 'constructive suicide' about Trotsky's insistence, against all advice, to keep in his entourage his eventual assassin 'Jacson' (aka Ramón Mercader, who also remarked on this fact), but it is difficult to square this with the titanic struggle he put up when mortally wounded by 'Jacson'. Ibid., pp. 503–5.

18. Guillermo Lora, *Historia del Movimiento Obrero Boliviano*, vol. II, La Paz 1969, p. 349.

19. Ibid.

20. Durkheim, *Suicide*, p. 353.

21. It is impossible to give a figure for the entire region because of omissions for certain countries (normally the rate per 100,000 people rather than the absolute number) for certain years. However, the rates in three countries sharply affected by repression in the 1970s – Argentina, Chile and Uruguay – remain remarkably constant

with those of earlier years. The only countries that register a clear shift are Guatemala and El Salvador. Guatemala reported only five suicides in 1976 and eighteen in 1977 (0.1 and 0.3 per 100,000 people) when the average over the previous five years had been 175 (3.75 per 100,000 people). Rates only slightly higher than those for 1976 and 1977 were reported for the period 1979–82, also years of considerable violence when very few death certificates were issued and many deaths went uninvestigated. By contrast, El Salvador reported a major increase in the 1980s in both suicide and homicide rates, the former averaging 11.9 per 100,000 people between 1980 and 1985 and the latter 64.2 – more than double the rates of a decade earlier. United Nations, *Demographic Yearbook*, New York, annually, for the years 1974, 1980, 1985 and 1986.

22. Bruno Bettelheim, *The Informed Heart*, London 1961, shows vividly the dangers of assuming a basic survivalism and the scope for 'choosing a different way to die'. One should also note Primo Levi's observation on the suicide in 1978 of a fellow victim of Auschwitz, Hans Mayer, that, 'like other suicides [it] allows for a nebula of explanations'. *The Drowned and the Saved*, London, 1989, p. 110. For a magisterial survey, see his *If this is a Man*, London 1966. One of the most memorable and moving passages of Jorge Semprún's memoir-mascarading-as-a-novel about Buchenwald relates to the influence of spring on his Russian fellow-prisoners: 'There was that light, sweet-smelling mist. The Russian looked up. The woods were green over there, the copses decked out in tender shoots. The Russian could no longer stay there, shifting soil with his shovel, it was too stupid. He took off.... He ran madly towards the immense, distant plains of his country, in the spring sunlight.

Sometimes the Russian got a bullet in the back of his neck before he'd gone a few steps. But death had been sweet, it had had the smell of spring about it, at that last moment when his face was buried in the ground. Sometimes the escapee was caught after a few hours of woodland freedom, and his face still wore the expression of an unbounded childish joy when he was hanged in the Appellplatz.

As soon as the fine weather returned, the Russians took off, it was well known.

"They're mad, the Russians!" Henk said.

No doubt they were, but that Russian madness made my heart beat faster.' *What a Beautiful Sunday!*, London 1984, p. 82.

23. Camus, *Myth of Sisyphus*, p. 13; A. Alvarez, *The Savage God. A Study of Suicide*, London 1971, pp. 67–8. I suspect that Alvarez at least would not have treated the suicide of the Marxist theorist Nicos Poulantzas as 'political' although he threw himself to his death clutching copies of his books, clearly inviting the interpretation that he wished to eradicate them as well as himself. It is remarkable how non-Asiatic commentators on the 1968 Tet offensive in Vietnam tend to dismiss it as the product of some kind of pathological impulse on the part of Vietcong militants and ignore the qualities of political commitment and valour required for mounting such a 'suicidal' operation, which, of course, General Giap was quite correct to identify as marking a turning-point in the war, for reasons that had little to do with formal logistics.

24. Carlos Manuel Pellecer, *Caballeros sin Esperanza*, Mexico 1973, pp. 159–63; Stephen Schlesinger and Stephen Kinzer, *Bitter Fruit. The Untold Story of the American Coup in Guatemala*, London 1982, pp. 230–2.

25. Alvarez, *Savage God*, pp. 99–109; Lukes, *Durkheim*, pp. 203–4.

26. Alvarez, *Savage God*, pp. 104–6.

27. The problem of inadequate reporting, especially in times of social and political conflict, has already been mentioned in note 21. It is likely to be particularly acute in rural populations, which dominated Latin America until the 1960s, because of the dearth of doctors. Equally, one must give full weight to the objection that under-

reporting is liable to be particularly high in Catholic countries because of the stigma, which is often extended to the refusal to give a mass for a suicide. (In Protestant countries suicides were sometimes buried to the north of the church, but this was apparently more out of superstition than as a mark of condemnation.) Still, emphasis on stigma should not lead us to assume that it necessarily leads to cover-ups, especially on the part of doctors. It is just as likely that the exigencies of practising an autopsy, as required in such cases, reduce reporting. In the one unresolved case I have investigated in detail, the final death certificate was signed by a doctor who had not seen the corpse and not by two others who were noted in the records of interment as having attended the '*levantamiento del cadaver*' whilst the police colonel reported in the press as having investigated the case denied having done so, and no record of the death was held in either the local police station, the central criminal archives or the embassy of the country of which the victim was a citizen. All the accounts of the death are, apparently, secondhand and certainly contradictory. And yet an identifiable grave exists. It is my impression that although this case is extraordinary because it involves the suspicion of murder, obfuscation of a comparable degree attends many suicides. On the other hand, Borda and Arbenz are peculiar cases in that they did not use a firearm, employed by all five cases considered below in more detail. It is probably easier to have an accident with a pistol than a bottle of tranquillizers, but it is arguably less easy to avoid an autopsy as a result of gunshot wounds, and once a corpse has escaped the control of the family, a cover-up, at least for the purposes of reporting to the World Health Organization, is much less easy.

28. Durkheim, *Suicide*, pp. 353–4.

29. Costa Rica; Guatemala; El Salvador; Mexico; Chile; Ecuador; Uruguay; Venezuela; Argentina; Brazil. Insofar as any sample of countries can be said to be illustrative of the region this one is adequate and determined by the availability of figures in the UN *Demographic Yearbook*.

30. Based on the same countries and using the same source for the first four years of the 1980s.

31. For a brilliant study of the duel, see V.G. Kiernan, *The Duel in European History. Honour and the Reign of Aristocracy*, Oxford 1989. Although Kiernan does not directly address the question of suicide, it naturally recurs in the text, and his treatment of the 'irrational' defence of honour provides many suggestive links. It is notable that Kiernan identifies a much greater proclivity for duelling in the 'north', including the USA, than in the 'south': 'No need seems to have been felt, as in Britain, of an accompaniment of duels. Cabinets came and vanished, the public remained profoundly indifferent.' Ibid., p. 300. This may perhaps be ascribed to the absence of a genuine aristocracy in Latin America as well as the mores of republicanism (consolidated everywhere by 1898). However, duels between politicians and army officers were held quite regularly well into the twentieth century, and I am not sure that I would entirely concur with Professor Kiernan's estimation of a low incidence of duelling in the region even if it is hard to dispute his point about public indifference (not that this need have much bearing on politicians' sense of honour). Duelling, unlike suicide, is prone to moments of comedy, and the following anecdote (which escaped Victor Kiernan's typically rigorous researches) may provide a modicum of relief from the tragic atmosphere surrounding this essay, showing the notion of honour to be no less demonstrative of the ridiculous than of the sublime. This example comes from 1958 but it could just have readily derived from the age of Don Quixote. It concerns a fight between the 72-year-old Chilean the Marquis de Cuevas, who, despite his rank, was an impresario by profession, and the French choreographer Serge Lifar.

The Marquis de Cuevas won his first duel yesterday by wounding the choreo-grapher Lifar in the forearm, but he immediately fainted in the arms of his second. After striking the blow, Cuevas, trembling and tearful, said: 'We will do a ballet together that will be called "The Duel".' Lifar, one of whose best-known works is entitled 'David Triumphant', did not reply. The duel was the result of an exchange between the two men days earlier over a ballet that Lifar had choreographed but did not wish Cuevas to use. During the conversation Lifar cast a handkerchief at the Marquis's feet, and Cuevas accepted the challenge. Both men took intensive fencing lessons during the week before the fight, which took place at noon yesterday some 65 kilometres from Paris. The two appeared to be most upset. On the first three assaults of the duel – in which four were to be fought – they dedicated themselves to crossing swords, but on the fourth Cuevas nervously wounded Lifar in the arm. 'Blood has been shed,' declared Jean Fournon, the ex-fencing champion who acted as referee. 'Halt the duel,' he added, 'and attend to the wound immediately.' While the doctors attended to Lifar the Marquis collapsed into the arms of his second, the Deputy Jean-Marie Le Pen. Lifar insisted upon kissing the Marquis, who appeared to be on the edge of an attack of hysteria, and down whose cheeks poured large tears. When the Marquis recovered he said, 'I am so sad! It is as if I wounded my own son.' Lifar, for his part, declared, 'I love the Marquis, but I never expected him to be so quick, as if he were full of youth.'

El Diario, La Paz, 1 April 1958. It is perhaps unsurprising to find the following comment in an obituary of Cuevas (whose 'first duel' appears to have been his most celebrated if not his last): 'From start to finish the affair was accompanied by the maximum publicity which neither of the two protagonists went out of his way to discourage.' *The Times*, 23 February 1961. If legal prohibition required that the theatrical impetus of duelling – taken here to risible lengths – be qualified by prudent secrecy, no such constraint inhibits the suicide, as is well known to travellers on the London Underground who are frequently informed in careworn tones that delays are 'due to a person under a train'. It may well be that for the desperate Londoner this is the most ready means of self-destruction, but it certainly has the effect of maximum advertisement, the distress of passengers being negligible compared to that of drivers (for whom the unions had to struggle long and hard against a singularly callow and infamously inefficient management in securing rights to leave in order to recover from the trauma).

32. For an interesting study, see William F. Sater, *The Heroic Image in Chile. Arturo Prat, Secular Saint*, Berkeley 1973.

33. This is particularly relevant to two national heroes: Augusto César Sandino of Nicaragua, who is perhaps the most potent political martyr in twentieth-century Latin America, and Víctor Raúl Haya de la Torre of Peru, who, after years of proscription, died a revered elder statesman. For their 'mystical' beliefs, see Donald C. Hodges, *Intellectual Foundations of the Nicaraguan Revolution*, Austin 1986; Frederick B. Pike, *The Politics of the Miraculous in Peru. Haya de la Torre and the Spiritualist Tradition*, Lincoln, Nebraska 1986.

34. This, of course, also applies to many of the indigenous religions of the Americas, particularly strong in the Andes and Mesoamerica, where their influence on the beliefs of non-Indians, such as Haya and Sandino, is more extensive than generally admitted. I remember being impressed at the distress felt by a Bolivian scholar of international reputation upon learning of the death in Mexico of her colleague René Zavaleta. It was sad enough that René had died in his prime but even worse that he had done so in such

a distant place, leaving his *ajayo* ('little soul', one that cannot itself determine life or death) forever sundered from its homeland, where the dead co-exist with the living in spirit or other forms. For an excellent illustrative study, see Thérèse Bouysse-Cassagne, *Lluvias y Cenizas. Dos Pachacuti en la Historia.* La Paz 1988. Such beliefs are quite distinct from those which have motivated reburial – as in the cases of Rosas, Torres and Allende – primarily for secular and political reasons, although it is also hard to imagine this practice taking root in Protestant societies.

35. The testimony is that of Dr Patricio Guijón Klein, a member of Allende's entourage, whose account was first presented by the military immediately after his capture as proving Allende's death. In 1990 Klein published a book on the subject which I was unable to consult at the time of writing. Amongst the many analyses and polemics over Allende's death, see Robinson Rojas Sanford, *The Murder of Allende*, New York 1976; Marta Sánchez and Lillian Calm, 'El Once, hora por hora', *Qué Pasa*, 10 September 1974, and *Qué Pasa*, 2–14 September 1977; Florencia Varas and José Manuel Vergara, *Coup! Allende's Last Day*, New York 1975; Paul E. Sigmund, *The Overthrow of Allende and the Politics of Chile, 1964–1976*, Pittsburgh 1976. All these sources are cited and some discussed in detail in Nathaniel Davis, *The Last Two Years of Salvador Allende*, London 1985, in which the author, the US ambassador to Santiago at the time of the coup, devotes much space to analysing the question of the president's death. His account is less biased and more generous than might be expected, but it still contains some notable lapses of consistency as well as a number of passages that mesmerize and depress with their irredeemable folksiness at the service of candour.

36. Davis, *Last Two Years*, p. 244.

37. Helios Prieto, *Chile: The Gorillas are Amongst Us*, London 1972, p. 72.

38. Camilo Taufic, *Chile en la Hoguera*, Buenos Aires 1974, p. 91. See also Régis Debray, *Conversations with Allende*, London 1971, which is worth reading to get a sense of Allende's outlook even if this means exposing oneself to Debray's limitless self-esteem.

39. For left-wing criticisms, see Prieto, *Gorillas*, where the term 'farce' is employed, p. 78; Jorge Palacios, *Chile. The Real Story of the Allende Years*, Chicago 1979; Michel Raptis, *Revolution and Counter-Revolution in Chile*, London 1974. For an account by a leading government adviser that contains self-criticism, see Joan Garcés, *Allende et l'Expérience Chilienne*, Paris 1976.

40. Sigmund, *Overthrow of Allende*, p. 186.

41. Quoted in Davis, *Last Two Years*, p. 246.

42. Quoted in ibid., pp. 253–4.

43. Ibid., pp. 255; 258–9; 265; 267, based upon a variety of cited sources.

44. This issue depends quite centrally upon an interpretation of the role and motivations of General Ernesto Baeza, who made the most tangible offer of safety to Allende and subsequently resigned over the junta's presentation of the president's death. Ibid., pp. 259; 302.

45. Pablo Neruda, *Memoirs*, London 1978, p. 350. For a traditional biography of Balmaceda, see J.M. Yrazzabal, *El Presidente Balmaceda*, Santiago 1940; for a 'revisionist' account, Harold Blakemore, *British Nitrates and Chilean Politics, 1886–1896*, London 1974. The socialist leader Luis Emilio Recabarren also killed himself, in 1924, following the imposition of a dictatorship and schism in the Communist Party.

46. For a less than flattering portrait of Allende painted by radical shop stewards, see Peter Winn, *Weavers of Revolution. The Yarur Workers and Chile's Road to Socialism*, Oxford 1986, pp. 70–5.

47. Gabriel García Márquez, *El General en su Laberinto*, Bogotá 1989; 'The Death of Salvador Allende', *Harper's*, March 1974. For a review of this and other 'political'

accounts, see Davis, *Last Two Years*, pp. 286–303.

48. For a succinct analysis of the collapse of the Grenadian revolution, see Manning Marable, *African and Caribbean Politics*, London 1987. Some sectors of the international Trotskyist movement drew parallels between the roles of Coard in Grenada and Carpio in El Salvador, but these are dangerously superficial. *Intercontinental Press*, 23 January 1983. For obvious reasons, the following paragraphs rely as much on personal information as on published sources.

49. For a description of the left, see James Dunkerley, *The Long War. Dictatorship and Revolution in El Salvador*, London 1985. For an unsympathetic analysis derived from the Dalton affair, see Gabriel Zaid, 'Enemy Colleagues: A Reading of the Salvadoran Tragedy', *Dissent*, Winter 1982.

50. See, in particular, Carpio's speech of 1 April 1983 to the FPL, reproduced in *Punto Crítico*, Mexico, July 1983.

51. Reprinted in Adolfo Gilly, 'El Suicidio de Marcial', *Nexos*, Mexico, no. 76, April 1984, pp. 31–2. It is notable that Carpio does not mention Bazzaglia in his letter, and he makes no specific charges against any individual. Bazzaglia had the authority and ability to liquidate 'traitors' and he was known to dislike Ana María personally as well as politically.

52. Statement of FPL, 9 December 1983, reproduced in *Barricada*, Managua, and *Granma*, Havana. See also *Bohemia*, Havana, 23 December 1983. The FMLN issued a separate declaration on 16 December supporting that of the FPL.

53. Gilly's demand for a clarification of the charges against Carpio was rejected, and an alternative interpretation of events presented, in a number of articles, particularly Gilberto Rincón Gallardo, 'El Asesinato de Ana María', *Nexos*, no. 78, June 1984. For a view close to that of Carpio, see Cuauhtémoc Ruiz, 'La crisis de la guerrilla y la solución política', *El Bolchevique*, Mexico, May 1984.

54. See, for example, Eduardo González, *Cuba under Castro: The Limits of Charisma*, Boston 1974; Victor Nuñes Leal, *Coronelismo: the Municipality and Representative Government in Brazil*, Cambridge 1977.

55. For a highly suggestive critical analysis of the attempts to produce typologies of modern Latin American politics, see Ian Roxborough, 'Unity and Diversity in Latin American History', *Journal of Latin American Studies*, vol. 16, part 1, 1984. For a 'traditional' view of populism, see G. Ionescu and E. Gellner (eds), *Populism*, London 1969. For a 'discourse approach', see E. Laclau, *Politics and Ideology in Marxist Theory*, London 1977.

56. For biographies, see Richard Bourne, *Vargas of Brazil, 1883–1954: Sphinx of the Pampas*, London 1974, and John W.F. Dulles, *Vargas of Brazil. A Political Biography*, Austin 1967.

57. Examples include the Costa Rican 'Olympians' Cleto González and Ricardo Jimenez; Alessandri in Chile; Velasco Ibarra in Ecuador; Belaúnde in Peru; Víctor Paz and Hernán Siles in Bolivia; Perón in Argentina; Pérez in Venezuela.

58. Quoted in J.V.D. Saunders, 'A Revolution of Agreement Among Friends: The End of the Vargas Era', *Hispanic American Historical Review*, vol. XLIV, no. 2, May 1964, p. 204.

59. F. Zenha Machado, *Os ultimos dias do governo de Vargas*, Rio de Janeiro 1955, pp. 81–2.

60. Thomas E. Skidmore, *Politics in Brazil*, New York 1967, p. 142.

61. The text quoted below is from a typewritten statement containing a number of grammatical errors. Vargas could not type and was most punctilious in his use of language. A separate, hand-written and signed note stated, 'To the wrath of my

enemies I leave the legacy of my death. I carry with me the sorrow of not having been able to do for the humble all I desired.' The authority of this note is not questioned. The longer statement may have been dictated, drafted for Vargas or possibly written after his death, although the details of its discovery do not support the idea of a deliberate concoction. This would, of course, detract from the president's own identification with the cult of his personality but not from the cult itself.

62. Quoted in Dulles, *Vargas*, pp. 334–5.

63. For the Chaco, see James Dunkerley, *Orígenes del Poder Militar en Bolivia*, La Paz 1988. For the post-war period, see Herbert S. Klein, *Parties and Politics in Bolivia, 1880–1952*, Cambridge 1969.

64. *El Diario*, 25 April 1939.

65. At a banquet for reserve officers of the Chaco campaign shortly after issuing the decree Busch improvised a speech that, as reported by Augusto Céspedes, captures the Bonapartist at his zenith: 'I have not reached the presidency to serve the capitalists. They have to serve the *Patria* and if they will not do so voluntarily then they will be made to do so by force. I swear to you, Comrades, that I, Germán Busch, will show the Patiños, Aramayos and Hochschilds, all these exploiters of Bolivia, that he is a president who will ensure respect for the *Patria*. This should have been done by my predecessors, very clever men, for sure; but now it is up to me, and I will do it with courage. I cannot defraud you, the officers, the soldiers, the people with whom I fought in the Chaco, the veterans who have returned from the war to make a better nation. If it is necessary to give my life I will give it, happy that my life might be of some use to this poor country. I do not fear death. You know me ...' *El Dictador Suicida*, La Paz 1968, p. 218.

66. Ibid., pp. 222–8.

67. Luis Azurduy, *Busch, El Martir de sus Ideales*, La Paz 1939, pp. 33.

68. Augusto Céspedes, *El Presidente Colgado*, La Paz 1975.

69. For a sympathetic biography that considers the suicide in detail, see Luis Conte Agüero, *Eduardo Chibás, el Adalid de Cuba*, Mexico 1955.

70. '... it was becoming evident that despite his great gifts, his strong mesmeric wireless personality, the streak of irrationality in him was growing with age; he would often fast, he would invite women to lunch with him and appear at five o'clock, he would remain in the bath under water for long periods, his telephoning of friends was frenetic, his speeches had more and more the hysteria of madness as much as of genius.' Thomas, *Cuba*, p. 751.

71. Peter Sloterdijk, *Critique of Cynical Reason*, London 1988.

2

El Salvador, 1930–89

During the first three decades of the twentieth century the economy of El Salvador became the most dynamic in Central America. Unlike the rest of the region, El Salvador had no banana enclave, but the success of its coffee economy was such that the country gained a reputation as 'the Ruhr of Central America'. The efficiency of the coffee sector owed a great deal to the capacity of a new generation of landlords to exploit the comprehensive alienation of communal lands in El Salvador's central zone in the years which had followed the Liberal revolution of 1871. The altitude and fertility of these lands was particularly well suited to the crop, and because El Salvador is by far the smallest Central American state (21,040 square kilometres) while possessing a large population – even in 1930 it was approaching 1.5 million – the density of settlement was extremely high and the opportunities for peasant migration correspondingly low. As a result, large numbers of rural inhabitants were not so much physically displaced as deprived of their status as small freeholders or members of the municipal commune and converted into waged harvest labourers or *colonos* paying labour rent for subsistence plots on the edges of the new coffee *fincas*. Thus the Salvadorean agro-export sector was unique in the isthmus in that it was blessed with a high availability of local labour. Moreover, the remarkably rapid and all-encompassing alienation of common land – the Church, that other traditional target of nineteenth-century liberalism, possessed very little rural property – encouraged an early concentration of commercial estates and propelled the formation of one of the most compact and confident landed oligarchies in the world.[1] The landed oligarchy of El Salvador is often referred to as 'the fourteen families', although in 1930 there existed sixty-five large commercial enterprises and some three hundred and fifty estates of more than 100 hectares, which is large by Salvadorean standards. Four decades later, well into an era in which agrarian reform had elsewhere ceased to be 'subversive' and was included in the mildest of political programmes, the distribution of land was still the most inequitable in Latin America while the economic power of the oligarchy remained concentrated to an impressive degree: twenty-five firms accounted for 84 per cent of all coffee exports and forty-nine families possessed farms of more than 1,000 hectares.[2]

The conversion of El Salvador into an oligarchic state and an agro-export economy based on private property was by no means a smooth process. It depended as much upon the exercise of class and ethnic violence as it did upon the entrepreneurial zeal and political confidence so celebrated in the opening years of the new century. Indeed, it was in El Salvador that Liberalism had first been challenged by Indian resistance in the aftermath of Central American independence; in 1833 the popular uprising led by Anastasio Aquino had required the deployment of troops from outside the province and widespread repression before social order was restored and the *ladino* state secured. In the 1870s and 1880s the expropriation of common land provoked a series of local revolts, residual violence being higher than that attending similar measures in the rest of the region. This conflict prompted the formation of a powerful army that simultaneously provided some protection against Guatemala, with which relations were always strained, and supported the regional designs of Liberalism, for which El Salvador had long been a spiritual home. Internal and external dependence upon armed force sustained for a while a political culture based upon the coup d'état, yet if the Salvadorean landlords lagged behind those of Costa Rica in subduing upstart army officers and introducing government by civilian grandees, they were not far behind. Within a decade of its establishment by coercive means, the Liberal state was provided with a comprehensive legal apparatus; and by the turn of the century, political life had been freed from both military intervention and the instability this cultivated. The economic resource and political confidence of landed capital was fully manifested in the monopoly over office held by the Melendez and Quiñonez families, who passed the presidency calmly between each other through formal elections and in a manner comparable to that of the Costa Rican 'Olympians'.

So assured was this regime that even after the Mexican revolution, towards which it displayed a notably unflustered attitude, the oligarchy was prepared to sanction a degree of popular organization, in the towns, at least, albeit of a severely supervised nature. In the 1920s artisanal guilds were permitted to operate, legislation was introduced to regulate the conditions of urban workers, and reformist opponents of the Liberal order were allowed to compete for office. When the boom years of the 1920s were brought to an abrupt end, however, the Salvadorean oligarchic regime was revealed not as a stable and organic means of social control capable of mutating into 'tradition' but as an extraordinarily fragile construction which had been built upon the exceptional performance of the agricultural economy, the termination of which it was unable to survive.

The distinctiveness of the Salvadorean agricultural system, in contrast to that of Costa Rica, for example, lay in the absence of a buoyant class of medium-sized farmers and the abundance of land-poor harvest workers. The dominance of the *finqueros* was based less on their indirect control of an internal market in coffee than on the direct control they exercised over land and production. This system may also be contrasted with that in Guatemala insofar as labour control in El Salvador depended much less upon moving large numbers of temporary Indian labourers to the plantations from separate zones of peasant settlement and subsistence agriculture, than upon supervision of workers living on or near to *fincas* where they were employed, either for the harvest or throughout the year. On the one hand, the weakness of what might be termed a 'middle peasantry' made landlord domination less the product of a negotiated hegemony than that of direct and emphatic control. On the other hand, both the relatively low importance attached to the 'Indian question' – by 1930 indigenous culture in El Salvador was limited to the regions around Izalco and Santiago Nonualco – and the marginal need for extensive coercive mechanisms to ensure a supply of labour reduced the tendency of the state towards centralism and authoritarianism. After the subjugation of the conflict that attended the first phase of appropriation, the role of the army in maintaining order was increasingly replaced by para-military forces – particularly the National Guard (Guardia Nacional) established in 1912 – which were often based near major farms and were more directly answerable to individual landowners than was the regular military.

This rural regime was marked by neither flexibility nor a philanthropy beyond that normally associated with an omnipotent but prescient *patrón*; wages and conditions on Salvadorean estates were among the poorest in the region and contributed towards the relative efficiency of the export economy. However, the maintenance of a coherent system of political control at the level of the state depended not only upon stable terms of competition within a very small capitalist class but also upon the restriction of social contradictions to the locus of the *finca*. By 1930 it was evident that this second condition no longer obtained as a peasantry in particularly onerous circumstances, even by Central American standards, began to manifest a widespread discontent. The Liberal order, already losing momentum, entered a period of crisis, and late in 1931 the landlord class withdrew from government, accepting the claims of the military to direct control of the polity. At the same time, the structure of the coffee economy ensured that the oligarchy continued to exercise the social power of a formidable ruling class, including that of veto over the economic policy of regimes which remained in the hands of the army, with one short break, from 1932 to 1982. Nowhere else in the isthmus was such a division of power so clear and systematized, or so much in contrast with the pattern of politics up to the 1930s. One of its characteristics – evident from the late 1970s as much as in the early 1930s – was a marked incidence of conflict within the dominant bloc in times of social crisis when the concession of political power by the landed bourgeoisie to the military could no longer be guaranteed to support their economic interests.

The origins of this singular division of power may be located in the turbulent weeks between November 1931 and February 1932, when the failure of a reformist Liberal administration to contain popular discontent caused by the collapse of the economy in the world depression led to a military coup and then, at the end of January 1932, to insurrections in both San Salvador and the western regions of the country. The suppression of these rebellions was of such ferocity that what became known as La Matanza could be described as the single most decisive event in the history of Central America until the overthrow of Somoza in Nicaragua in July 1979. It traumatized both the peasantry and the oligarchy, laying the basis for a fifty-year regime that, notwithstanding prolonged periods of general tranquillity, drew its underlying strength from the memory, both real and cultivated, of the violence of 1932 and the fear that it might recur. When this fear was realized in the civil war of the 1980s, some of the vestiges of 1932 were still plainly visible in the low level of armed conflict in those areas where the revolt had taken place, as well as in the extreme reluctance of the landlords to accept a civilian regime pledged to reform and strongly sponsored by Washington in preference to proponents of open militarism and unabashed conservatism.

In 1930 the Salvadorean economy was more narrowly based on coffee than any other in the region. During the 1920s high prices had prompted both an extension of the agricultural frontier close to its limits – 90 per cent of land under coffee in 1960 was under coffee in 1930 – and concentration on a single crop that was considered risky by more than cultivators of sugar, *henequen* and cotton. The fall in the price of coffee – from 25 cents a pound in 1925 to 9 cents in 1935 -- as a result of the world depression had, therefore, a catastrophic effect and generated wider and more directly politicized social conflict than that witnessed elsewhere in Central America. Income from exports in 1932 was less than half of that in 1926, the average annual growth rate for 1930–34 was −0.7 per cent, and by 1939, after several years of gradual recovery, GDP per capita was still below that of 1929. Although there is evidence that the *cafetaleros* (commercial coffee farmers) held back from collecting the harvest of 1930, the most logical response to the crisis was to maximize the volume of exports, cutting wages to the increased harvest labour force required by expanded production. Thus, despite lay-offs of permanent workers, some extension of plantation lands, the calling-in of debts and tightening of terms of tenantry, the principal economic cause of popular unrest in the countryside appears to have been the sharp reduction in pay, which was cut from 75 to 15 centavos per day in two years. This measure provoked a series of rural strikes in 1931, markedly increasing political tension and providing growing support for the Federación Regional de Trabajadores de El Salvador (FRTS), which had been established in 1924 but which from 1930 was sharpening its activity under the direction of the newly formed Partido Comunista de El Salvador (PCS) led by the veteran agitator Agustín Farabundo Martí. The party itself, however, was very much less popular than the Partido Laborista (PL) recently founded by Arturo Araujo, a maverick member of the ruling class whose adoption of a vague but robust reformism had enabled him to win the presidency in 1931 despite profound oligarchic misgivings as to the outcome of an open poll. The greater advance of trade-union organization in El Salvador than elsewhere in the region during the 1920s had already obliged the Liberal governments to engage in some pre-emptive populist activity, but Araujo took this tendency to its limit in economic circumstances which precluded the possibility of both meeting popular expectations and safeguarding the interests of the landlords. Hence, although the president retained a strong personal following, his government soon lost its sense of direction and authority in the face of strikes and demonstrations, while the military began to manifest unfamiliar signs of disquiet and the oligarchy chafed under its failure to secure a devaluation of the currency. When, in December 1931, the army finally rebelled, principally because it had not been paid for months, few were surprised. Only Araujo loyalists were completely dismayed because even the PCS, which had strenuously opposed the government, did not believe that the coup presaged any major change in the political system as a whole. This view soon proved to be gravely mistaken when the new head of state, Araujo's minister of war, General Maximiliano Hernández Martínez, withdrew his promise to hold elections in January 1932 after the voting lists had been drawn up and campaigning was well advanced. One persuasive interpretation of Martínez's timing in this manoeuvre was that it enabled the army to identify supporters of the PL and PCS, drawing them into the open before embarking upon their repression. In all events, the cancellation of the poll gave the proponents of insurrection within the PCS support for a hastily planned and several times postponed urban revolt. It also drove the leadership of the peasantry around Ahuachapán and Izalco towards a rebellion that had some links with the PCS but was at root an independent movement in pursuit of both immediate economic amelioration and a more deeply seated defence of the region's embattled communal culture.[3]

The urban uprising of 22 January 1932 was suppressed within a matter of hours because news of its preparation had already reached the high command; isolated mutinies by radical conscripts had already been contained and several important communists, including Farabundo Martí, detained some days previously. The subsequent campaign of persecution in San Salvador was extended to supporters of Araujo and members of artisanal guilds who often had nothing to do with the rebellion. The adoption of a policy of summary execution of known opposition elements and extensive incarceration of suspects effectively decapitated the radical movement – Farabundo Martí was shot after a brief court martial – and was emphatic enough to eradicate all vestige of independent popular organization for a dozen years and to hamper its progress for a further two decades thereafter. In the west of the country – there was no fighting in the east – the jacquerie led by Indian *caciques* managed a somewhat less fleeting existence in that it exercised control over a number of small settlements for up to forty-eight hours. It was, nonetheless, directed without strategic ambition and in the traditional mode of peasant revolts, devoid of the 'Bolshevik' characteristics often ascribed to it, manifesting a notable reluctance to damage religious property, and generally preoccupied with imposing justice on individual representatives of the state and the landlord class in a brief flurry of disorganized and almost carnival repudiation of the regime of the *cafetaleros*. The level of violence inflicted by rebel forces almost entirely bereft of firearms was, however, quite low; fewer than fifty people died at their hands.

Apprehension over the consequences of both the economic collapse and the cancellation of elections had prompted the US and British governments to dispatch warships to Salvadorean waters. Some Canadian marines were briefly disembarked. But this outside force was rapidly ordered to retire following Martínez's insistence that the army and civilian vigilantes had the revolt under control within two days. In the light of subsequent developments, this proved to be something of an understatement because the retreat of the rebels began on the first full day after their insurrection and was rapidly converted into a rout as the troops and 'fraternities' of irregulars organized by landowners exacted an awesome revenge for the challenge to a social order based not only on the coffee *finca* but also on a belligerently *ladino* republic. Given the summary and extensive nature of this repression, it is not surprising that assessment of its human cost has become the subject of rather macabre debate; but if the figure of 40,000 deaths presented by the opposition movement of the 1980s is often deemed too high, it is evident that the razing of villages and liquidation of many of their inhabitants throughout February 1932 produced a death toll that may reliably be said to be in the tens of thousands. The impact of such attrition was no less cultural than political; it threw the peasant *cofradías* (socio-religious brotherhoods) into confusion and effectively suppressed the wearing of Indian clothes, which was now considered by the rural population to be a provocative act of cultural resistance – and rightly so since although the revolt was denounced as communist by the regime, for many local *ladinos* it was a revolt of primitive *naturales* against whom a genocidal solution was not beyond the realm of reason.

Although much of the violence of the spring of 1932 was undertaken by civilian vigilantes – the forebears of the death-squads of the 1970s – its political outcome was the confirmation of the army's claim to office; and because the army remained a backward, garrison-based force lacking an institutional system for political decision-making, power stayed firmly in the hands of its commander, Martínez, who consolidated a regime of pronounced personalism. The decisiveness of the general's direction of operations enabled him to impose a number of limited constraints upon the oligarchy. He readily accepted its demands for a devaluation and weathered the difficulties of suspending the external debt within weeks of coming to power, but he later cut interest rates, established a central bank and withdrew rights of issue from private institutions, imposed exchange controls and provided for state participation in a credit bank. None of these measures severely prejudiced entrepreneurial interests, but some restricted short-term profitability and laid the basis for a modest state intervention in the economy, albeit usually in close collaboration with the powerful corporate associations of the bourgeoisie such as the Asociación del Café, which was transformed in 1942 into the Compañia Salvadoreña del Café and subsequently remained little less than a parallel economic cabinet through its control of the coffee market. By the end of the 1930s this process of modest qualification to a completely free-market model had proved to be sufficiently advantageous to the landlords and their commercial partners that they tolerated Martínez's introduction of some protectionist measures on behalf of an artisanate bereft of corporate representation and still in need of tariffs to assist recovery from the effects of the depression. There was nothing particularly adventurous in such initiatives – the exceptional economic conditions of the 1930s drew similar measures from equally conservative regimes in the region – and they never reached the point at which the landowners' control of economic policy, through the relevant cabinet portfolios, or its capacity for non-compliance, through its representative bodies, came under serious challenge. (Indeed, this did not occur until the tabling of a bill for agrarian reform in 1976.) There was no further agitation over the exchange rate, which was maintained at its 1935 level of 2.5 colones to the dollar for more than fifty years.

Martínez ruled El Salvador for more than twelve years (1932–44) in a style broadly comparable to that of his peers in the neighbouring states, through a cycle of unopposed re-elections and with the retention of no more than a veneer of democratic procedures. It should, however, be noted that over time this became a formality of some consequence insofar as the Salvadorean military, unlike their counterparts in many South American countries, never fully jettisoned the protocols of the Liberal constitutional system. Under Martínez the survival of this political form was both ensured and yet evacuated of substance by a narrow concentration of personal power combined with a no less marked eccentricity of character that was later lampooned for its ostentatious mysticism -- the president was an ardent advocate of theosophy and did not lack confidence in his ability to tap super-natural powers – but which also served to create an aura of unpredict-ability and distinctiveness around the person of a *caudillo* who could by no means be considered a mere cipher of the oligarchy. The predict-ability of his electoral successes sometimes provoked ill-fated stabs at revolt by disgruntled senior officers, but even before Washington reversed its refusal to recognize de facto regimes in 1936, Martínez's position was extremely secure. Thereafter it appeared little less than unassailable until the final stages of the Second World War. By this time the enforced expansion of trade with the United States had compensated for the very low level of direct US investment and bestowed upon Washington an unprecedented degree of influence in El Salvador, albeit more circumscribed than in any other Central American state except Costa Rica. This influence was employed to reinstate a modicum of popular participation in the political process without at the same time undermining the landlords or threatening the army. Such an objective in the mid 1940s (as in the 1970s), pursued by Roosevelt by means short of direct intervention, was exceptionally difficult – arguably impossible – to achieve, but it nonetheless greatly debilitated a dictatorship which had declared war on the Axis on the basis of geographical necessity rather than ideological repudiation and increasingly at odds with the democratic sentiments of the 'Four Freedoms' propounded by the Allies.

57

By the time Martínez's authority appeared to be slipping in 1943 – a year in which, on the one hand, a tax on coffee exports agitated the *finqueros*, and, on the other, the railway-workers managed to revive their union – his dalliance with the Fascist powers in the late 1930s had become but a minor feature of growing discontent with a longstanding and narrow autocracy, most forcefully expressed in the middle class, which had been hit particularly hard by the sharp rise in consumer prices induced by the war. By Central American standards the urban middle sector in San Salvador was large and, despite a dozen years of obligatory absence from public life, not lacking in political traditions. Moreover, agitation over the corruption and bureaucratic inefficiency stemming from the favouritism inherent in Martínez's personalist regime found a strong echo in the ranks of the army, where many officers felt threatened by the president's growing patronage of the paramilitary forces, which were commanded by regular officers but not answerable to the minister of war. When, early in 1944, the inflexible *caudillo* instructed a compliant congress to amend the constitution to allow him yet a further term in office, he succeeded in maximizing antipathy towards his government. In April a section of the officer corps staged a revolt that was subdued only with difficulty by the National Guard and the execution by firing squad of the ringleaders, none of whom could be described as radical. Such a move, unprecedented in the history of the modern Salvadorean army, increased hostility between the various security forces, and outraged not only the victims' colleagues but also the urban populace at large. The students and doctors of the capital declared a civic strike, which did not last long but engendered enough support to persuade the president that he could no longer rely upon the army, Washington or popular acquiescence. However, both the cautious approach of the US embassy, which refused to support either side, and the desire of a majority of officers for a conservative and institutional succession restricted the immediate outcome of the anti-dictatorial movement to Martínez's replacement by a trusted colleague, General Andrés Ignacio Menéndez.

The strike of April 1944 was staged in support of the military dissidents and against Martínez rather than the ruling class as a whole; there was no significant movement in the countryside, and the working class played only a subordinate role. Although this was the first of a series of popular anti-dictatorial mobilizations in Central America during 1944 and opened a short but active period of political competition, there was no instant upsurge in radical activity once Martínez had gone and Menéndez had announced new elections for the autumn. The initially cautious mood appeared to confirm expectations of a restitution of the system that had obtained up to 1931. However, the accumulating impetus of the candidacy of Dr Arturo Romero, who gained the endorsement of the communist-backed and rapidly expanding Unión Nacional de Trabajadores (UNT) despite his espousal of a programme less radical than that of Arturo Araujo's Partido Laborista, raised fears inside both the military and the oligarchy of uncontainable mobilization following an almost certain victory for Romero at the polls. Such apprehension was deepened by the removal of General Ubico in Guatemala in June and the popularly backed military coup of October. Thus, when a large crowd gathered in the central plaza of San Salvador on 21 October 1944 precisely to celebrate the Guatemalan revolution, Menéndez finally bowed to the pressure from his colleagues and permitted a pre-emptive coup by Colonel Osmín Aguirre, one of the leaders of the repression in 1932. The resulting massacre in the city centre within six months of Martínez's departure not only marked a return to the methods of the ex-president but also underscored the extreme vulnerability of any effort to sustain a civilian political system without the unambiguous imprimatur of the army. Attempts to stage a second general strike and then to invade the country from Guatemala were suppressed without quarter even, as in the case of the ill-organized student invasion, when the opposition was middle class and far from extremist. Aguirre's coup imposed unity on the military apparatus and ensured that no civilian candidate stood in the elections of January 1945, the 'overwhelming majority' of votes being cast in a manner quite distinct from that envisaged by the United Nations, for an old ally of Martínez, General Salvador Castañeda Castro, heading the aptly named Partido Agrario (PA).

Castañeda presided over a four-year holding operation during which time the Cold War set in and the international conditions for a return to democracy deteriorated under the weight of a pervasive anti-communism. The same period also witnessed a steady economic recovery as coffee prices were freed from war-time agreements, opening possibilities of agricultural diversification and encouraging ideas of some industrial development. This encouraged a degree of differentiation within a capitalist class which, although exceptionally tight, was not fully integrated and had always incubated some tension between landlords and merchants. Competition rarely went much beyond sectoral tussles over positions in the markets, but within such a compact community it had enough resonance to disturb unity over the prospect of a simple retreat to the restrictions of the Martínez years. This was politically reassuring yet also out of keeping with the new phase of economic growth. Moreover, many junior officers who had supported the coup of April 1944 considered that of October, with its personalism and rejection of an institutional system of apportioning office and regulating policy, to have defrauded them. Hence, when Castañeda endeavoured in 1948 to prolong his lacklustre regime, he was overthrown in what became known as 'the majors' coup', which marked both a consolidation of the military around the objectives of the 1944 revolt and a clear shift towards modernizing the style of control. A regime of complete political prohibition and economic conservatism moved towards one that promoted an increased level of state intervention in the economy, tolerated a number of closely watched-over urban unions and civic associations, accepted some political competition within the middle class as well as the oligarchy, and gave a degree of support to those elements of capital seeking to invest in new sectors of agriculture, particularly cotton, and the manufacturing industry. The principal figure in this movement was Colonel Oscar Osorio, who manoeuvred diligently and forcefully to establish the Partido Revolucionario de Unificación Democrática (PRUD) in 1949 as the military-sponsored official party of government that would in 1961 mutate with little change beyond that of title into the Partido de Conciliación Nacional (PCN), which ruled until 1979.

The junta that held power until 1950 was young, middle-class and technocratic, initially attracting widespread sympathy for the military in what was seen as a reprise of April 1944. But the *apertura* that many expected was never granted. Anti-communism remained resolutely at the centre of a system that replaced Martínez's narrow autocracy with a more dynamic style of domination predicated upon the belief – as expressed by Colonel José María Lemus – that 'the only truly efficient way to achieve [social and economic] equilibrium and avoid the evils of dangerous doctrines is to promote broad transformative doctrines within the framework of co-operation between government, the capitalists and the workers'.[4] *Transformismo* was a much-used term in Central America at this time, yet although the constitution of 1950 included stipulations in favour of agrarian reform and the 'social function' of all property, the Salvadorean officers desisted from implementing the former in the countryside and implemented the latter only with great caution in the towns. The new regime could be described as anti-oligarchic only insofar as it confirmed Martínez's exclusion of civilians from political power and adjusted the terms of that exclusion to incorporate some statist and developmentalist currents. This fully assuaged Washington, while absolute prohibition of popular organization in the countryside and tight control of the urban unions through both co-optation and direct coercion ensured that, for the mass of citizens, the system was only marginally different from its predecessors.

The governments of Oscar Osorio (1950–56) and José María Lemus (1956–60) consolidated military power in a period of generally buoyant coffee prices, agricultural diversification and some modest growth in manufacturing. The election of 1956 was, as usual, contested by parties of the civilian right, but the PRUD received 93 per cent of the votes once a reshuffle in military appointments had ensured full institutional support for the official candidate. Such a reassuring result enabled Lemus to start his period in office with great confidence and to relax some of the controls imposed by Osorio. However, towards the end of the decade coffee prices began to fall and the example of the Cuban revolution excited the enthusiasm of the students, who subjected the government to increasingly vociferous opposition through their union, and the newly established reformist party named after the movement of 1944, the Partido Revolucionario de Abril y Mayo (PRAM). At first Lemus attempted to field this challenge with some flexibility since the alliance built around the PRAM won the mayoralty of the capital and five other towns in the spring 1960 elections. Nevertheless, government refusal to permit any opposition victories in the congressional polls only encouraged their campaign to the point at which, in August 1960, Lemus declared martial law and sent the army into the university. These measures, and the vigorous clampdown that ensued, signalled a refusal to accept a genuinely independent and active opposition. Although communist influence and the economic slump certainly caused consternation within the officer corps, there was a lack of unanimity over the wisdom of restricting political participation so tightly. Hence, when a section of the army overthrew the now highly unpopular president in October 1960 and established a junta with civilian technocrats and sympathizers of democratic reform, there was apprehension but no immediate resistance from more conservative elements. Yet, once it became clear that the junta would permit the left to stand in new elections, this caution was rapidly reversed and the counter-coup led by Colonel Julio Rivera in January 1961 received majority military support for its restitution of institutional government. Just as in 1944, when open elections and civilian government emerged as a tangible possibility, political concessions by the military were soon curtailed. However, Lemus's precipitate prohibition of all authentic opposition not from the right was henceforth adjusted by the newly formed PCN to permit some congressional and municipal representation as a form of safety-valve and to refurbish the image of the regime within the Alliance for Progress. The Partido Demócrata Cristiano (PDC), established in 1960, was permitted to win fourteen congressional seats against the PCN's thirty-two in 1964, and in 1966 one of the party's young leaders, José Napoleón Duarte, was allowed to take the mayoralty of San Salvador, which he soon converted into a platform for the PDC's policy of social rapprochement and measured reform.[5] On the other hand, the Partido de Acción Renovadora (PAR), which had had a tenuous existence since the late 1940s to be revived under a new leadership in the early 1960s, was banned in 1967, having won 29 per cent of the vote on the basis of a much more extensive programme of reforms. Its effective successor, the Movimiento Nacional Revolucionario (MNR), led by Guillermo Manuel Ungo, was allowed to contest the poll of 1968 on a social-democratic platform that included the call for an agrarian reform – not a leading item on the PDC agenda – but it lacked great popular appeal and failed to win any seats in 1970, which may well have guaranteed its continued existence.

The presence of an opposition was integral to the PCN regime, which continued to exploit its control over elections to maintain a 'continuist' system of government under the presidencies of Colonels Julio Rivera (1961–67), Fidel Sánchez Hernández (1967–72), Arturo Molina (1972–77) and General Carlos Humberto Romero (1977–79). Although the more devout and philanthropic aspects of Catholic social policy promulgated by the PDC, or demands for redistribution emanating from the social democrats, were at times unsettling and threatened to attract considerable support, their mere existence served to sustain the appearance of democracy and kept the system from being a full-fledged dictatorship, even though it was guaranteed by the regular army at elections and more generally upheld by the paramilitary forces. From the end of the 1960s these were assisted by a powerful, semi-official organization known as ORDEN, which functioned principally as a vigilante force in the countryside. In contrast to previous bodies of this type, ORDEN was designed to have a mass membership, and many who joined it were less attracted by its reactionary ideology than by the possibility of minor official favours or often simply the need to protect themselves against persecution, usually at the hands of the National Guard, which firmly suppressed dissident activity and ensured the prohibition of independent rural unions.

In the 1960s, rural unions often originated from the co-operatives and communal associations sponsored by the Church, posing little ostensible threat to the established order until rising violence and support for the 'preferential option for the poor' in the pastoral work and theological convictions of many rural priests engendered potent currents that acquired organizational autonomy in the 1970s.[6] Radical Catholicism was perhaps stronger in El Salvador than elsewhere in Central America, and it matched the influence of the secular left in politicizing rural labour and the students, if not the urban working class. By the mid 1970s this was plainly depleting the rank-and-file support built up by the PDC, but it did not deprive the party of large numbers of tactical votes in elections where the left either could not or would not stand. The strength of the movement was nowhere more clearly signalled than in the positions adopted at the end of the decade by Archbishop Oscar Arnulfo Romero, a cleric of hitherto conservative persuasion who, on the basis of his forceful condemnation of violence, was considered by the military and the right to be a major hindrance and, with somewhat less justification, an active supporter of the left. The shock caused by Romero's volte-face paralleled that generated by the scale of rural organization, which, because it remained largely outside the pattern of formal national politics, diffuse, and almost by definition absorbed with local tactics, was not for a long time perceived by the military as posing a markedly greater threat than the tame co-optational entities out of which it grew. As a consequence, efforts to establish an agrarian reform against landlord opposition were pursued with minimal energy and the demands of the centrist opposition for a strategic resolution to the rural question generally dismissed as demagogy. When, however, it was recognized that an authentic challenge existed in the countryside, the political instincts of the armed forces were permitted to run free in a repressive campaign that frequently compounded rather than cowed opposition.

In the towns, particularly San Salvador, the marked growth of manufacturing and regional trade in the 1960s prompted by the Central American Common Market (CACM) provided some space for trade-union expansion. Moreover, although the number of organized workers remained very low and many of these were enrolled in federations controlled by government supporters, independent action such as the general strike of 1967 reflected an erratic trend towards militancy and away from the mutualist traditions of the artisanate.[7] That this was still vulnerable to co-optation as well as coercion may be seen in the wide support for the government's invasion of Honduras in the 'Soccer War' of 1969, when nationalist fervour captured the PDC, which enjoyed appreciable support among workers, and elicited minimal opposition from the Communist Party (PCS), which was the major leftist force inside the unions.

This conflict had little to do with clashes during various football matches in the first round of the World Cup, and was aggravated less by border disputes than by El Salvador's considerable commercial superiority over Honduras and the large number of Salvadorean migrant workers in that country. The imbalance in trade resulted from Salvadorean exploitation of its already existing advantages under the more favourable commercial climate given by the CACM, but emigration from densely populated and intensively farmed El Salvador had provided its oligarchy with a valuable safety-valve for many years. More than half a million people had left the country since 1930, the majority to Honduras. This population provided a ready target for the embattled Honduran regime of Colonel Osvaldo López Arellano, which sought both to resist Salvadorean economic hegemony and to reduce popular opposition by appropriating the lands of Salvadorean settlers for redistribution. At least 100,000 migrants were driven back to their homeland, and this produced long-term problems that far outweighed the short-term political gain of a momentary boost to Salvadorean nationalism. Many of these refugees had trade-union experience from working the Honduran banana plantations, and most necessarily sought to re-establish their lives in the capital since the prospects for rural labour were now far worse than when they had left the country. The size of the influx was in itself a problem, but many of the refugees were less inclined to be grateful for their deliverance than discontented by the absence of opportunities that attended it, which was also a factor of some consequence. The capacity of the urban economy to absorb more labour was already exhausted, and the war effectively ended the CACM. More immediately the regime's resettlement programme provided little or no relief.

Thus, not only was a strategic outflow of poor Salvadorean workers brought to an abrupt halt by the war with Honduras, but a large number of displaced and dispossessed people were added to the expanding population of the shanty-towns around the capital, accelerating an already visible process of 'marginalization'. Between 1950 and 1980 the country's urban population grew from 18 per cent to 44 per cent of the total – an average increase by regional standards – and that of the city of San Salvador from 116,000 to 700,000 – this, too, by no means exceptional in Central America. However, by the mid 1970s the department of San Salvador, containing more than a fifth of the national population, had a population density of 843 per square kilometre against a national average of 170, itself five times the Central American average. Thus, although the social conflict of the 1970s and 1980s could not be explained plausibly just by population density, which had been high for centuries, it was the case that this phenomenon was reaching chronic proportions and creating in the political centre of the country conditions of settlement that both exacerbated the economic difficulties of the mass of the people and promoted extra-occupational patterns of unrest and organization. As with the rapid expansion of the student population – by 1974 more than 30,000 were enrolled in the Faculty of Humanities alone – a major new political constituency came into being and unsettled the familiar socio-political balance between town and country.

The war with Honduras generated a crisis within the PCS, which was seen by many radicalized youth as incapable of providing a decisive challenge to the regime. Continued devotion to the 'peaceful road to socialism' through elections and cautious work in the unions were in keeping with Moscow's advice – increasingly harmonious with that issuing from Havana – and the organizational instincts of a party that had been all but destroyed by the adoption of an insurrectionary strategy within two years of its birth. Critical of this approach and of the 'idealist' belief that democracy could be obtained with the support of a 'national bourgeoisie' of anti-oligarchic entrepreneurs, the secretary-general, Salvador Cayetano Carpio, together with several

important union and student leaders, left the party to establish a
'politico-military organization', the Fuerzas Populares de Liberación –
Farabundo Martí (FPL), in 1971. This guerrilla organization did not
begin operations immediately, because it rejected the *foco* theory
derived from the Cuban example as well as notions of rapid insurrection in favour of a strategy of 'prolonged people's war' on the
Vietnamese model. In 1972 a more middle-class and adventurous
group of disenchanted PDC supporters broke from legal politics to set
up the Ejército Revolucionario del Pueblo (ERP) on the basis of a more
militarist *foquismo*. Internal disputes over the validity of this model of an
elite vanguard bringing the masses to revolutionary consciousness
through example more than organizational collaboration reached a
bloody apogee in the execution by the ERP leadership of the distinguished writer Roque Dalton in 1975. Supporters of Dalton's criticisms
of the ERP subsequently formed the third major guerrilla force, the
Fuerzas Armadas de Resistencia Nacional (FARN) on more cautious
political and military lines. The relatively late emergence of these
groups in El Salvador compared with the rest of Central America may
be attributed in large part to the fact that although there appeared to
be some prospects for democratic progress in the 1960s, these were
progressively reduced over the following decade as the PCN prevented
the reformist opposition from obtaining office despite, or more
probably because of, their growing popular support.

Since the principal mechanism for this containment continued to be
government manipulation of the polls – particularly flagrant in those
for the presidency in 1972 and 1977 – the pattern of polarization
tended to follow the electoral calendar, popular discontent at scarcely
credible opposition defeats provoking significant breakdowns in public
order as well as accumulating a more general disenchantment with the
political system as a whole. Although the parties of reform might be
criticized for a misguided belief in their ability to take office or cajole
the regime into introducing progressive change, they acted with
appreciable skill in seeking to exploit the opportunities available to
them. By forming the Unión Nacional Opositora (UNO), the PDC,
MNR and the Unión Democrática Nacionalista (UDN) – effectively a
front for the outlawed PCS – not only suppressed what were little more
than tactical and confessional differences between themselves but also
presented the government with an impressive challenge behind the
candidacy of the able Duarte, supported by the less colourful but more

intellectual Ungo. Indeed, so high were expectations of a UNO victory in 1972 that when Colonel Molina was finally declared the winner by less than 10,000 votes after a suspiciously abrupt suspension of public information on the count, a section of the officer corps was prompted to stage a coup. Although the rebels refused to distribute arms to civilians, they were defeated only after troops from neighbouring states organized in the Central American Defence Council (Consejo de Defensa Centroamericana, CONDECA) were flown in to assist the disorganized loyalist forces and the ever-faithful paramilitary police. Duarte had hesitated to support the rising and held back UNO followers from staging their own street protests, but he was deemed too threatening an opponent to be afforded further guarantees and was arrested, severely beaten and exiled to Venezuela. The treatment administered to one of the most talented leaders of Latin American Christian Democracy enhanced his profile abroad and greatly increased his popularity at home.

The Molina regime, though shaken by the events of 1972, did not thereafter impose markedly tighter control than had its predecessor. It even reduced pressure on the formal opposition in an effort to maintain its participation in the system. This temporary relaxation was most evident in the regime's preparedness to acquiesce in opposition control of some congressional committees. Although this was won more by tactical skill than official concession, such acquiescence enabled the presentation in 1976 of a bill for limited agrarian reform which the government did not immediately block. However, the oligarchy staged a resolute resistance through its principal pressure groups – the Asociación Nacional de Empresas Privadas (ANEP) and the Frente de Agricultores de la Región Oriental (FARO) – thwarting the proposed legislation and signalling to the high command that the limits of concession had been exceeded. This stance was brutally supplemented by the growing activity of right-wing vigilante groups (death-squads) such as FALANGE and the Unión Guerrera Blanca (UGB), which undertook selective assassinations and established a pattern of repression that was henceforth to be a sadly persistent feature of Salvadorean life.

Both the ground yielded to the opposition and the Molina regime's own disposition to countenance some form of reform in the rural sector drove the military farther to the right. The PCN candidate for the 1977 poll, General Romero, was an extreme conservative. In an effort to protect its candidate against a reprise of the events of 1972, UNO put forward a retired officer, Colonel Ernesto Claramount, who represented a minority liberal current within the military. This forced the hierarchy to carry out a frantic reorganization of army commands in order to assure support for an official candidate more resolute in his convictions than skilled in defending them. However, the scale and clumsiness of the machinations employed to return Romero both before and during the poll provoked the occupation of the capital's centre by his opponent's followers, widespread street violence and a short-lived general strike. Although the guerrillas were responsible for some of this activity, much of it stemmed from popular organizations and trade unions whose members had voted for UNO but were inclining to direct action in pursuit of both economic and political objectives. The post-electoral repression of 1977 assisted the growth of this tendency because President Romero, unlike his predecessor, maintained and increased coercive control, courting a rupture with the Carter administration as official government forces, ORDEN and the death-squads embarked upon a violent campaign against both the orthodox left and the Catholic radicals, which had already begun to construct broad-based popular organizations, fronts or 'blocs' around the much smaller guerrilla groups: the Bloque Popular Revolucionario (BPR) (1975) for the FPL; the Ligas Populares – 28 de Febrero (LP–28) (1977) for the ERP; and the Frente de Acción Popular Unificada (FAPU) (1974) for the FARN.[8] These bodies were still in fierce dispute over political and military strategy and unable to stage more than small-scale operations, usually against individuals connected with the oligarchy or military. But in the wake of UNO's manifest failure to secure reform through constitutionalism, the extension of the left's influence and growing acceptance of armed struggle were not without a certain logic. This, combined with continued sectarian divisions, gave rise to a string of organizations which were to compete for popular support until, with the country standing on the verge of civil war early in 1980, they were forced into unification.

It is certainly true that the final collapse of the PCN regime as a result of the coup of 15 October 1979 was influenced by developments at a regional level, particularly the Nicaraguan revolution of July but also the poor and deteriorating relations between the Romero regime and Washington as a result of Romero's suspension of constitutional guarantees and reluctance to halt escalating violence by the military and its informal allies, who were not afraid to promise the liquidation of the country's entire Jesuit order unless its members left. However, the momentum of domestic conflict had reached such a point by mid 1979 that a major political crisis appeared inevitable in any event. The acquiescence of the United States in a change of regime merely facilitated a relatively bloodless and essentially pre-emptive coup initiated by reformist junior officers but soon captured by less ambitious conservative rivals to Romero anxious to meet the accumulating radical challenge with both a more resourceful strategy and badly needed US economic and logistical support. Romero had been obliged to lift his state of siege earlier in the year, yet this proved insufficient to stem the tide of strikes, demonstrations and guerrilla operations; both the suspension of the constitution and its restitution in unaltered circumstances confirmed the exhaustion of the PCN strategy of combining repression with formal liberties. Neither was adequate by itself, and when organized separately they simply cancelled each other out. An essentially tactical arrangement had decomposed into confusion whereby the populace was aggrieved at the absence of proclaimed freedoms and insufficiently cowed by the violence. The younger officers behind the October coup generally associated with Colonel Majano sought to provide space for negotiation (although, unlike their forebears in 1944 and 1961, they held back from promising immediate elections). In this they enjoyed the tacit support of Washington, still shocked by the overthrow of Somoza and concerned to avert open military rule. Nonetheless, the reformists remained a minority inside the army and enjoyed even less support in the powerful paramilitary forces; and since the radical left refused to halt popular mobilization or abdicate armed activity – only a truce was agreed – on the basis of changes in the military hierarchy, conservative officers were able to harness the logic of maintaining public order to their rapidly organized campaign to sabotage economic concessions. For both internal and external reasons it proved impossible to resolve these tensions inside the dominant bloc with any speed. As a result, although the reformists progressively lost authority, political conflict within the military and ruling class endured long after El Salvador had entered a low-level but prolonged and very brutal civil war in which the military and oligarchy were ranged against a popular bloc composed of the majority of the erstwhile legal opposition and the organizations of the radical left.

In economic terms the outbreak of major social conflict in El Salvador in 1979 was perhaps more predictable than even the Nicaraguan revolution; the steady increase in production and agro-exports during the post-war period had been matched by a no less impressive tendency to reduce access to land for subsistence, prompting increased unemployment and underemployment and a regressive distribution of income in the countryside more pronounced than in the rest of Central America and certainly beyond hope of significant alleviation from growth in the urban economy. Between 1950 and 1980, GDP grew from $379.6 million to $1,526 million at an annual average rate of 5.2 per cent while the population expanded at 3.3 per cent. The increase in GDP per capita from $185 to $289 over this period appeared to indicate an improvement in the wealth of the population at large, consonant with a threefold increase in the number of vehicles, a fourfold rise in paved roads and in the number of telephones, and other infrastructural advances of a similar order. Yet if the global stock of wealth had increased faster than that of people and the forces of production had advanced considerably, the impression of a comprehensive modernization was belied by the indices for income distribution and land tenure. In 1977 the wealthiest 6 per cent of the population earned as much as the poorest 63 per cent. In 1975, 41 per cent of rural families were completely landless, 34 per cent farmed less than one hectare (insufficient for subsistence) and 15 per cent possessed less than two hectares.[9] Moreover, although since before the turn of the century, the Salvadorean peasantry had been much more restricted in its access to plots of land than had small farmers in neighbouring states, land poverty had accelerated appreciably since the late 1950s as commercial estates dedicated to both coffee and new crops such as cotton and sugar as well as cattle-ranching occupied greater space within a virtually static agricultural frontier. The rise in production that supported the post-war growth in GDP may be explained in part by better yields – that for coffee rose from 655 kilos per hectare in 1950 to 1,224 in 1977 – which also had the effect of at least maintaining demand for harvest labour. However, while the expansion of land under coffee was relatively modest – from 112,000 in 1950 to 147,000 hectares in 1977 – that under cotton more than trebled (to more than 60,000 hectares) while sugar increased by comparable degree (to 38,000 hectares) and the area in pasture for cattle – the sector that demanded

70

least labour and most land per unit – rose by 50 per cent. In many cases this expansion was achieved at the direct cost of peasant holdings on the periphery of established coffee country and outside the traditional zones of large estates. Although cotton was an established crop and could be extended on the basis of existing patterns of tenure, the rise in cattle-raising trespassed deep into the less fertile and marginal lands that had hitherto provided a modicum of space for subsistence. This expansion did not produce an absolute stasis in the domestic food-crop acreage – which may be broadly but not exclusively associated with peasant agriculture – but it did impede growth in land cultivated for the domestic market. Between 1948 and 1978 land given over to maize expanded by 30 per cent; to beans, by 2.3 per cent; and to rice, by just 12 per cent. Modest improvements in yield assisted increases in production of 75 per cent, 43 per cent and 67 per cent respectively over a period when El Salvador's population nearly trebled in size.[10] Thus, while harvest labour demand was maintained and agro-exports grew in both volume and value, the subsistence economy declined relative to both the commercial estates and the population. The import of increasing quantities of basic grains was necessary to maintain levels of consumption. Lacking virgin lands in which to settle or even a culture of socio-economic 'refuge' comparable to that sustained by the Indian farmers of Guatemala, the expanding Salvadorean peasantry was caught in a pincer movement between loss of opportunities for direct cultivation and those for temporary waged labour. This by no means compelled a breakdown in rural order, still less open revolt, but it did aggravate discontent with the landlord regime while dislocating large numbers of rural labourers from the economic and social controls of the *finca*, opening the traditionally cautious political consciousness of the peasantry to the unsettling influence of local priests, schoolteachers and lay activists opposed to the established order. The sharp contrasts in the human condition in El Salvador, where the wealth of the landlord class was as impressive and as ostentatiously paraded as anywhere else in Latin America, were naturally prone to excite sentiments of Jacobin egalitarianism as much as resignation to an historic and unremovable order.

As we have seen, a significant proportion of the rural population moved either permanently or temporarily to the towns as the manufacturing sector began to grow. Between 1950 and 1977 industry expanded by an average of 6.3 per cent a year. The share of GDP attributable to manufacturing production rose from 12.9 per cent to 18.7 per cent, which was high by regional standards. Much of this growth took place under the CACM in the 1960s when the share of foreign, principally US, investment in manufacturing rose from 0.7 per cent in 1959 to 38.1 per cent in 1969.[11] Such progress was not of the type envisaged by many planners in the period after the Second World War insofar as there was very little heavy industry – capital goods accounted for 8.6 per cent of production in 1978 – and the bulk of output (64.7 per cent) was of perishable commodities frequently related to agricultural production. Neverthelesss, the amount of locally produced inputs was lower than this structure might suggest, the textile industry importing 45 per cent of its raw materials and the paper industry nearly 90 per cent. This, combined with the 'assembly and finishing' character of many of the new enterprises, limited the trickle-down effects of sectoral growth to the rest of the economy. Further-more, since much of the new industrial plant was foreign-owned and capital-intensive, the overall rise in the labour force (from 87,300 in 1962 to 118,000 in 1975) was much more modest than that in produc-tion and masked a fall in the size of the working class relative to the economically active population as a whole (from 10.2 per cent to 9.3 per cent), as well as the fact that nearly half of this manufacturing labour force was still employed in artisanal workshops of five employees or less.[12] Thus, not only did industrial growth fail to supply alternative employment for most of those leaving the countryside, it also resulted in the properly 'proletarian' character of the urban labour force being diminished from the early 1960s onwards – a matter of no little importance for sociological theories of revolution. The influence of assembly-line and factory syndicalism cannot by any means be excluded from the urban unrest of the late 1970s, but these were often subordinate in terms of both numbers and political impetus to the role of radicalized white-collar and skilled workers (particularly the teachers and power workers), the impoverished 'self-employed' in the informal sector, and locally based community organizations that usually dominated the plebeian fronts to the fore in popular mobiliza-tion until open activity was halted by repression following the general strike of August 1980. Nonetheless, it is of some consequence that once a modicum of public organization and activity again became possible after the elections of 1984, the trade unions, particularly those in the white-collar and public sectors, revived remarkably quickly, suggesting that urban discontent could not be reduced simply to a revolt of a marginalized lumpen proletariat.

It is evident that neither economic stagnation nor mere poverty caused the social conflict of the late 1970s, the former because it simply did not occur until the civil war had begun – and the international economy entered recession – and the latter because poverty in itself was no novelty in Salvadorean society nor as great as in Honduras, which remained relatively free of violence, although undoubtedly people were getting poorer faster than ever before. What lay behind the collapse of a social order established a century before was a process of concerted growth dominated by the export sector that dislocated tens of thousands of rural labourers from the security of both their lands and harvest wages but failed to replace this disaggregation of the peasantry with a process of socially stable and economically compensatory urbanization. This imbalance not only accelerated impoverishment but also created a significant population devoid of 'pure' class character, often geographically as well as socially mobile, outside established circuits of control, and subjected to decreasingly efficacious strategies for survival. This population cannot be accounted as exclusively urban or rural since the symbiosis between town and countryside is too strong in El Salvador, as later became evident in the relatively fluid exchange between the two spheres in terms of military operations. In this respect, at least, the crisis was as 'modern' as it was traditional, combining features of the late twentieth century (the guerrillas' use of video for propaganda and education) with those familiar for centuries (the struggle over land; cultural antipathies; inter-communal violence).

Between October 1979 and January 1980 there was considerable confusion in Salvadorean politics as a junta combining both reformist and conservative officers, representatives of the legal opposition (including the PCS), the oligarchy, and some sectors of the radical bloc endeavoured to agree upon policy while the military continued to attack popular demonstrations. By the end of 1979 those reforms the progressive elements had managed to introduce were plainly being stalled by the right, and the refusal of the military to accept government control over its operations resulted in the resignation of all the reformists except members of the PDC. In January 1980 the plebeian fronts held a large demonstration in the capital to mark the anniversary

of the 1932 rising and the formation of the Coordinadora Revolucionaria de Masas (CRM), which unified the popular organizations and
was joined two months later by most of the reformist parties and many
unions to form the Frente Democrático Revolucionario (FDR). Henceforth the FDR acted as the principal political body of the opposition.
This consolidation of the popular bloc was hastened by the assassination of Archbishop Romero in March, a crime widely attributed to the
paramilitary forces nurtured on the periphery of the army and publicly
lauded by extremist politicians of the right, such as Roberto
D'Aubuissón, who considered as subversives even those depleted and
cowed representatives of reform still in government. Romero's death
indicated how far such forces were prepared to go in their campaign
against reform, and it split the PDC, a minority leaving both government and party on the grounds that it was no longer politically possible
or morally acceptable to collaborate with the right in order to fortify
the centre against the left. The majority of the party, however, continued to support their leader José Napoleón Duarte, who was
receiving support from Washington for his vehement campaign against
his old UNO allies for being the dupes of communism. The opposition
retorted with equal predictability that he had made common cause
with those who not only oppressed the people but had also tortured
and exiled him when he championed democratic rights.

Although Duarte was henceforth vilified by the left and centre as a
puppet, he maintained a position independent of the extreme right and
most of the military in that he insisted upon an agrarian reform as a
necessary means by which to reduce polarization in the countryside.
Since the Carter administration supported this strategy and the high
command was now prepared to accept it as the price for much-needed
US logistical backing, a still disorganized oligarchy failed to impede its
formal introduction in May 1980. The reform subsequently underwent
a very chequered history in that redistribution of large coffee estates
either fell outside its compass or was postponed *sine die*, and the
conversion of a number of less efficient and 'over-sized' haciendas into
co-operatives often amounted to little more than an alteration of deeds,
since sabotage and violence impeded a genuine adoption of control by
the labourers. There was some progress in granting title to small plots,
but this proceeded far more slowly than planned and certainly did not
produce the stratum of small capitalist farmers envisaged by the US
planners in charge of the programme. Harried particularly by the

forces of the right but also sometimes by those of the left, the recipients of long-awaited lands were largely incapable of realizing a significant change in their circumstances, while the great majority of the rural population remained excluded from the reform. Yet even those limited steps that were taken proved anathema to the landlords, who began to exercise their de facto powers of veto with the help of officers who accepted the reform as a requirement of US support but whose political instincts were to hinder any change in the traditional order. The exceptions to this rule were notable for their small number, but as the war became more extended some of the more able commanders not known for their progressive views began to accept the programme on purely logistical grounds.

Even before this attitude began to take root, the oligarchy was being obliged by the thrust of the junta's policies to move beyond spoiling operations and stage a political challenge for formal office. This was compelled both by the fall of the PCN and Washington's strategy of making military support conditional upon at least the promulgation of some social reforms, a quid pro quo greatly facilitated by the PDC's presence in the junta but justifiably viewed by the extreme right as susceptible to adjustment should it gain power and the left-wing challenge continue to perturb the US administration. The establishment of the Alianza Republicana Nacional (ARENA) under the leadership of the reactionary populist Roberto D'Aubuissón may, therefore, be seen as the first genuinely independent intervention of the landlord class in open political competition since 1932, a development that was somewhat obscured by the adoption of modern methods of campaigning in the style of US parties to complement the power of patronage and retribution over voters employed by, or vulnerable to, the party's leading supporters. ARENA's unqualified repudiation of economic reform and advocacy of a purely military solution to the conflict was nothing if not simple and coherent – the electoral appeal of which was often underrated by its opponents – and it effectively obliged Washington to desist from any major challenge to the landed bourgeoisie. Yet if D'Aubuissón's well-publicized connections with the death-squads and chilling proclamations engendered diplomatic embarrassment, his opposition to the government lent some credibility to the notion that formal political competition existed in El Salvador, thereby facilitating the presentation of both the government and its legal opponents as constituting a democratic system worthy of protection against communist subversion.

The programme drawn up by the Coordinadora Revolucionaria de Masas (CRM) in January 1980 and adopted by the Frente Democrático Revolucionario (FDR) a few weeks later was not a charter for communism, but it did include a comprehensive agrarian reform and the nationalization of strategic economic infrastructure as well as the banks and foreign trade. (These last two measures were, in fact, implemented in part by the junta on rational capitalist grounds, and although they were resisted by the oligarchy, were allowed to stand when the right was in control of the constituent assembly and presidency in 1982–84.) Although the FDR contained a number of powerful and openly Marxist bodies seeking some form of socialism through revolutionary change, none of its members was in a position to impose a programme of socialist transformation or indeed considered it viable in even the medium term, and the alliance had been made possible only through agreement on a 'popular democratic' platform that postulated a social policy comparable to that held by UNO in the early 1970s. Yet under the conditions of extreme violence obtaining from early 1980 the political methods of the FDR predictably took on a more radical tone, and opposition strategy increasingly came under the influence of the guerrilla groups. This shift began following the failure of the general strikes of June and August 1980 when the reformists were obliged to accept that there was no alternative to armed struggle.

The establishment of a combined military command in the Frente Farabundo Martí para la Liberación Nacional (FMLN) in the autumn of 1980 marked the end of a period of ambiguity in opposition tactics and the beginning of a civil war in which some 70,000 people lost their lives over the following six years. The precipitate attempt by the FMLN to stage a 'final offensive' in January 1981 not only provoked greater US intervention but also obliged the guerrillas to alter their tactics from a predominantly urban and insurrectionary approach to a more rural and low-level campaign punctuated with occasional large-scale attacks, particularly in the north and east of the country. The rebels were strongest in Chalatenango (where the FPL was dominant), Morazán (ERP-dominated) and around the Guazapa volcano to the north of San Salvador (where all the groups possessed forces), although a total force of perhaps 7,000 combatants had the capacity to harass an army over 30,000-strong beyond these zones and particularly in the rich farming country around San Miguel and San Vicente. Under the

Reagan administration military assistance to El Salvador was substantially increased but also limited in its efficacy by the army's lack of experience in combat, the low quality of the officer corps, and the proclivity of the paramilitary forces for killing unarmed peasants. Such resort to the traditional methods of control greatly prejudiced the international image of the regime and prompted the French and Mexican governments to recognize the FMLN-FDR as a representative political organization. Yet even though the Salvadorean military acquired a formidable reputation for both inefficiency and brutality, the waging of a war of attrition did eventually reduce the inhabitants of combat zones to strategies for survival beyond that of supporting the guerrillas. Thus, by the end of 1982 it was evident that although it had established a remarkable capacity for resistance, the rebel army lacked the ability to defeat the military in the foreseeable future.

In the spring of 1982 elections were held for a constituent assembly which produced a working majority for a revived PCN and ARENA over the PDC, which had dominated the junta under Duarte's provisional presidency. Unable to halt the poll, the guerrillas were now faced with a regime that was certainly more conservative than its predecessor but could also claim to have a popular mandate. Even though such claims were rebutted with evidence of electoral irregularities that appeared convincing to many beyond the rebel ranks, and despite the fact that the change in administration barely affected military operations, the poll did mark a shift in political conditions insofar as it opened up a second sphere of contest. This was boycotted by the FDR on the plausible grounds that since so many of its leaders and supporters had been killed there was no possibility of its being permitted to participate without precipitating a massacre. The notion that a political competition between parties of the right under the conditions of a civil war constituted a genuine democratic process was subjected to much scepticism both within the country and abroad, especially given El Salvador's questionable electoral traditions. On the other hand, it was apparent that however insufficient a reflection of public opinion, the restitution of the formalities of democratic government was a major development. This opened tensions inside the opposition on both tactical and ideological grounds, differences inside the left only finally being resolved following the death of two veterans of the FPL – Cayetano Carpio and Mélida Anaya Montes. As a result of these disputes, early in 1984 the FDR issued a new programme that was appreciably less radical than that of 1980; it suppressed concrete economic and social objectives and concentrated upon the mechanisms for a ceasefire and the establishment of a provisional government combining representatives of both the existing regime and the FDR. The opposition continued to denounce the formal political system as a charade, but the Reagan administration's decision to stage a concerted campaign against the left in Central America and the retreat of the embattled Sandinista government in Nicaragua from its early logistical support for the rebels indicated that expectations of a victory achieved in the short term and by military means were misconceived. The shift towards negotiation was further encouraged when, in May 1984, Duarte narrowly beat D'Aubuissón (by 54 per cent to 46 per cent of the vote) in an election that, although neither free of suspect practices nor reflective of the sympathies of a considerable section of the population, did nevertheless indicate a widespread desire for peace. By campaigning in the name of rapprochement, Duarte was able to match the well-funded and agile anti-communist crusade staged by D'Aubuissón, and although Washington made no secret of its preference for the PDC, the extent of the slaughter, economic crisis and forced migration undoubtedly convinced many to vote for what seemed the quickest and least terrifying path to terminating hostilities. However, if the exhaustion of the populace stemmed the progress of the radical right, expectations that the war would now be halted dissipated rapidly as Duarte, threatened by the powerful and suspicious high command and lacking US support for negotiations, rejected proposals for a ceasefire and a new government, made by the rebels at the town of La Palma in November 1984. For the next two years peace talks foundered upon the president's insistence that the opposition lay down its arms without condition and the rebels' refusal to accept these terms as anything distinct from surrender. As the economy continued its steep decline, Duarte lost both popularity and authority, and the military failed to extend its containment of the FMLN to a decisive victory. The prospects of a government victory appeared as distant as those of a resolution that favoured the rebels who, confronted with absolute opposition from Washington, were unable to escape the logic of a *guerra popular prolongada* that offered their supporters no relief from violence and economic hardship.

Under such conditions, which produced a death toll of some 70,000 between 1980 and 1988, both sides had reason to consider the merits of the regional peace plan proposed by President Oscar Arias of Costa Rica in February 1987 and ratified, in amended form, by the regional heads of state in August of that year as the Esquipulas II agreement. Although both the armed forces and the FMLN remained profoundly reluctant to countenance concessions on the part of their political allies, President Duarte was unable to escape the logic of his earlier initiative to negotiate, while the left, now under pressure from Managua and Havana to display strategic flexibility, perceived the need to broaden its campaign on both domestic and diplomatic fronts.

The obstacles confronting a negotiated settlement were more substantial than in Nicaragua – where the Contra rebels had failed in their military campaign and remained almost entirely beholden to Washington – or, indeed, in Guatemala – where the Union Revolucionaria Nacional Guatemalteca (URNG) was too weak to expect reasonable terms from a civilian administration which was patently cowed by the military. Yet the political leadership of the Salvadorean opposition had never fully rejected the electoralist road or entirely dedicated itself to the capture of state power through insurrection. Equally, the civil war had greatly prejudiced the economic interests which challenged Duarte from the right and which now perceived some advantage in launching a nationalist campaign against the government's dependence on the United States, not least perhaps because this opened up the possibility of conducting an independent overture to the guerrillas. Although both the level of violence and the degree of ideological polarization underwent no diminution, it became apparent that US involvement in Salvadorean affairs had produced some unforeseen consequences.

The strength of ARENA's conservative challenge to the PDC was not immediately obvious because the Christian Democrats secured control of Congress in 1985 and their opponents remained tarnished abroad by D'Aubuissón's association with the death-squads. However, the Duarte administration was hamstrung by more than its extreme dependence upon US aid, which by 1988 amounted to half the national budget. Although the army was bolstered by US assistance, it was the government that suffered from its failure to translate this into victory over the guerrillas. At the same time, North American largesse provided ample opportunity for official corruption, which particularly damaged a confessional party that made much of its high moral purpose. Moreover, from the time that Duarte had obtained the provisional presidency his party had excused its failures in terms of the extreme right's control of the judiciary and, after 1982, the legislature; after 1985 such an explanation appeared threadbare indeed to those who had voted for the PDC, which failed to develop an organized popular movement based on its voters and then began to suffer from divisions within its elite. ARENA, by contrast, was able to stage a significant recovery as the government failed to realize the promises made between 1981 and 1984. As a result, the extreme right scored a sweeping victory in the legislative elections of 1988. Recognizing that this paved the way to ousting the PDC from the presidency in the poll of March 1989, the ARENA leadership turned its attention to improving its international image and making some gesture towards a negotiated settlement of the conflict so as to placate regional concerns as well as the preoccupations of many voters. These moves ran directly counter to the party's frequent calls for a 'final' military solution to the civil war, suggesting it had registered the importance of US influence but was unwilling to alter its fundamental outlook. This, certainly, was the interpretation of many when D'Aubuissón was replaced as party leader by Alfredo Cristiani, a mild-mannered coffee grower who, educated in the United States, soon proved to be an extremely adroit advocate of the 'modern' ARENA in Washington.

Faced with a number of important developments both within the country and in Central America as a whole in 1987–88, the left responded with some unexpected initiatives of its own. In the autumn of 1988 the FDR leaders Guillermo Manuel Ungo and Rubén Zamora returned openly to San Salvador, secured personal guarantees and announced that they would participate in the March 1989 election in the name of Convergencia Democrática (CD), which, they claimed, would win a free and fair poll. The military leadership of the FMLN effectively dissociated itself from this move but desisted from directly attacking it. Then, as the election campaign got under way, the FMLN itself took the lead by proposing a postponement of the poll for six months as the principal basis upon which a ceasefire might be established, the left reincorporated into legal political life, the military dramatically reduced in size, US military aid cut, and a true electoral test held. For a while the new Bush administration seemed prepared to consider discussion of this offer, and ARENA displayed even more willingness than the PDC to negotiate with its enemies. However, the FMLN's terms proved to be too steep and the initiative rapidly foundered. The guerrillas returned to their campaign to sabotage the poll but failed to impede Cristiani from easily beating the PDC candidate, Fidel Chávez Mena, while the CD predictably returned a very low vote.

In one sense these developments deepened the complexities of Salvadorean political life and appeared to open up possibilities not seen since the onset of the civil war in 1980–81. Yet even at the height of the manoeuvres it was difficult to envisage a stable resolution of the conflict in local terms. Indeed, ARENA's victory appeared to herald a return to the oligarchic mandate, uniting a fiercely reactionary dominant bloc under a reluctant but decisive North American imprimatur. A decade of bloody strife had failed to reduce political activity, but the practice of politics had equally proved incapable of putting an end to war.

Notes

1. For discussion of this process, see David Browning, *El Salvador: Landscape and Society*, Oxford 1971, and Rafael Menjivar, *Acumulación originaria y desarrollo del capitalismo en El Salvador*, San José 1980.

2. The character and development of the oligarchy have yet to be analysed exhaustively. However, much useful information and suggestive discussion may be found in Robert Aubey, 'Entrepreneurial Formation in El Salvador', *Explorations in Entrepreneurial History*, 2nd series, vol. 6 (1968–69); Everett Wilson, 'The Crisis of National Integration in El Salvador, 1919–1935', unpublished PhD dissertation, Stanford University, 1970; Eduardo Colindres 'La tenencia de la tierra en El Salvador', *Estudios Centroamericanos* 31 (1976); Manuel Sevila, 'El Salvador: la concentración económica y los grupos del poder', *Cuaderno de Trabajo*, no. 3, Centro de Investigación y Acción Social, Mexico 1984.

3. The events of 1931–32 are discussed in some detail in Thomas P. Anderson, *Matanza: El Salvador's Communist Revolt of 1932*, Lincoln, Neb. 1971; Rafael Guidos Vejar, *Ascenso del militarismo en El Salvador*, San José 1982; Roque Dalton, *Miguel Marmol*, New York 1987.

4. Quoted in Robert E. Elam, 'Appeal to Arms: The Army and Politics in El Salvador, 1931–1964', unpublished PhD dissertation, University of New Mexico, Albuquerque 1968, p. 146.

5. The origins and development of the PDC are analysed in one of the very few published studies of a Central American political party: Stephan Webre, *José Napoleón Duarte and the Christian Democratic Party in Salvadoran Politics, 1960–1978*, Baton Rouge 1979.

6. Carlos Cabarrús, *Génesis de una revolución*, Mexico 1983; Jenny Pearce, *Promised Land: Peasant Rebellion in Chalatenango, El Salvador*, London 1985.

7. See Rafael Menjivar, *Formación y lucha del proletariado*, San José 1982.

8. Latin America Bureau, *El Salvador Under General Romero*, London 1979.

9. Ministerio de Planificación, 'Distribución del ingreso y gasto por deciles de hogares', San Salvador 1981; Censo Agropecuario, 1975, cited in J. Mark Ruhl, 'Agrarian Structure and Political Stability in Honduras', *Journal of Inter-American Studies*, 26, no. 1 (1984), p. 47.

10. Edelberto Torres Rivas, 'The Beginnings of Industrialization in Central America', Working Paper no. 141, Latin American Program, Woodrow Wilson Center, Washington, DC 1984, p. 17.

11. Gert Rosenthal, 'El papel de la inversión extrajera directa en el proceso de integración', in *Centroamérica hoy*, Mexico 1976, p. 125.

12. Ramón Mayorga, *El crecimiento desigual en Centroamérica*, Mexico 1983, pp. 60–66.

3

Guatemala, 1944–54

The experience of Guatemala during the decade following World War II was exceptional within Latin America. As in most of Central America, an anti-dictatorial movement strongly influenced by the war took root in 1944. However, in contrast to all of the countries of the isthmus except Costa Rica, this movement succeeded in both overthrowing a dictatorship established in the wake of the Depression – that of General Jorge Ubico (1931–44) – and resisting the ensuing right-wing backlash. In distinction from the general pattern in the subcontinent the regimes of Juan José Arévalo (1945–51) and Jacobo Arbenz (1951–54) pursued policies of progressive socio-economic reform, accepted and sometimes encouraged the spread of unionization, and fostered a nationalist sentiment that increased pressure on foreign enterprise and tension with the US. These features were also evident in Argentina during the same period, but in contrast to the Peronist experience the Guatemalan governments desisted from taking a resolutely anti-communist line and came to rely upon the support of independent radical forces in the labour movement. As a result, the Arbenz regime was eventually overthrown – in perhaps the most open and emphatic example of US Cold War interventionism to be seen in Latin America – when the CIA organized a counter-revolutionary invasion from Honduras in June 1954.

The counter-revolution, or 'liberation', of 1954 may be seen as marking Guatemala's overdue reversion to the pattern of regional politics, although it was precisely by virtue of the long delay that the reactionary backlash was so singular in its degree of US backing and its consolidation of an anti-communist political culture that impeded even the most modest reforms for over three decades. Indeed, the differences in both local and international conditions between 1954 and 1945–48 – the context for the 'Cold War resolution' almost everywhere else – greatly reduce the usefulness of direct comparison. Equally, a survey of the immediate post-war years in Guatemala would yield a distinctly partial history and exclude many developments – the right-wing coup attempt of 1949, the agrarian reform and formal establishment of a national Communist Party in the Partido Guatemalteco del Trabajo (PGT) in 1952 – integral to the character of the reformist regime and to Washington's decision to eradicate it. One is, therefore, confronted with two problematic objects of study. On the one hand, a formally similar experience significantly dislocated in time. And on the other, the same period of time characterized by some distinctiveness from the rest of Latin America yet in itself providing little definition of events. A detailed study of either would undoubtedly reveal precise points of contrast and similarity with the rest of the subcontinent, but for our purpose it would seem most relevant to address in more interpretative fashion the broader question of why it was that Guatemala took the better part of a decade to conform to regional type.[1]

The political liberalization opened by the revolution of October 1944 and the project of socio-economic reform that emerged with increasing strength from 1947 can only be understood in the light of the national experience over preceding decades, in particular the 1930s. With the exception of Costa Rica, autocratic government based on the military prevailed throughout Central America during the years of the Depression. However, this was an essentially new form of regime for the region, and only in Guatemala had it been the established type of government since the early republic. Partly as a result of this, Ubico possessed greater autonomy from the landlord class than did most of his peers, even Somoza, whose fortune and power were consolidated in the 1940s. Equally, the presence of large US companies controlling a strategically vital banana enclave was unexceptional in regional terms. Yet nowhere else was the enclave both controlled by a single enterprise, the United Fruit Company (UFCO), and inserted into a buoyant coffee economy over which it could exercise considerable influence by virtue of an effective monopoly of rail transport.[2] Hence, whilst in 1929 coffee accounted for 77 per cent of export revenue and bananas only 13 per cent, the profile of UFCO within the economy was particularly high and it was the object of discontent amongst an appreciable local bourgeoisie frequently prejudiced by the company's differential freight rates.[3] These two long-term conditions – the strength of autocratic government and the singularly contentious character of a foreign enterprise – were to have considerable resonance in the late 1940s since they provided exceptional potential for the expression of political democracy and nationalist sentiment across class lines, thereby delaying for a short but critical period the appearance of social conflict and ideological polarization. On the one hand, liberal constitutionalism enjoyed unusual resilience due to the strength of anti-dictatorial feeling and the weakness of independent political traditions and organization on both right and left wings. On the other, core economic reforms were slow to generate major confrontation because they affected UFCO's interests more sharply than those of local capital. In a sense, then, it could be said of the post-war experience in Guatemala that it initially derived strength from the very weakness of domestic political forces and that it ultimately proved vulnerable precisely because of the strength with which foreign interests were confronted. The fact that the project of democratic reform was defeated primarily by external forces undoubtedly corresponds to Washington's local and international requirements in the early 1950s, but should also be seen in the context of long-term domestic developments.

Ubico was the heir to a formidable local tradition of personalist and autocratic government that began during the conservative epoch under Rafael Carrera (1838–65) and continued into the liberal free-trade era with the regimes of Justo Rufino Barrios (1871–85) and Manuel Estrada Cabrera (1898–1920). To some degree this proclivity for dictatorship derived from the fact that under the Spanish Guatemala City had been the centre of colonial administration of the isthmus, the local elite being accustomed to dominating the rest of the Captaincy General and possessing an armed force sufficient for this objective, which continued well into the republic. However, coercive government corresponded in more direct terms to the fact that the country had a very large indigenous population – at least 65 per cent of the population of 1.8 million in 1930 and an equal proportion of that of 2.4 million in 1945. This Indian population was split into some two dozen ethnic groups but it possessed powerful communitarian traditions that always coexisted uneasily with – and sometimes openly challenged –

the minority *ladino* population of all classes that upheld the Hispanic state. Following the expansion of coffee from the mid 1870s both class and ethnic tension was abetted by the expropriation of communal lands in the foothills and the need to supply the *fincas* with a seasonal labour force from the densely populated highlands. The provision of harvest labour was initially attempted through application of the colonial mechanism of *mandamiento* or direct obligation, but within a decade the liberal state shifted to reliance upon debt peonage, which operated through market forces yet continued to depend on a powerful military force that invigilated seasonal migration and pursued evaders under the direction of departmental *Jefes Políticos*. When occupying such a post early in the century Ubico had on occasions clashed with local landlords whose economic interests did not always elide with those of public order. In 1934, as president, he replaced debt peonage with a labour system based on a vagrancy law that made all landless and most subsistence peasants liable for plantation labour as well as unpaid work on road-building, which was greatly accelerated during the 1930s.[4] This important organizational alteration was presented by Ubico as a major democratic advance but appears to have been more onerous in economic terms for the rural poor whilst providing appreciable support for *finqueros* hit by the Depression and to whom Ubico refused to concede a devaluation, making only a modest overture in reducing export taxes. The authority of both the central state and Ubico himself may be seen in these measures, which were complemented by the abolition of traditional Indian municipal government (replaced by centrally appointed intendants) and all independent entrepreneurial associations, including the Chamber of Commerce.

Such suppression of the established vehicles for expression of two very different but highly important corporate interests was facilitated by the fact that the partial relaxation of political control and the economic buoyancy during the 1920s had failed to produce either a coherent system of oligarchic political parties or a strong popular challenge. This is somewhat surprising because the overthrow of Estrada Cabrera in 1920 had been achieved with the subordinate but significant participation of the urban middle class and poor whilst the subsequent regimes of generals Orellana and Chacón had permitted at least some competition and expression of opposition to the particularly leonine contract secured by UFCO in 1927. It should, however, be noted that the racial question divided the popular movement not only between town and country but also within the countryside, whilst the newly organized banana labour force was small and isolated from the highland communities that comprised the majority of the rural population. Significantly, Guatemala alone in Central America lacked a communist organization at the end of the 1920s, its urban trade unions were exceptionally weak, and social mobilization in the wake of the 1929 Crash was more easily contained than in the rest of the isthmus.[5] Equally, the landlord-dominated bourgeois forces failed to remedy their longstanding lack of political organization, in part simply because the requirements of coercive control of both Indian and peasant had not diminished one iota; in part because their economic vanguard lay in the very small community of German planters who accounted for over a third of coffee exports but resisted real engagement in political life; and in part because the anti-Estrada Cabrera campaign had rapidly collapsed into conflict over the idea of Central American union, which had once been integral to the psyche of the dominant class but was now rendered anachronistic by US hegemony. Moreover, the antagonism caused by UFCO was qualified by the absence of any real alternative to it, Washington's support for the company, and the fact that it had not yet secured complete control of and fully exploited the sole means of bulk transport to the Atlantic in the line owned by International Railroads of Central America (IRCA). Finally, the Guatemalan elite remained traumatized by the experience of popular revolution in neighbouring Mexico, its fears of mass mobilization, political radicalization and anti-clericalism greatly diminishing the desire to curb military authority or seek a political control based upon a modicum of popular participation akin to that visible for a while in the rest of Central America.

As a consequence, when Ubico was elected unopposed early in 1931 he was readily able to revive a longstanding dictatorial tradition rooted in a social system divided by race and an economy based largely upon coerced labour, curtailing in the process the particularly insecure democratic and reformist tendencies that had emerged in the 1920s. Although his election to all intents and purposes constituted a coup, its formality facilitated full and comparatively easy relations with Washington from the start. Similarly, Ubico's support for UFCO in the disputes of the late 1920s provided him with important company patronage and underpinned the unusually generous 1936 contract under which the enterprise was relieved of its previous obligation to build a Pacific port and thus enabled to consolidate its control over IRCA and influence through it.

Guatemala remained in political stasis throughout the thirteen years of Ubiquismo. Opposition to the general was rapidly eradicated; the left through a spate of executions, expulsions and imprisonment in the wake of the Salvadorean revolt of January 1932, and middle-class dissidents by similar means, and on a rather larger scale, some two years later. Ubico was subsequently untroubled by opposition above or below ground, experienced no difficulty in enforcing the prohibition of all independent political parties, trade unions and civic bodies, and suffered virtually no challenge from within the army even after the officer corps was expanded and a more modern institutional ethic engendered within it by the establishment of the Escuela Politécnica under a US officer.[6] True to the literary depiction of the Caribbean despots of this era, Ubico presided over all aspects of government with extraordinary zeal, employed a very small bureaucracy, a highly active secret police force, and enough eccentric behaviour to instil unusual awe in both the oligarchy and the lower orders.[7] Like his peers in the neighbouring states to the south, he never dispensed with the formal trappings of democratic procedure since his personal power ensured absolute compliance and rendered unnecessary any direct organizational emulation of the European Fascist regimes that he greatly admired.

Such comprehensive domination by a single man (who, together with a clique of minions, inevitably drew maximum pecuniary advantage from his power) was not as extraordinary as it might appear since it took place in a very small country where the Depression had exercised a sharp impact on a backward economy and a society still regimented along nineteenth-century – and sometimes sixteenth-century – lines. In 1930 Guatemala's GDP was a mere $449 million and its GDP per capita $245; agriculture prevailed as the overwhelming source of export and tax revenue, the value added by a manufacturing sector dominated by artisanal workshops amounting to a mere $70 million.[8] Urban culture was limited to the capital, which had a population of only 150,000 whilst the second town, Quezaltenango, had no more than 20,000 inhabitants.[9] Moreover, once the immediate discontent caused by the economic crisis in 1930–32 had been suppressed, Ubico's rule was fortified by a slow but constant economic recovery – GDP per capita rose from $197 in 1932 to $392 by

1940 – in which non-export agriculture proved to be especially buoyant whilst by the end of the decade the staples of coffee and bananas were returning a reasonable profit and upholding a domestic budget only slightly lower than that of the 1920s.[10] For the central forces in Guatemalan society – the coffee *finqueros* and the peasantry (both Indian and *ladino*) – the Depression did not produce rupture so much as contraction, stasis and then measured recuperation. Manufacturing grew much more slowly from a very low base whilst the urban middle class was sharply affected by budget reductions (by some 50 per cent between 1928 and 1932), reduced employment and inflation. Of all the social sectors seeking political expression in the 1920s, the *ladino* artisanate and middle strata were most directly prejudiced by Ubico's rise to power since they expected more than the historically subordinate *campesinado* and lost more than the bourgeoisie.

In most respects the impact of World War II in Guatemala conformed to regional type. Neither in 1939 nor in 1942 did Ubico relax or alter the internal regime, but having recognized Franco at the earliest opportunity he was now obliged to adjust foreign policy according to the needs of realpolitik rather than ideological enthusiasm. War was declared on the Axis in the wake of Pearl Harbor, bases provided for US troops, full collaboration offered to Washington over the Inter-American Highway (which bolstered Ubico's road-building plans) and to UFCO over cultivation of strategically important *abacá* (hemp). The closely regulated and extraordinarily sycophantic press provided coverage of the conflict but clearly sought to reduce discussion of the underlying ideological issues, with respect to which the oligarchy and right had – for once – to embrace geographic fatalism. All the same, the political cost of the war to the regime did not appear substantial until the spring of 1944, before which there was no sign of reorganization within the labour movement or middle class. Equally, the broad economic impact of the war proved to be less disastrous than at first feared once the Central American states were allocated generous quotas under the Inter-American Coffee Agreement of November 1940.[11] In 1932 Guatemala had sold over 28 per cent of her coffee to Germany and received 11 per cent of her imports from that country, but the Nazi regime's shift to paying for such commodities in Aski marks (which could only be exchanged at face value for German goods) meant that from 1935 Guatemala sought alternative markets with the result that although in 1939 27 per cent of imports derived from Germany (largely by virtue of accumulated Aski mark credit), only 12 per cent of coffee exports went to that country.[12] Equally, since trade with the UK in 1939 amounted to only 1.8 per cent of exports and 2 per cent of imports, Guatemala was less severely hit than some countries, such as Costa Rica, by the loss of this market. Unsurprisingly, the banana trade was most sharply affected, the volume of exports falling by some 40 per cent in 1939–40 although UFCO continued to make profits and issue a dividend throughout the war. Against this, a strictly modest fall in the volume of coffee sales following the quota agreement (to an average of 99.6 million lbs per annum in 1939–43 from 104.2 million lbs in 1934–38) kept the overall level of export revenue somewhat above that of the second half of the 1930s (an average of $87.5 million a year in 1939–43 against $82.6 million in 1934–38).[13] On the other hand, a sharp fall in imports fuelled inflation when prices had been falling since 1937 (1937 = 100; 1939 = 93; 1941 = 81; 1943 = 122; 1945 = 174) and contributed to a significant diminution of GDP per capita, from $392 in 1940 to $249 in 1944.[14] Import-substitution industrialization was barely perceptible, value added by manufacturing rising from $60 million in 1939 to only $70 million in 1944.[15] Under these conditions the urban artisanate continued to experience a very gradual recovery from its poor position of a decade earlier but mercantile interests and the salaried workforce remained under acute pressure, the latter especially so.

Perhaps the single most critical effect of the war was on the important German community. By the end of the nineteenth century immigrant planters had invested 200 million marks in the purchase of 300,000 hectares of prime coffee land, predominantly in the department of Alta Verapaz; at the outbreak of World War I their 170 estates accounted for 35.8 million lbs of a total coffee export of 52.5 million.[16] During that conflict Estrada Cabrera had placed restrictions on the Germans and their property but strenuously resisted imposing the outright controls eventually demanded by Washington, rapidly devolving property that had been 'intervened' after the armistice. Subjected at an earlier stage to greater pressure for the expropriation of all Axis-owned property on the 'Proclaimed List' during World War II, Ubico had little choice but to acquiesce in the deportation of German nationals to the US. Moreover, in 1941 the general did not resist the 'intervention' (temporary state management) of what became known as *fincas nacionales* since these still amounted to over 300,000 hectares, accounted for at least a third of the national coffee crop, and defrayed between 10 and 15 per cent of the national budget.[17] However, Ubico intended at all costs to avoid the outright nationalization of German property, a move which he viewed as 'communistic'. As a result, by early 1944 Cordell Hull was insisting that US Ambassador Boaz Long push the dictator to take this step, threatening to reduce the country's coffee quota if it was further delayed.[18] In the subsequent exchange Long effectively defended Ubico's position, noting the importance of the properties to fiscal revenue (although this was not the major issue at stake) and the constitutional difficulties involved.[19] Hull, however, remained insistent, and although in the wake of the Salvadorean revolt of April 1944 Long diligently reported Ubico's fears of the political dangers of full expropriation, the dictator was finally obliged to announce the nationalization just a few days before he was ousted from power at the end of June 1944.[20] In itself the issue cannot be accounted a central feature of the overthrow of the dictatorship but it does appear to have stiffened the resolve of the State Department – and even of the ambassador – to maintain a strictly neutral stance in the final mobilization against Ubico.[21] The exchanges between Guatemala City and Washington did not receive great publicity, and for the bulk of the population the precise status of German property already managed by the state could not have excited the degree of interest already directed towards the achievement of civil liberties. On the other hand, it is distinctly worthy of note that since Ubico's short-lived heir General Federico Ponce ratified the expropriation, the Arévalo and Arbenz regimes inherited a large amount of land (with a labour force in excess of 20,000) that first provided important revenue and then – in addition to Ubico's own expropriated estates – enabled an agrarian reform to be realized without a major assault on locally owned private properties. Under Arbenz's reform law of June 1952 some 365,000 acres of the 920,000 expropriated over the next two years belonged to the *fincas nacionales* whilst most of the remainder belonged to UFCO, and only 3.9 per cent of locally owned private land was affected.[22]

The transition from reactionary dictatorship to liberal constitutionalism took place over the last half of 1944. Continuous demonstrations in the capital in the final week of June forced Ubico to surrender office on 1 July. In October a relatively bloodless coup led by junior officers overthrew the tyrant's chosen successor General Ponce, established a short-lived junta, and in December called the elections that were easily won by Arévalo. Given the complete absence of popular organization, political activity and open military discontent over the previous ten years, this was an extraordinary period in which, for the urban population at least, the world indeed seemed to have 'turned upside down'. It was not, however, a time of constant mobilization or great ideological turmoil. The drumming of Ubico from office was almost exclusively a middle-class affair, lacking trade-union support for the simple reason that there were no unions in existence until 3 July, when the teachers established a national association (to be rapidly followed by the railway-workers' SAMF, labourers on UFCO's Tiquisate plantation, and a welter of small artisanal bodies). Equally, it was the captains and majors who dispatched Ponce in October, and while the rebel officers did distribute arms to the students, there was minimal participation in the revolt by members of the new Confederación de Trabajadores de Guatemala (CTG), formed less than three weeks earlier. On neither occasion was there any organized left-wing presence, although a number of individuals later prominent in the PGT – José Manuel Fortuny, Alfredo Guerra Borges, Carlos Pellecer – were to the fore in the anti-dictatorial campaign centred on the University of San Carlos (USAC). The very smallness of USAC (less than 700 students) meant that these individuals were subsequently able to establish a personal as well as political identification with the con- stitutionalist movement – a matter repeatedly stressed (and often exaggerated) by State Department reports in the early 1950s: 'Com- munist political success derives in general from the ability of individual Communists and fellow travellers to identify themselves with the nationalist and social aspirations of the Revolution of October 1944.'[23]

Neither in June nor in October 1944 did the US embassy take undue fright at events or note the presence of any dangerous radical elements beyond suggesting that Arévalo might be supported by leftists.[24] Indeed, if in July Boaz Long proved to be somewhat misguided in his optimistic assessment of General Ponce's popularity and his observation that 'the first ten days of the new Government augur well for the future', the October coup's emphatic demonstration of his error did not dissuade Chargé William Affeld from cabling Washington within a week of the revolt to indicate that the junta represented 'the establishment of democratic ideals and procedure'.[25] Such a response is not surprising in view of the fact that three weeks earlier Long had received a letter from the Acting Director of the Office of American Republics, Norman Armour, in reply to his concerns about the burgeoning autocratic tendencies of Ponce's regime:

a number of us in the Department are deeply concerned at political developments in Guatemala and elsewhere in Latin America. The problem of support for democratic processes is not an easy one and was discussed at some length this morning. The idea was advanced that we might have President Roosevelt or the Secretary include in an early address a statement more or less along the following lines: 'We wish to cultivate friendly relations with every government in the world and do not feel ourselves entitled to dictate to any country what form of government best suits its national aspirations. We nevertheless must feel a greater affinity, a deeper sympathy and a warmer friendship for governments which effectively represent the practical application of democratic processes.'[26]

The effective adoption of this policy by the embassy towards Ponce in mid-October amounted to a distinct cold shoulder although there is no evidence to suggest that what was still a small and unimportant legation offered any encouragement to Majors Arana and Arbenz to stage the coup of the 20th when the sensitivity of US policy to such an event would be particularly high, especially in the wake of the confusing and bloody events in neighbouring El Salvador.[27] Moreover, only three days before the revolt Affeld reported that 'the embassy does not on the basis of present evidence look for any immediate widespread violence'.[28] It can, then, be said with some confidence that during 1944 Washington stuck closely to protocol, which in practical terms meant leaving both Ubico and Ponce unprotected against the forces of democratic reform by more than formal recognition. At no subsequent point – even in the weeks prior to the June 1954 intervention – did the State Department stray from its view that the events of 1944 were positive, progressive and popular. Instead, in a fashion remarkably similar to the more recent case of Nicaragua, Washington's perception was of an initially laudable development that later degenerated. In an inter-departmental memorandum of May 1950 it was noted that

In 1944 one of the most ruthless of all Guatemalan dictatorships was overthrown by what amounted to a truly popular uprising supported by all segments of the population. Popular elections followed, and Juan José

Arévalo, a liberal and progressive-minded ex-teacher, was elected President by an overwhelming popular vote. Shortly thereafter Guatemala embarked on a social, economic and political program which in general terms aimed at improving the standard of living of the masses, protecting them from the abuses of the old feudal system, and achieving freedom and democracy for the Guatemalan people. This program was at its outset commendable.[29]

At the end of 1944 it would have not required undue prescience to predict the 'pro-labor attitude', 'nationalist tendency' and 'deep-seated mistrust' of UFCO that the document goes on to attack, but the events of that year offered few signals of future difficulties for Washington. The June campaign against Ubico had begun on a simple platform of autonomy for USAC and owed much to the example of the mobilization against General Martínez in El Salvador in April. Even when Ubico's police repressed the demonstrations and killed a teacher the offensive remained within purely constitutionalist parameters and was conducted in an eminently civic manner, the UN charter being proclaimed to the masses and Ubico subjected to a petition signed by 311 professionals who requested application of the Four Freedoms on the grounds that 'Guatemala cannot remove itself from the democratic imperatives of the era. It is impossible to frustrate with coercive means the uncontainable impulses of that generous ideology which is being reaffirmed in the world's conscience by means of the bloodiest of struggles between oppression and liberty.'[30]

Once Ubico was out and Ponce installed there was a discernible lull in political momentum, as if the urban populace was shocked by the relative ease of the operation. Ponce was sufficiently astute to convene elections for October and cancel the most draconian of the dictator's edicts. However, as soon as it became apparent that the general's intended *continuismo* was endangered by the candidacy of Arévalo, a military leadership that had undergone few changes since Ubico's departure simply staged a fraud whereby Ponce won, in Affeld's words, 'by a handsome, not to say fantastic margin, garnering 48,530 votes out of a total of 44,751'.[31] As has been seen, such a manoeuvre could no longer be guaranteed North American indulgence, and although popular opposition was temporarily cowed by the truckloads of Indians brought into the capital by Ponce, it was evident that 'Ubiquismo without Ubico' lacked any future. The constitutionalist agenda remained open, at a higher level of popular expectation, and beyond the point of repudiation of a specific individual. Moreover, between June and October the high command had failed to subborn the junior officers, who by dint of their position, pay, training and family ties had been influenced by the democratic movement as well as fortified by the replacement of their longstanding *caudillo* by nondescript figures deprived of political skills by his concentration of power. As a result, whereas elsewhere in Central America the army halted the constitutionalist tide, in Guatemala it acted to guarantee its success.

This close association of the officer corps with the establishment of democratic government was central to the capacity of the reformist regime to secure the general neutrality of the military over the following years. The army acquired uncommon popularity from its leadership of the October revolt, and despite receiving a reduced share of the (increased) budget under both Arévalo and Arbenz, it lost little influence in policy-making compared to that held under the dictatorship whilst retaining the bulk of its prior administrative powers, particularly in the provinces. No less importantly, it encountered very little anti-militarism from the left.[32] Of course, the momentum given by this unusual convergence in the anti-dictatorial movement was subsequently placed under considerable stress. From 1948 new arms supplies were withheld by Washington – a policy which, as military envoys continually pointed out, reduced both logistical capacity and institutional esteem.[33] Equally, the existence of even modest and informal groups of armed civilians – first in the shape of the Caribbean Legion patronized by Arévalo, and then in the popular militias organized by the left early in 1954 – challenged the army's formal monopoly, if not its real exercise, of military power. Furthermore, as vividly illustrated by the abortive coup of July 1949, consensus over the desirability of constitutionalism by no means extended to the social reforms – still less the popular mobilization – that followed in its wake. Nonetheless, the failure of the army to lead a counter-revolutionary movement when it had the coercive means to do so owed a great deal to the fact that the bulk of the officer corps had accepted the violent displacement of the Ubiquista old guard that both removed the leading conservatives from the scene and constituted an institutional trauma sufficient to make support for the ethos of democracy a necessity as well as a virtue. As in the case of the State Department, the celebration of 1944 by the military was never subsequently foresworn, even by the right after 1954, and until that date the palpable absence of a coherent political alternative to progressive reform outside of regression to a dictatorship led by one of Ubico's acolytes – the *caudillo* died in New Orleans in 1946 – made the regime tolerable to most as well as desirable to some.[34] The purely generational aspects of the 1944 revolution may have been exaggerated, but it is significant that what may be dubbed 'right-wing' and 'left-wing' interpretations of it were contested within the ranks of those who had staged the revolt – Arana championing the former and Arbenz the latter – whilst the post-interventionist regime was led by officers associated with the dictatorship. Nor should one ignore the fact that although Arbenz was on the left of the political spectrum, he was also a highly respected officer who safeguarded institutional interests from the presidential palace, receiving in return a high degree of loyalty. In sum, whilst UFCO and those elements in Washington considering the overthrow of reform – the State Department itself apparently resisted serious investigation of this course until late 1953 – could identify sympathetic officers, they could not find enough support to make a major move.[35]

Washington's inability to depend upon the military as a counter-revolutionary force was not made fully clear until July 1949, when army commander Colonel Francisco Arana was assassinated. For the first four years of the Arévalo regime Arana seemed the obvious candidate to lead any thermidor, and in all probability his control over the military misled the US as to the ideological reliability of the officer corps as a whole. Arana's ambition to succeed Arévalo in the presidency lay behind his defence of the civilian administration against a plethora of ill-organized rightist plots, this distinctly interested loyalty obscuring substantial political differences with Arbenz and the reformist current in the army. It was only from late 1948, when it was clear that Arana's candidacy would not be supported by any political party, that he himself was perceived – from all the evidence, correctly – to be preparing a coup.[36] His assassination can, therefore, be viewed as a pre-emptive strike to defend the regime – whether Arbenz was directly involved is less evident – and a decisive act inasmuch as a successful coup by Arana would almost certainly have followed the Salvadorean path in eliminating all but the rhetoric of reform.[37] Nevertheless, the failure of the military uprising in response to Arana's death strongly suggests that by that stage matters depended upon far more than the initiatives of individuals. Arana's own fatal delay in staging a challenge and the subsequent collapse of his supporters' effort owed much to the fact that Arévalo had hitherto acceded to military invigilation and tabled a set of strictly modest reforms that were applied with notable caution. By this stage the State Department had begun to modify its assessment of Arévalo as a weak and vacillating character who survived largely by shifting with the tide.[38] It was, in fact, moving to the view that the president had deliberately lulled both his army commander and Washington into a false sense of confidence. After all, the 'hidden agenda' approach to reform in this period was avidly pursued by the Costa Rican PLN (as Figueres's group was to become) and Acción Democrática in Venezuela, both of which organizations were closely allied to Arévalo. There is, however, no evidence that the 'spiritual socialism' espoused by the president was not as anti-communist and social democratic in substance as he repeatedly declared it to be.[39] Furthermore, unlike his regional peers, Arévalo was not a member of any party, and he owed a great many of the 255,000 votes cast for him in December 1944 (out of a total of 295,000) precisely to his independence, the political 'purity' gained by years of exile in Argentina, and his personification of the liberal democratic values thrown up by the anti-dictatorial movement. Whilst his support for the Caribbean Legion – the source of appreciable concern in Washington – was somewhat anomalous within his generally cautious and legalistic approach, this was realized independently of the parties, depended upon military acquiescence, and in no sense amounted to patronage of radicalism per se.[40] Arévalo was undoubtedly a more adept politician than has been generally recognized, but he remained throughout his period in office a solitary and highly vulnerable figure whose moderate programme survived primarily because it cohered with the objective limits and possibilities of the time. The right, by contrast, sought a decisive settling of accounts before conditions were given.

In the political sphere Arévalo's programme was effectively condensed in the constitution of 1945, which replaced the charter of 1879 in a manner fully consonant with other constitutions of this period. Property was identified as possessing a 'social character', thereby providing a legal resource for state intervention, and the franchise was extended to all adults except illiterate women, still a substantial proportion of the population. The university was granted both autonomy and an increased budget, but parties with international affiliations were proscribed in line with the standard continental form for outlawing communist organizations (although none yet existed in Guatemala). In the same vein, vagrancy was abolished – without major effect on either rural order or agricultural production – whilst the restoration of municipal government in 1946 returned autonomous administration to the Indian communities. None of these measures upset the US or any but the most ultramontane domestic forces; they met the central demands of the broad anti-dictatorial movement and yet altered the balance of social forces to a strictly limited degree. Moreover, their introduction greatly drew the sting of the newly formed parties, three of which – the Frente Popular Libertador (FPL); Renovación Nacional (RN); and the Partido de Acción Revolucionaria (PAR) – came to dominate formal politics. All publicly backed Arévalo and served in his cabinets. Yet whilst the FPL possessed a congressional majority and the PAR advocated more radical policies, none ever managed to establish a clear monopoly on either the 'legacy' of 1944 or government patronage, still less popular support.[41]

This weakness, which encouraged sectarianism and impeded all attempts to establish a single 'revolutionary party', may be ascribed in good measure to the lack of middle-class political tradition and the rapid, 'bipartisan' manner in which the central political reforms were introduced; it was also encouraged by the fact that the virtues of Arévalo's independence were followed by the necessities of Arbenz's similar status, derived from his position in the army. Its effects were to dilute the identification of government policy with the pronouncements of any single organization, particularly the ebullient PAR, diffuse the clientelist links of the nascent labour movement, and provide cover for communist activities, allowing the Marxists to remedy some of their own weaknesses by exploiting those of the PAR, entering it and eventually dominating its leadership. The corresponding debility of oligarchic political organization meant that while in practice the FPL pursued a quite conservative line, there was no constant and clearly defined polarization of ideological positions. Instead, Arévalo presided over and Arbenz arbitrated between a stream of claims to patronage, parliamentary competition failing to produce a viable challenge for the presidency, as was evident from the absence of significant opposition in the November 1950 poll.[42] As a result, party politics became a secondary activity, buoyant in expression but feeble in organization. At one level the stridency of competing claims to revolutionary bona fides alarmed Washington simply because it was conducive to a radicalization of the general nationalist sentiment from which no party could afford to stray. Yet until the formation of the PGT in late 1952 no single organization incarnated this line, the fluidity and ambiguity of both policies and personnel shifting the locus of 'real' politics to the much less tangible sphere of 'influence'. This lack of organizational resolution eventually permitted the attribution of positions and sympathies to Arévalo and Arbenz on the basis of the guilt by association and 'duck test' methodology of the McCarthy era, but until that course was made imperative it confused the picture and complicated the characterization of the regime.

If the absence of a finite 'representation' of the radicalism immanent in the 1944 revolution was in itself a key factor in delaying a reactionary response, it possessed more than symbolic importance and accurately reflected the slow and erratic manner in which the 1944 agenda of political democracy elided into that of economic nationalism and social reform. Perhaps the most critical factor in this process was the over-bearing presence of UFCO, which provided the reformists with a target of exactly that definition which the conservative forces lacked. Yet even in this case Arévalo advanced slowly and with moderation, incorporating the nationalist issues at stake within the democratic and legal agenda in his insistence that the labour question be resolved by enactment of a new code and UFCO's position be dealt with by negotiation. Although a series of strikes and invectives in congress during 1946 convinced UFCO that the IRCA might be expropriated, Arévalo permitted Arana to contain the railway-workers, whose union leadership (SAMF) had already signalled its independence from the radical tendencies emerging within the CTG by splitting with it early in 1945. Moreover, in August 1945 Arévalo prohibited any unionization of rural workers until the promulgation of the labour code, and in January 1946 he ordered the closure of the Marxist-dominated Escuela Claridad workers' night-school. Indeed, when the code was finally introduced early in 1947 it appeared to ratify this conservative approach; although it provided the expected clauses as to union rights (eight-hour day, etc.), it also restricted the existence of rural unions to those enterprises with a labour force of at least 500 workers where a minimum of 50 wished to form a union, 60 per cent of whose members would have to be literate in order to receive registration. However, UFCO claimed that this was deeply discriminatory and aimed directly at the corporation, which had refused to renegotiate its 1936 contract and now threatened to withdraw from the country. Whilst the State Department sought to modify some of the company's claims – most notably that it was the only enterprise affected – Washington applied considerable pressure on Arévalo.[43] The final result of this was that the code was amended to permit unions on all rural estates so that whereas early in 1948 there were only eleven organizations, by 1953 at least 345 were in existence.[44] In effect, by challenging the supposedly nationalist element of a markedly conservative law, UFCO and the State Department had contrived to make the legislation much more extensive whilst failing to relieve the company of its unprecedented vulnerability to labour organization, which began to flex its muscles in a series of strikes in 1948--49. There is a certain irony in the fact that the final code was more democratic than the original version and that the whole affair deepened the conviction of the State Department as well as UFCO that Arévalo was decidedly, if not dangerously, 'pro-labour'.[45]

This belief was further hardened when, in December 1949, the president introduced the 'law of forced rental', which realized the social property clauses of the 1945 constitution in obliging the leasing of uncultivated estate lands at a rent of no more than 5 per cent of harvest value. This act was not, though, used to a significant degree against UFCO and indeed was never extensively applied. As was the case with the proposed (and eventually thwarted) income tax law, the measure stood to prejudice local capital more directly than foreign interests, and perhaps for this reason it was never zealously employed. In fact, US investment in Guatemala rose during this period, albeit modestly, from $86.9 million in 1943 to $105.9 million in 1950, the climate for entrepreneurs being supported by the establishment of the National Institute for the Development of Production (INFOP) that provided state credit to the private sector, the investment of which accounted for 8 per cent of GDP in 1950 compared to 3.8 per cent in 1944.[46] Wages also rose appreciably, in the urban sector by as much as 80 per cent and in the countryside to around double the level of the late 1930s, although rates varied and were seldom paid fully in cash.[47] In the five years following the war the economy was buoyant rather than booming – although banana exports rose 34 per cent between 1944 and 1949 – and much of the increase in pay was determined by the establishment of formal minimum rates together with a significant expansion of government expenditure upon services and the freeing of the labour market in the coffee sector. Consequently, one should neither discount the pressure on capital nor overemphasize the role of organized labour in obtaining economic gains.

The development of an organizationally coherent and politically pugnacious labour movement was markedly uneven, even after the introduction of the code. The early establishment of unions on UFCO plantations placed the company under pressure that was unprecedented yet qualified by three years of state restriction on labour activity. There was effectively no organization elsewhere in the countryside until after 1947 whilst the urban unions were constrained by the small size and artisanal character of industry – in 1953 1,070 enterprises with a total labour force of 20,500 at an average of 19 workers per plant – the absence of virtually any syndicalist tradition, and ideological differences that combined the essence of disputes witnessed elsewhere in the 1920s with those determined more directly by contemporary developments. As a result, no rural confederation was established until May 1950, the urban movement remained divided until October 1951, and the two coexisted uneasily even after the introduction of the agrarian reform in June 1952. Both the recent formation of plantation and sectoral unions and the comparatively long delay in national unification and political activism served to shield the labour movement from precipitate repression and provide the small communist group with the opportunity to deepen its organizational influence in a manner similar to that undertaken within the political field inside the PAR. Hence, whilst there was no open Marxist organization in Guatemala until the end of 1952, by 1947 communists were acting as the general secretaries of the PAR (José Manuel Fortuny) and the CTG (Víctor Manuel Gutiérrez). Once again, polarization was impeded by a form of parallax.

The division between the CTG and the SAMF-dominated Federación Sindical de Guatemala (FSG) began over the question of affiliation with Lombardo Toledano's CTAL, which the CTG joined at the earliest opportunity. This link with the Mexican unions, and particularly with Lombardo, proved to be of enduring importance, in a sense compensating for the previous decades of isolation. After 1948, when the conditions for union politics underwent a sharp change in Mexico, relations did not diminish despite the fact that Lombardo now lacked the authority of earlier years. This was partly because the Mexican left could support a popular anti-imperialist cause in Guatemala without major risk on either side of the border, and partly because many Central American and Spanish exiles found the country's provincial but politically uplifting climate preferable to the uncommon chill of post-*charrazo* Mexico.[48] Arévalo was periodically prevailed upon to expel clutches of foreign radicals whose political credentials were more manifest than those of local activists, but his own experience of exile, sympathy for the Spanish republic and Central American union, together with the fact that the foreigners bolstered the state's administrative skills as well as those of the left, ensured that the 'alien question', which had, of course, been at the heart of J. Edgar Hoover's original US anti-communist drive in 1919–20, never developed into the campaign sought by Washington and the indigenous right. It is unclear to what extent the experience and advice of Mexican radicals prompted the Guatemalan communists to embrace the entryist strategy. Until 1950 there existed few feasible alternatives and when, in November 1949, Gutiérrez's radical union militants broke with Fortuny's predominantly middle-class group and left both the clandestine Partido Communista Guatemalteco (PCG; formed in September 1949) and the PAR within which it was operating, Lombardo's efforts at mediation came to nought.[49] At the same time, it is possible to overestimate the importance of CTAL in determining the division between the CTG and the FSG that impeded labour unification for five years. Under the control of Manuel Pinto Usaga SAMF, which effectively controlled the FSG, was not so much 'apolitical' as opposed to the 'adventurism' of the communists with whom its leaders battled for influence within the PAR.[50] Pinto Usaga was a persistent thorn in the flesh of IRCA, and since he facilitated the 1949–50 truce with Gutiérrez and the eventual unification of the urban unions in the Confederación General de Trabajadores de Guatemala (CGTG) he was particularly odious in US eyes (a 'veiled communist' – one step up from a 'pro-communist' and in some senses more reprehensible than the full-blooded, overt variety), but the railway-workers' prolonged resistance to the communist influence clearly implied by unification was a key factor in restraining union radicalism.[51]

At the time of the counter-revolution the CGTG claimed to have more than 100,000 members in 500 affiliated unions. Because this was a very considerable proportion of the urban working population and since the general secretaryship of the confederation was held by Víctor Manuel Gutiérrez, it could be said that the Guatemalan working class was under communist control. That this was not the case was due not simply to the fact that numbers on paper bore only an approximate relation to the practice on the ground but also to the intrinsic limits of national union leadership – abetted by the overwhelmingly rural and unintegrated character of the economy – together with the deeply uneasy relations between the 'workerist' Marxists headed by Gutiérrez and the 'politicians' led by Fortuny. This division took place almost immediately after the clandestine PCG was formed inside the PAR in the autumn of 1949 – that is, once the communists were moving towards a more than purely cellular form of existence – and lasted until March 1952. It therefore covered a particularly critical period of labour activism during which both the urban CGTG and the rural Confederación Nacional Campesina de Guatemala (CNCG) were established and when Arbenz was elected with union backing. At this time the State Department estimated the number of communist activists to be between 500 and 1,000 – in all probability it was closer to the lower figure, which would also have included many *simpatizantes* – a relatively small group that had only four deputies in congress, no representatives in the cabinet, and less than two dozen militants in senior administrative posts.[52] However, US perceptions of a much greater Marxist influence were not mere flights of fancy, and the fact that this political community was divided precisely over the question of union work (the entryist issue was an extension of this dispute) when one leader headed the country's largest confederation gave the debate a more than purely sectarian character. The tension between Gutiérrez and Fortuny certainly enabled the SAMF/FSG bloc to move towards the CTG, and once Gutiérrez established the Partido Revolucionario Obrero de Guatemala (PROG) independently of both the PCG and the PAR he created a third pole in left-wing politics in a manner that signalled distance from the communist core and yet did not lead to significant competition with it. The effect of this was to enhance Gutiérrez's own reputation with the broad union membership and to thwart the threat of an anti-communist current within the new CGTG. Gutiérrez returned to the fold shortly before the establishment of the PGT – pressure from Moscow seems to have been instrumental – but for three years his autonomous line kept union politics simultaneously fluid and radical.[53] In the eyes of the right and Washington these comings and goings made little difference – Gutiérrez remained a committed Marxist and the CGTG an avowedly radical organization – yet they demonstrate both the organizational weakness of Guatemalan communism and how that weakness proved to be an advantage by averting a major rupture within the radical labour bloc at a time when politics as a whole was rapidly polarizing.

The key point in this polarization was the assassination of Arana on 18 July 1949 and the subsequent abortive coup of his followers that left some 150 dead and 300 wounded – a toll far higher than that of October 1944. Arbenz's distribution of weapons to the students and workers, together with the call for a general strike thwarted the uprising, converted the colonel into the undisputed protector of the reformist regime, and provided the labour movement with both increased confidence and a clear alliance. It may be stretching matters to suggest a parallel with the events of October 1945 in Argentina, but some underlying similarities are certainly evident. Following debate within the unions over tactics, Arbenz's candidacy in the November 1950 elections was fully supported and the right wing's 'minute of silence' on the first anniversary of Arana's death was the object of enough opposition to indicate that this support would be militant and consequential. Sealed four years into the regime, within the parameters of liberal democracy, at a point where the unions were acquiring organizational resources and demands for economic reform were on the rise, the military–labour alliance was forged in peculiarly advantageous circumstances at a local level whilst the international context was equally unpropitious. Internally, the fact that Arévalo was able to serve out the last eighteen months of his term unassailed from either the right or the left provided an aura of continuity and, despite the fact that he did not endorse Arbenz (or any other candidate), effectively bestowed the democratic mandate of October 1944 on the decidedly more Bonapartist regime that succeeded it.

This sense of legitimacy was heightened by the fact that Arbenz's principal opponent at the polls was General Ydígoras, who was closely associated with the Ubico dictatorship and seen to repudiate the revolution *tout court* rather than simply dispute its terms from within. Arbenz's decisive victory – by 267,000 votes to 74,000 – was not challenged by Washington, which had pursued a policy of extreme caution during the campaign so as not to excite nationalist fervour. Moreover, at this stage the State Department still perceived the colonel as an opportunist with whom it could treat.[54] Such a policy of 'watchful waiting' may have been encouraged by the fact that the State Department's labour officers and the embassy staff remained embroiled in a dispute over the legal and political acceptability of the 1947 labour code and its ramifications for UFCO.[55] Equally, whilst North

American sensibilities continued to be aggravated by such matters as the playing of nationalist tunes instead of the 'Star-spangled Banner' to greet the Puerto Rican team to the Central American Olympics in Guatemala City, it remained a fact that in the wake of the Chinese revolution and at the onset of the Korean war Guatemala voted with the US on most issues in the UN whilst its new government – as distinct from certain political elements within the country – showed and admitted to no disposition to alter existing external policy, meddled in the affairs of its neighbours less than any prior regime, and desisted from promoting communism to the same degree as it asserted its right to exist as a national force.

The argument as to whether it was a general 'Cold War logic' or the more direct interests of UFCO that prompted the shift from 'watchful waiting' and discreet pressure in 1951 to indirect armed intervention in 1954 is somewhat artificial in that these factors are only partially distinguishable. As has been indicated, the professional diplomats continued to be cautious and upheld the strategy of diplomatic pressure and economic isolation (although this never came to include a boycott of coffee and bananas) until late 1953.[56] Yet by then the general panorama was quite distinct from that prevailing when Arbenz assumed office. The replacement of Truman by Eisenhower (and Acheson by Dulles) must be accounted a factor of significant – if not decisive – importance, both in general terms and because senior officials of the new administration possessed especially close ties with UFCO.[57] The degree to which Eisenhower's election condemned the Guatemalan revolution is open to discussion at least insofar as the new administration continued Truman's policy of negotiation with the revolutionary regime that came to power in Bolivia in April 1952. But Eisenhower was prepared to tolerate nationalization of the tin mines and an agrarian reform in Bolivia because they did not greatly affect US capital, whereas in Guatemala less radical measures did so directly. In view of the high and growing US pressure over both the 'persecution' of UFCO and alleged indulgence of communism by Guatemala City since 1947, Arbenz's introduction of an agrarian reform law in June 1952 – when the US presidential campaign was underway – and his legalization of the PGT in December – when Eisenhower had already defeated Stevenson – show every sign of corresponding to local requirements and little, if any, effort to alter what had seemingly become an irretrievable impasse with Washington. There is no indication

that the Guatemalan authorities subsequently relaxed their determined efforts to come to terms with the US or that they considered
their policies to constitute a decisive provocation. Of course, they had
relatively few precedents upon which to draw in assessing the likely
consequences of their acts, which fell clearly within the parameters of
the constitution and far short of, say, Cárdenas's nationalization of the
oil industry in Mexico. They may well, therefore, have adjudged such
moves as unlikely to prejudice in a critical fashion already poor
relations with Washington whilst greatly improving domestic support.
(The question of how far Latin American regimes tailored their policies
to shifts within US political life is of relevance here, but the scope for
this was discernibly more limited in the early 1950s than it was even a
decade later.) The agrarian reform indubitably enhanced the local
popularity of the government, but both measures, and particularly the
registration of a Communist Party, gave the advocates of counter-
revolution exactly those substantive targets for condemnation and
mobilizing issues that had previously been lacking. They served to give
the initiative to those both inside Guatemala and abroad who believed
that, in the words of US Ambassador John Peurifoy, 'if [Arbenz] is not
a Communist, he will certainly do until one comes along ... normal
approaches will not work in Guatemala'.[58]

The agrarian reform, Decree 90 of 27 June 1952, was a deliberately
modest measure defended by Arbenz as the best means by which to
promote capitalism in the countryside. All farms under 90 hectares
(219 acres) and those of up to 300 hectares (488 acres), two-thirds of
which were under cultivation, were exempted, as were all forests,
communal lands and completely cultivated properties.[59] Equally,
redistribution of the *fincas nacionales* absorbed much of the shock
anticipated by the landlord class, which was not severely hit but
responded with vehemence to Central America's first modern agrarian
reform. Such repudiation was entirely predictable for a deeply reactionary sector sustained by forced labour until seven years earlier
and determined to avoid the 'Bolshevik path' of Mexico. It may,
indeed, have been more concerned by the level of peasant mobilization
than distribution per se. By 1952 the rural labour movement was
organized at a national level, that in the towns finally unified, and the
two acting in erratic but unprecedented concert. Thus, although
mobilization in the countryside did not approach the levels witnessed
in Bolivia at the time (still less those in Mexico of earlier decades), the

issue was profoundly worrying for landed capital, which was quick to denounce the existence of openly-declared communists in the CGTG and the Departamento Agrario Nacional (DAN) that administered the reform. In fact, the PGT possessed an exceptionally weak apparatus in the countryside, and while both the Church and the landlords railed against the 'Bolsheviks' in the CNCG, the domestic anti-communist scare campaign never took firm root or seriously challenged the regime. However, the reform was hotly denounced by UFCO, which, with some 15 per cent of its 650,000 acres of plantation under threat, was by far the most prejudiced party and particularly vulnerable to the device of assessing compensation on the basis of tax returns since these had always been exceptionally modest.[60] The threat was, therefore, far greater than that proffered by the labour code, and the State Department now rallied to the corporation's defence without qualification. Although Arbenz's complementary economic policies of building a road to the Caribbean coast to break the monopoly of the IRCA railway and developing a state-owned electricity plant to compete with US-controlled supply had been recommended by the 1950 World Bank mission, these measures were now perceived as constitutive of a coherent and dangerous nationalist project. In sum, by the end of 1952 the US had come to oppose Arbenz's economic programme in itself, the interpretation that it was conducive to radicalization now being of secondary importance.

The 'problem' of communism projected to the US public in terms of an uncomplicated 'Red Conspiracy' was, in fact, always discerned in Washington less in terms of a Bolshevik takeover − the evidence for which was negligible − than in those of Moscow and the PGT edging Guatemala into a 'neutralist' stance.[61] Whilst it might be argued that Mexico at least had been able to approximate to this position over the previous three decades, the terms of that country's 'relative autonomy' were quite distinct and required persistent policing, which had always included restricting Mexican influence in the isthmus. The general political conditions of 1953−54 made any reduction of US hegemony implied by 'neutralism' particularly dangerous, and the Mexican government was in any case entirely unwilling to defend Guatemala's shift towards such status beyond reaffirmation of the principles of non-intervention and sovereignty in the diplomatic sphere. Lacking the support of a 'non-aligned' bloc in the UN, let alone in the OAS where the US concentrated its campaign, the Arbenz regime was far too weak to resist Washington's offensive for any length of time. The Guatemalan defence necessarily had to focus on the rule of law, and this created a number of subordinate difficulties for Washington, in that it was confronted with a case where a properly constituted government in control of national territory was supported rather than subverted by a communist organization. Nonetheless, neither the terms of the Rio treaty nor the *modus operandi* of the OAS depended upon strict observance of constitutionality. Furthermore, the US conviction that the difference between the real and 'hidden' agendas in Guatemala was now a matter of mere formality determined that realpolitik would prevail, even if Dulles took care to employ surrogate forces as the public actors in Arbenz's downfall. The colonel's second line of defence – that his domestic policies were intrinsically desirable and fortified capitalism whilst the issue of foreign relations provided no basis for concern whatsoever – was of little avail abroad, and it is noteworthy that he did not, in fact, embrace the notion of a developmentalist 'third way' to the degree evidenced by Perón or the Bolivian MNR, still less Mossadegh in Iran or Jagan in Guyana.

These two elements – constitutionalism and the modesty of economic reform – may be deemed purely marginal in the context of US management of the hemisphere. Yet Washington's inability to cleave the military from the regime simply on the basis of anti-communism should be viewed in such terms. Even after Colonel Monzón, Arbenz's minister of the interior, was impeached and removed from office for suppressing the communist paper *Octubre* in 1952, the army resisted staging a coup that would have greatly eased the US position by rendering the extensive domestic and diplomatic campaign of the first six months of 1954 unnecessary. Such reluctance certainly enabled Washington to make a virtue of necessity and undertake an operation that had a considerable 'demonstration effect' well beyond the Caribbean Basin; but the matter should not be taken lightly since after the formidable effort at destabilization and use of CIA bombers, the invasion from Honduras led by Colonel Castillo Armas very nearly failed to achieve its objective and was in palpable danger of collapsing in ignominious defeat. In the event, the army's refusal to repeat its actions of October 1944 and July 1949 in withholding weaponry from the civilian population extinguished the possibility of further deviance from Washington's mandate. The inability of the unions and *campesinado* to stage independent resistance demonstrated that, even after the accelerated mobilization of 1950–54, the popular forces still lacked the power to enforce a domestic stalemate. This absence of a decisive struggle at the moment of external intervention highlights the degree to which the politics of the previous decade depended upon the shifting and fragile terms of local equilibrium that were as difficult to assess from the outside as they were to manipulate from within.

For a number of days after Arbenz's departure the officer corps continued to operate on the assumption that these conditions still obtained, senior officers disputing Ambassador Peurifoy's designation of Castillo Armas as the new president. However, the mass of Guatemalans were rapidly and violently disabused of any notion that there was further room for manoeuvre. Within a matter of months most unions had been dismantled, almost all redistributed land returned to its former owners, left-wing organizations effectively proscribed and their leaders either exiled, jailed or, less often, executed. UFCO's contracts were restored at only slightly less than their earlier levels of generosity, and the apparatus of liberal democracy was evacuated of any substance. All this did not exactly amount to a return to the status quo ante – neither debt peonage nor the vagrancy laws were restored – but the counter-revolution was enforced with such determination that the Guatemalan left subsequently remained deeply suspicious of legal and electoralist strategies (and was amongst the first to adopt the 'Cuban road' that its own experience played no small part in encouraging) whilst a traumatized and profoundly relieved right wing henceforth viewed reformist policies as inherently conducive to Bolshevism, resisting for three decades all but the most superficial amendments to the free market and dictatorial rule. 'Cold War politics' persisted far longer in Guatemala than almost anywhere else in Latin America. Its polarities were long delayed but finally established with such a vengeance that the subsequent influence of the Cuban revolution, which engendered significantly new terms in hemispheric politics, was always overshadowed by that of 1954. The price of one period of exceptionalism was another, of much greater length and incomparably greater human suffering.

Notes

1. This approach, of course, reverses that normally taken with respect to post-war Guatemala, namely how and why did Washington overthrow the Arbenz regime? Studies of the 1954 intervention and its immediate background are now sufficiently detailed to render a further account unnecessary. The standard contemporary account, written from an unbending anti-communist position, is Ronald M. Schneider, *Communism in Guatemala*, New York 1958. For a more moderate and critical appraisal, see Richard H. Immerman, 'Guatemala as Cold War History', *Political Science Quarterly*, vol. 95, no. 4, 1980–81, and *The CIA in Guatemala. The Foreign Policy of Invervention*, Austin 1982. A less scholarly if equally detailed study that attributes a much greater role to the United Fruit Company is provided in Stephen Schlesinger and Stephen Kinzer, *Bitter Fruit. The Untold Story of the American Coup in Guatemala*, London 1982. José M. Aybar de Soto, *Dependency and Intervention: The Case of Guatemala in 1954*, Boulder 1978, adopts a rather more schematic perspective.

2. There was no banana enclave in El Salvador, where the coffee oligarchy was, if anything, stronger than that in Guatemala. UFCO faced subordinate competition from Standard Fruit in Honduras, but that country continued to lack a significant dominant class based upon export agriculture and only adopted coffee in the 1940s. Banana production was never established on a stable basis in Nicaragua whereas in Costa Rica UFCO possessed a monopoly of neither cultivation and export nor the railway network.

3. Victor Bulmer-Thomas, *The Political Economy of Central America since 1920*, Cambridge 1987, pp. 37; 77.

4. Kenneth J. Grieb, *Guatemalan Caudillo. The Regime of Jorge Ubico*, Athens, Ohio 1979; David McCreery, 'Debt Servitude in Rural Guatemala, 1875–1936', *Hispanic American Historical Review*, vol. 63, no. 4, 1983. Between 1932 and 1943 the country's roads were extended from 1,375 to 6,375 miles. Bulmer-Thomas, p. 71.

5. It is frequently asserted that a Communist Party was established in 1922 on the basis of the Unión Obrera Socialista (1921), but this organization never took root despite receiving informal Comintern recognition. In 1928 two militants of the Federación Regional Obrera de Guatemala (FROG) participated in the Sixth Congress of the International, and in 1929 the FROG was recognized by the Red Trade Union International. Claims for the establishment of a Communist Party in 1929 are also made, but there is no evidence that this took organizational shape beyond informal meetings of FROG militants, and the PGT recognizes its origins to go back no further than 1949. Víctor Manuel Gutiérrez, *Breve Historia del Movimiento Sindical de Guatemala*, Mexico 1964; Huberto Alvarado Arellano, *Apuntes para la Historia del Partido Guatemalteco del Trabajo*, Guatemala City 1975. For the weakness of the labour movement at the end of the 1920s and in the early 1930s, see José Luis Balcarcel, 'El Movimiento Obrero en Guatemala', in Pablo González Casanova (ed.), *Historia del Movimiento Obrero en América Latina*, vol. 2, Mexico 1985; Brian Murphy, 'The Stunted Growth of Campesino Organisations', in Richard H. Adams, *Crucifixion by Power. Essays on Guatemalan Social Structure, 1944–1966*, Austin 1970.

6. Kenneth J. Grieb, 'The Guatemalan Military and the Revolution of 1944', *The Americas*, vol. XXXII, no. 1, July 1975.

7. Grieb, *Guatemalan Caudillo*, suggests that Ubico cultivated a popular following within the peasantry although this is doubted by McCreery and Jim Handy, *Gift of the Devil. A History of Guatemala*, Toronto 1984, not least because such observations are based on official papers. Ubico, a lover of motorcycles, was constantly on the move and

would frequently make unannounced visits to the provinces. Although an amateur drummer and admirer of Napoleon, he was less eccentric than General Hernández Martínez in El Salvador.

8. Bulmer-Thomas, pp. 308; 312; 322.

9. Carol A. Smith, 'El desarrollo de la primacía urbana, la dependencia y la formación de clases en Guatemala', *Mesoamérica*, no. 8, December 1984.

10. Bulmer-Thomas, pp. 81–2; 312.

11. Ibid., pp. 91–2; 350.

12. Ibid., p. 79.

13. Ibid., pp. 93; 330.

14. Ibid., pp. 95; 332.

15. Ibid., p. 322.

16. Ralph Lee Woodward, *Central America. A Nation Divided*, New York 1976, p. 165; Julio Castellanos Cambranes, *Coffee and Peasants in Guatemala. The Origins of the Modern Plantation Economy in Gautemala, 1852–1897*, Stockholm 1985, p. 145.

17. Mario Monteforte Toledo, *Guatemala. Monografía Sociológica*, Mexico 1959, p. 429; Leo A. Suslow, *Aspects of Social Reform in Guatemala*, New York 1950, p. 66.

18. Hull to Long, United States National Archive (hereafter USNA), 740.00112A European War, 1939/36499a, 28 February 1944.

19. Long to Washington, USNA, 740.00112A European War, 1939/36572, 18 April 1944.

20. Long to Washington, USNA, 740.00112A European War, 1939/36610, 16 May 1944; Long to Washington, 740.14112A/89, 13 June 1944.

21. 'A confidential American informant was sent to the Embassy this morning by a Cabinet Minister to report that a group of doctors and nurses are planning a sitdown strike along Salvadoran lines and to inquire whether American doctors and nurses could be counted on to handle emergency cases. I replied that this would constitute intervention in internal politics in violation of our well known policy.' Long to Washington, USNA, 814.00/1464, 21 June 1944. 'The Department assumes that the "good offices" referred to in your telegram ... relate exclusively to the transmission of messages between the contending factions and do not involve the preparation and submission of formulas of settlement etc.' Washington to Long, 814.00/1470, 21 June 1944. See also Washington to Long, 814.00/7–744, 7 July 1944; Long to Washington, 814.00/7–1444, 14 July 1944.

22. Long to Washington, USNA, 814.00/7–1444, 14 July 1944; Mario Monteforte Toledo, 'La Reforma Agraria en Gautemala', *El Trimestre Económico*, vol. XIX, no. 3, 1952; Neale J. Pearson, 'Guatemala: the Peasant Union Movement, 1944–1954', in Henry A. Landsberger (ed.), *Latin American Peasant Movements*, Ithaca 1969, p. 343; Nathan L. Whetten, *Guatemala: the Land and the People*, New York 1961, p. 163.

23. National Intelligence Estimate, USNA, 11 March 1952, UNA, NIE-62.

24. Long to Washington, USNA, 814.00/10-1344, 13 October 1944.

25. Long to Washington, USNA, 814.00/7-1444, 7 July 1944; Affeld to Washington, 814.01/10-2644, 26 October 1944.

26. Armour to Long, USNA, 814.00/9-2644, 3 October 1944.

27. In April 1944 junior officers staged an abortive coup against General Hernández Martínez, the Salvadorean dictator who subsequently shot the rebel ringleaders, causing such a popular outcry and loss of control that he was obliged to flee the country in early May. There then followed five months of popular mobilization in an election campaign, which was halted in a reactionary coup headed by Colonel Osmín Aguirre y Salinas on 21 October – one day after the Guatemalan revolt, the celebration of which

in San Salvador was savagely repressed by Colonel Aguirre's troops.

28. Affeld to Washington, USNA, 814.00/10-1744, 17 October 1944.

29. Memo by the Director of the Executive Secretariat, 29 May 1950, USNA, Under-Secretary's Meetings, Lot 52 D 250.

30. Quoted in Manuel Galich, *Por Qué Lucha Guatemala. Arévalo y Arbenz. Dos Hombres contra un Imperio*, Buenos Aires 1956, pp. 334–6.

31. Affeld to Washington, USNA, 814.00/10-1744, 17 October 1944.

32. In August 1949, a month after the assassination of Colonel Francisco Arana and the abortive coup attempt by rightists, the Partido de Acción Revolucionaria (PAR) issued a manifesto calling upon the masses to support the army and praising the military as a professional institution at the service of the people. *Nuevo Diario*, 19 August 1949. At the time the PAR's leadership was still under the strong influence of the Marxists of Vanguardia Democrática Guatemalteca (VDG), which operated inside the party as a clandestine 'entryist' group. After the counter-revolution the PGT recognized that it had been 'far too soft' with the military leadership. PGT, *La Intervención Norte-americana en Guatemala y el Derrocamiento del Regimen Democrático*, n.p. 1955, pp. 3–4; 30–6.

33. In a typical case, Colonel Oscar Morales López insisted, when visiting the State Department in December 1950, that the renewal of arms sales was necessary for the containment of communism. USNA, 714.562/12-2950. Morales was politely rebuffed although the US was no longer able to defend its policy on the grounds that Guatemala had not ratified the Rio treaty, duly undertaken in September 1950 but complicated by the country's claim on Belize. In an internal policy statement of May 1951 the State Department identified the army as weak and indicated that the US unofficially provided support to the Guatemalan military although no details were given. USNA, 611.14/5-251.

34. In one of his first speeches after the intervention Castillo Armas went out of his way to distinguish 'the social gains' made in the wake of October 1944 from the practice of communism. *El Imparcial*, 6 July 1954.

35. A detailed assessment of US policy is beyond our scope here but it should be mentioned that in May 1950 the State Department warned UFCO executive Thomas Corcoran not to pursue his idea of influencing the November 1950 election. USNA, 714.00/5-1550. Equally, in October 1952 it acted to impede a planned overthrow of Arbenz by Somoza, who, it was recognized, would not have entertained taking on the Guatemalan military had he not been encouraged (supposedly in error) by Truman's assistant military aide, General Neil Mara, to believe that Washington would offer support. USNA, 714.00/10-352. A CIA memo of December 1952 to the State Department scrupulously noted that the Agency had given 'no overt or covert' assistance to the anti-Arbenz plot. 714.00/12-1252. In May 1953 the Department recognized that Arbenz's hold over the junior officer corps was not so strong as his hold over the high command yet reiterated that in the event of an invasion Guatemala would have a clear case for complaint in the OAS. National Intelligence Estimate, 19 May 1953, reprinted in *US Foreign Relations. American Republics, 1952–54*, vol. IV, p. 1071.

36. See, for example, USNA, 814.00/7-846; 814.00/11-1248 on Arana's discontent with Arévalo and possible links with a coup.

37. Even Ronald Schneider stops short of directly accusing Arbenz. *Communism in Guatemala*, pp. 28–31. The report of the US airforce attaché is more direct but still only refers to a 'strongly suggested implication'. USNA, 814.00/2-1049.

38. Early in 1945 the State Department, suspicious of Arévalo's 'radical tendencies', cabled the embassy in Buenos Aires to check up on his politics. It was informed that, 'it

is my considered opinion that anyone reasonably well informed about his teachings, writings and general activities would be inclined to pass over such suspicions as being so utterly without foundation as to call for no response.' USNA, 814.00/1-1345. At the beginning of 1947 the embassy in Guatemala said the president was 'far more of a student than a politician'. 814.00/1-247. Even after the controversy of the labour code the embassy considered that 'he appears to have a realistic approach to the problem' although 'inherent sympathy for the laboring classes may swing him at the crucial moments'. 814.504/12-1947. By the end of his term Arévalo was described to Truman as 'an extreme leftist rather than a Communist'. 611.14/9-950.

39. Arévalo described himself as an admirer of the New Deal, and in advocating 'spiritual socialism' he fused motifs of that secular mysticism common amongst the Central American middle class with a less familiar developmentalist vision: 'We are socialists because we live in the twentieth century. But we are not materialist socialists. We do not believe that man is primarily stomach. We believe that man is above all else a will for dignity.... Our socialism does not aim at an ingenious distribution of material goods or the stupid economic equalization of men who are economically different. Our socialism aims to liberate man psychologically and spiritually ... the materialist concept has become a tool in the hands of totalitarian forces. Communism, Fascism and Nazism have also been socialist. But theirs is a socialism that gives food with the left hand while the right mutilates the moral and civic values of man.' Juan José Arévalo, *Escritos Políticos*, Guatemala City 1945, p. 199.

40. The State Department viewed the Caribbean Legion and Arévalo's support for it as 'one of the principal causes of unrest and instability ... in the Caribbean'. USNA, Under Secretary's Meetings, Lot 53 D250, 'Current Relations with Guatemala', 29 May 1950. It is interesting that late in December 1952 a CIA memo stressed Arbenz's support for the presidential campaign of Figueres in Costa Rica as an 'un-American' activity. 714.00/12-1252.

41. The activities of the parties are too labyrinthine to discuss here. There was an almost constant series of ruptures and alliances between 1945 and 1948, general unity during the crisis of 1949, renewed conflict from 1951 to 1954 qualified only by resistance to Arbenz's attempt to foster an officialist party, which never got off the ground. In the 1949 congressional elections the FPL won 30 seats, the right-wing alliance 15, the PAR 11, RN 5, and independents 3.

42. In the election Miguel García Granados, formerly of the FPL, won 29,000 votes. The FPL was the only party to campaign against Arbenz and Ydígoras but ran two candidates and eventually withdrew.

43. At the end of July the Guatemalan foreign minister was visited by the State Department's chief of Central American affairs (Robert Newbegin) who requested a precise response to the claims of discrimination. In August and September the US ambassador visited Arévalo to press the point home. USNA, 814.504/8-447; 814.504/8-847; 814.504/9-2247. By the end of the year Arévalo had agreed to present most of the required revisions to congress, 814.504/12-1947.

44. Pearson, p. 350.

45. See note 38 above. In an exchange with US Ambassador Richard C. Patterson in January 1950 Arévalo stressed that Guatemalan 'labour troubles' were the result not of communist influence but of that emanating from the US coal and steel strikes, which, he indicated with unusual use of irony, instilled little faith in North American management techniques. *US Foreign Relations 1952–4. American Republics*, pp. 865–6.

46. Bulmer-Thomas, p. 120.

47. Handy, p. 108; Pearson, p. 336.

48. Schneider provides a detailed account of the activities of foreign militants. Early in 1947 the US embassy reported, 'every opportunity has been taken to bring to the president's attention the changed position with regard to relations between the Mexican government and labor subsequent to the inauguration of President Alemán'. USNA, 814.00/1-247.

49. Schneider, pp. 66–7.

50. Ibid., p. 63.

51. Ibid., pp. 171–2.

52. In March 1952 the State Department figure was 500; two years later it was put at between 2,000 and 3,000. National Intelligence Estimate, 11 March 1952, *Foreign Relations 1952–4*, p. 1033; USNA, 714.00/4-1954. According to Mario Monteforte Toledo, the party had 1,300 activists at its peak, *Guatemala*, p. 316.

53. Schneider, p. 67, notes that Gutiérrez visited Moscow in December 1951 and that upon his return in February 1952 the PROG voted to dissolve itself in the name of unity.

54. *Foreign Relations 1950*, vol. II, p. 877; USNA, 714.001/11-1560.

55. USNA, 611.14/5-1750, Memo Fishburn to Miller, 19 April 1950; 611.14/5-1750, Wells to Washington, 17 May 1950.

56. USNA, 711.04114/2-2850; 611.14/5-251.

57. For details of the links, see Schlesinger and Kinzer, *Bitter Fruit.*

58. USNA, 611.14/12-1753.

59. For details of the agrarian reform, see Guillermo Paz, *Guatemala: Reforma Agraria*, San José 1987; Handy, pp. 126 ff.; Pearson; Mario Monteforte Toledo, 'La Reforma Agraria en Guatemala', *El Trimestre Económico*, vol. XIX, no. 3, 1952.

60. Handy, p. 142.

61. National Intelligence Estimate, 'Probable Developments in Guatemala', 19 May 1953, *Foreign Relations 1952–4*, vol. IV, p. 1061.

4

Reflections on the Nicaraguan Election

Following the defeat of the FSLN in the Nicaraguan elections of February 1990, the state of that country's politics remains unclear and unpredictable. Although there can be no doubt that Violeta Chamorro's victory represents a major setback not only for the Sandinistas but also for the Latin American left as a whole, it would be wrong to depict it as a categorical defeat of the Nicaraguan revolution. The revolution may indeed be over in many senses, but the FSLN's loss of governmental office has to be weighed against the fact that this was incurred through a fair poll freely convoked by the Sandinistas, whose vote massively outstripped that of any other single party. Equally, the FSLN remained undefeated on the military front, and in the immediate aftermath of Chamorro's inauguration it was able to secure the effective integrity of the armed forces that had defended the revolutionary state for over a decade. These two factors alone possess a historical singularity, and underline the need for caution in assessing a situation that is as fluid and confusing in its detail as it is difficult to place in comparative context. Nonetheless, it is possible to make some broad observations as a first step beyond the tributes and expressions of resolution that immediately followed the election.

The poll of 25 February 1990 produced one simple, indisputable result: the opposition UNO alliance led by Violeta Chamorro won 55 per cent of the ballot against 41 per cent for the FSLN. Although the Sandinistas' share of the vote came close to that which had provided a 'landslide victory' for the British Conservatives, it was far lower than anticipated by most participants and observers, increasing the sense in which the election had not just produced a change in government but delivered a historic political defeat. The reaction abroad (considered below) sharpened this image, and it may well prove to be the case that the election has greater consequence beyond Nicaragua's frontiers than within them. In all events, the predictable projection of the matter as absolutely decisive is in need of quite substantial qualification. This is especially so since it forms part of a global political scenario in which what is seen to be is as contagious as what is. Moreover, not all of those affected are court appointees of whose findings it is sufficient to ask '*cui bono?*'. In such a mood it is, more than usual, necessary to insist upon respect for matters small as well as great, and to challenge those who would see this as nothing more than a strategem to alleviate distress. A little scrutiny of the case of Nicaragua produces a very mixed picture, but it is assuredly not one that damns the left to extracting virtues from necessities.

The Result: Shock at the Obvious

To ask why the result of the election was such a surprise is to pose a question that extends well beyond the immediate circumstances of the poll, although these were undoubtedly important. The key factor here is less the fact that the FSLN was confronted by truly formidable forces – this was widely recognized prior to the election and lay at the heart of subsequent explanations of its results by Sandinista supporters – than the overestimation of the party's capacity to resist these forces. Whilst such an attitude on the part of sympathizers may be understood in good measure by the depth of their commitment, it would seem that the FSLN leaders themselves shared this belief well beyond the allowable limits of political conviction. After all, they studiously eschewed a short-term reflation of the economy prior to the campaign – a decision that would seem to reflect their confidence far more accurately than the necessary presumption of success once they got on the stump.

In November 1984, the FSLN had gained a very comfortable victory with 66 per cent of the vote in a poll that Washington chose first to denigrate and then to ignore, but which was widely judged to be fair in itself and a reasonably accurate reflection of popular sympathy.

Although this success was assisted by the last-minute withdrawal of the leading opposition candidate, Arturo Cruz, its root cause lay in the extensive sympathy and authority enjoyed by the Frente because of its leadership in the overthrow of the Somozo dictatorship, the barbarism of which was keenly remembered. The FSLN justifiably received electoral ratification of its revolutionary valour and promise, notwithstanding a rapidly sharpening economic recession, two years of escalating counter-revolutionary activity, and the invasion of Grenada – the latter seeming to presage a major US offensive to follow the widely anticipated re-election of Ronald Reagan a few days after the Nicaraguan poll.

Conditions in 1984, then, were decidedly tough, but those in 1990 were incomparably worse. In May 1985 the USA had imposed an economic boycott, and this, combined with a world recession and discrete but important government mismanagement, had plunged the country into a catastrophic state of hyperinflation, shortages, indebtedness and general disorganization. Confronted with a situation that threatened the survival of the revolution, the FSLN first halted most of the social programmes that had been implemented in the early years of the revolution and lay behind much of the support won in 1984. Then, in February 1988, it introduced an economic stabilization plan that was very close in nature to those prescribed by the IMF. Over the next eighteen months inflation was indeed reduced significantly but at an extraordinarily high cost. In 1988 GDP fell by nearly 10 per cent, and government revenue by 60 per cent. Subsidies were scythed back as average wages fell to the levels of the 1950s. At least 50,000 public employees lost their jobs. At the same time, counter-revolutionary violence had caused direct damage estimated at $1 billion whilst its indirect economic cost was assessed at $3 billion. Aside from this, of course, it had led to the loss of some 30,000 lives and the introduction of military conscription, causing palpable discontent amongst that rising portion of the populace that respected the Sandinistas but did not owe them strong allegiance. Furthermore, although the FSLN had from early 1986 bowed to peasant pressure and accelerated the distribution of lands to individual small farmers, the passage of time alone had dimmed much of the revolution's original lustre and shifted popular hopes from change to consolidation.

Despite this profoundly adverse scenario, there was broad expectation that the FSLN should readily gain at least 50 per cent of the vote.

When this did not occur, the Sandinistas' shortfall was persuasively explained in terms of a 'tactical vote' by a significant sector of the electorate which perceived UNO as having a better chance of fulfilling the FSLN campaign slogan of 'Everything Will Be Better' than did the Sandinistas themselves. This perception owed much – if not everything – to the fact that UNO was backed by the USA, and only the USA was able to lift the economic embargo, end the war and provide aid. In short, the difference between the real and the expected Sandinista result was the product of an instrumentalist vote that reflected over-bearing need before innate sympathy. Understood in such terms, it could be described as 'tactical' and far more the result of North American aggression than of the merits of UNO's campaign or of the FSLN's shortcomings.

The Politics of National Radicalism

Few would dispute the strength of this analysis, but it still leaves open a number of questions, not least that of surprise at the scale of the UNO vote. Here, there are several factors of varying importance that deserve more attention than they have understandably received in the im-mediate wake of the election. First, and least consequential, was the influence of the opinion polls, which were, with rare and barely honourable exceptions, spectacularly inaccurate (as has been the case in almost every recent Latin American election except that in Chile). The fact that almost all the polls showed a significant Sandinista majority provided FSLN supporters with a plausible argument that a good part of an inexperienced electorate only took a disagreeable decision at the last possible moment. Equally, of course, one must allow for sheer technical ineptitude by pollsters, at sea in a country bereft of electoral tradition and psephological skills. Furthermore, it would be foolish to discount completely opposition assertions that the conditions of the campaign made it more difficult to express support for UNO than for the official party.

Of greater substance is the failure, in my view, of the FSLN leader-ship to comprehend the gravity of the problem facing it. Here I should stress that I am not privy to inside information, and neither was I in Nicaragua during the campaign. Moreover, I believe that the FSLN had fully accepted the consequences of adopting the core features of a liberal-democratic system at least in 1986 and probably in 1984. It follows, then, that the party would only have countenanced a cancellation of the poll in the most extreme circumstances, which were effectively removed by the Iran–Contra scandal and the Arias regional peace plans of 1987. If this is so, we should accept that the FSLN was not only prepared to risk electoral defeat, but may also have recognized that it was a real possibility, albeit by a much slimmer margin than finally transpired. There is, however, precious little evidence that the Frente anticipated the degree to which exhaustion and the desire for peace would be converted into votes for UNO. Of course, 'tactical voting' is essentially unpredictable, and Chamorro's campaign was, by all accounts, extremely unimpressive. Yet I believe that there were at play other factors of rather greater importance to the left as a whole.

Because of its efforts to secure economic recovery at undeniable cost to the urban poor, public sector employees and the social measures introduced early in the revolution, the FSLN was compelled to base its campaign on what we might call the politics of radical nationalism. Under the prevailing circumstances this required a high degree of commitment, which in turn depended upon mobilization to stir spirits and still despondency through the excitement and comforts of mass demonstration. The Sandinistas have always been very good at this, and had latterly undertaken a nimble shift in approach away from stentorian evocations of valour to more typically populist celebrations, Daniel Ortega dispensing with his camouflage fatigues and spectacles to lay on salsa and dish out prophylactics and polaroid snaps of supporters in his company. Yet, as Adolfo Gilly has written in a poignant reflection on these events, 'a people cannot be mobilized for an entire lifetime'.[1] The effort was necessary but insufficient.

Moreover, despite its notable flexibility with respect to policy, in organizational terms the FSLN was poorly positioned to gauge the scope of this insufficiency. Here it should be recognized that an organization called a Front was at its core a vanguard party, and one that had neither held a congress nor conducted internal elections during its entire existence. Whilst it had evaded many of the traits commonly associated with orthodox Leninism, it retained a strong *dirigiste* impetus, not least because the executive features bred of its guerrilla origins had been upheld by the need to fight a war against counter-revolution. The Sandinistas had made substantial efforts to curb the dangers of this producing isolation in power, and they had registered clear signals of discontent – as distinct from opposition – in the operation of the Comités de Defensa Sandinista and the criticisms voiced at the 'Cara al Pueblo' meetings addressed by government leaders. Yet they manifestly had difficulty in ridding a prescriptive politics of those presumptions that are essential to fighting a revolution but prejudicial to winning elections.

Perhaps the most important of their misconceptions was that nationalist sentiment can be exhausted but not fulfilled in adversity. Although this may seem to be a strange and contradictory observation, it is surely the case that resistance to the USA had by 1990 not only depleted the reserves of popular energy but also established an unprecedented national identity and instilled sufficient pride for many thousands of Nicaraguans to feel that the 'imagined community' had become real. This was a positive achievement that could outgrow a given form of Sandinismo. Put bluntly, the most transcendent element of national sovereignty – the will to defend it – had been proved. In the sense that many people could now feel proud of being Nicaraguan and still vote against Sandinismo, the party was victim to the success of its ideology. If, as Eric Hobsbawm has recently emphasized – in a text that looks more askance at nationalism than many on the Latin American left will find acceptable – nationalism necessarily precedes the nation, then it is not so perverse, as it might at first glance appear, to suggest that the tangible establishment of a nation represents fulfilment as well as demanding adjustment.[2] The 'tactical voting' argument stresses the question of adjustment but tends to depict fulfilment in celebratory before historical terms. It does not know its own strength.

History Before Ideology

Both the Nicaraguan revolution of 1978–79 and the poll of 1990 incorporated less ideological conflict than is often attributed to them. Although the FSLN directed the overthrow of Somoza, it could only do so in alliance with those anti-Somocista forces now leading UNO. The Sandinistas determined the terms of this alliance, pushing it constantly to the 'left' in so far as they successively repudiated compromises designed to protect the apparatus of the dictatorship. This adamant attitude on the question of power also permitted the cohesion of the popular forces around a platform of radical social change; but it was always governed by the need to maintain the support of liberal constitutionalists. The political importance of the latter should not be underestimated simply because they were later outmanoeuvred, and subsequently scurried off into the arms of Uncle Sam.

Amongst the many attributes of the concatenation of forces in 1978–79, particular note should be taken of the fact that, at the end of the day, the bourgeois opposition to Somoza provided the key in luring a distraught and impotent Washington into tight-lipped acceptance that whilst it could control the outer limits of the conflict, it was unable to achieve a local resolution to its precise liking. There is something of an echo of this situation in 1990 involving the same basic forces and the same relation between the FSLN's insistence on the military question and its tractability on most issues beyond it. Now, of course, the boot is on the other foot; but one should not underestimate the degree to which past as well as present conditions commend engagement between Sandinismo and the traditional currents of Conservatism and Liberalism as a means of keeping the Yanqui and his mercenaries at one remove from the negotiation of a local accord. In many respects the 1990 election brought into the open the suppressed competition of 1978–79 within the anti-Somoza bloc. This was and is a very real contest, but it is not one that pits two diametrically opposed political systems against each other.

In the first place, UNO contains the pro-Moscow Communist Party (PSN) and the supposed Maoists of the Partido Comunista de Nicaragua (PCN), the presence of which in the alliance secured pockets of workers' votes, diluted the association of class interests with its anti-authoritarian platform, and precluded the espousal of nakedly neo-liberal economic policies. Secondly, the FSLN had itself already introduced a quite orthodox stabilization plan that denied UNO much mileage in either inveighing against collectivism or embracing a free market alternative that might prove alluring to an electorate yet to experience its social costs. UNO promised the opening of North American coffers and very little else. Equally, Washington's decision to impose Chamorro as the leader of UNO – over the hard-nosed *caudillos* of the Liberal (Godoy) and Conservative (Calero) currents, which had been steeped in anti-communist vitriol after a decade nursing their wounds in Honduras and investments in Florida – was born of a prescient choice to milk the *simpatía* of the frail, awkward widow of the man whose assassination by Somoza had opened the revolutionary offensive. Yet, although Doña Violeta was never intended to be more than a figurehead, the logistics of the campaign, the precarious unity of UNO, and the need to keep its association with the military forces of the Contra as loose as possible, meant that the leadership of the opposition to the FSLN was delivered to a person who lacked both the disposition and the resource to give an ideological core to a campaign designed to exploit discontent with hunger and war. She had, after all, felt compelled to excuse her politically inspired departure from the revolutionary junta in 1980 on grounds of ill-health; she patently failed to grasp the point behind Fukuyama's 'end of history'; and there was a certain beguiling predictability in her exploitation of the collapse of the Berlin Wall as an image of happy reconciliation, rather than a metaphor for the termination of tyranny. It is not entirely supercilious to suggest that Chamorro's inability to speak English – unusual amongst the Central American elite – protected her from full programming as a 'unilaterally controlled Latino asset' and encouraged her US sponsors in the belief that she was intellectually dim and lacked political savvy.

In fact, Chamorro possesses a smiling insouciance of almost Reaganite proportions, and this may well have compounded FSLN convictions that the ramshackle UNO campaign required a resolute *machista* response rather than the patient listening and diligent cultivation of village and *barrio* elders that might well have produced a better result. However, as demonstrated by her subsequent skill in securing the formal disarmament of the main Contra forces, Chamorro had the ability to conjure a great deal more than sympathy out of the artless innocence of her persona. Furthermore, the team that was assembled to provide support and protection for those numerous areas of policy where she made no pretence at skill stood at a critical distance from the mainstream of the Contras. Latching on to the clear personalist factor in the UNO victory, this group was able to exploit the factionalism that broke out immediately after the result, and consolidate what their opponents denounced as a cabal of dangerously independent *técnicos* around the new president. The traditionalists were ambushed in their initial efforts to grab a quota of executive power through the guise of a ministry of all the talents, since these were overwhelmingly concentrated in a younger generation of US-educated pragmatists.

The presidential clique's dedication to obtaining a viable bureaucratic transition complemented Chamorro's personal preference and served as a bridge with the FSLN in a manner not dissimilar to that undertaken in 1977–78 by the twelve nominally independent figures known as '*Los Doce*'. Equally, the role of family connections should not be ignored, particularly because this traditional ingredient of Nicaraguan politics had only been partially suppressed under the FSLN. Certainly, the ties between the Sandinista leader Joaquín Cuadra and Chamorro's minister of the presidency and son-in-law, Antonio Lacayo, greatly assisted progress over the most immediately taxing issue of control of the army. This, though, is only the start; family politics are, if anything, more mercurial than most.

The Challenge of Transition

The two-month period between the poll and Chamorro's inauguration was one of hyperactivity as the FSLN and UNO negotiated the terms of an extraordinary transition. At the same time, while Washington adopted a low profile, the Contras opened what was effectively an independent campaign of pressure on both parties, accentuating the importance of the military question, which was from the start the central political issue at stake. On the economic front, the main area of contention was the agrarian reform, on which Chamorro initially made obscure and contradictory declarations, but which, by virtue of the extent of land expropriated since 1979, was bound to exercise the traditional parties as well as the large number of beneficiaries for whom this was the most tangible gain made under the revolution. However, since 1980 the reform had passed through several distinct phases and established different types of agricultural enterprise. This provided a degree of flexibility in making alterations, which were initially targeted on the collective state-owned farms established at an early stage largely on the basis of alienated Somocista property. These could be privatized as coherent units on a secure ideological basis and with a relatively modest risk of provoking a backlash.

However, the cooperatives and those individual plots distributed since 1986 posed much more taxing difficulties for UNO in terms of both consistent policy and political danger. It was in this area that the FSLN had established a firm constituency which could be expected to put up staunch resistance if the new government attempted to placate dispossesed landlords with a significant offensive against the reform.

Consequently, the government sought to hold back the UNO hard-liners whilst endeavouring to square their demands with the prospect of considerable opposition, not only in the countryside but also in congress, where the FSLN could expect to gain the votes of important UNO currents on this question. Here, then, the heterogeneous nature of UNO, the substantial Sandinista representation in the legislature, and the pragmatic character of the presidential group, combined to impede reactionary advance on a core issue: that of property. Whatever the eventual outcome, it is highly unlikely to produce the type of scenario that might be expected in the wake of an unencumbered counter-revolutionary conquest of power.

The government's problems in the urban sphere were made manifest in sharper and more immediate form, when, in May, civil servants staged a largely successful strike for a wage rise to compensate for the devaluations rapidly introduced by the new administration. The political aspects of this action were accentuated by the FSLN's declaration that henceforth it would 'govern from below', and the threat of the government to fire the strikers, who were mostly Sandinista supporters. It should also be noted that the conflict occurred when the Contras were still resisting demobilization, and the threat of revived clashes with the army appeared high. This undoubtedly weakened Chamorro's nerve. Nevertheless, the swift reaction of the public labour force clearly showed the strength of the Sandinista rank and file, and suggested that the FSLN was, in one sense, better able to protect them against UNO than against itself. The coming period will surely see this ability subjected to much sharper tests, not least because the UNO parties can be expected to demand posts for their followers and the firing of civil servants whose working conditions have so far only been altered by Chamorro's matronly prohibition of 'provocative clothing'. In Nicaragua's climate such a reimposition of bourgeois formality is rather less petty than it appears, but it stands as nought compared with the purges and patronage battles looming on the horizon.

The delays in disbursement of US aid also underlined the precarious nature of expectations of a bonanza. (The experience of Grenada provides a sobering example in this respect.)[3] The economy remained in a thoroughly calamitous state, and despite James Baker's assurances, there were now contesting claims on North American largesse from new mendicants whose gratification promised greater political reward. As a result, the government could anticipate growing popular dissatisfaction. Nevertheless, the extent to which the Nicaraguan populace had been driven to use survival tactics within the 'informal economy' limited any expectations of such discontent developing into a union-based mass campaign, despite the strength of the Sandinista organizations. Equally, if the promise of bread began to look threadbare, UNO still stood in a good position to deliver peace, which was arguably as important to its popularity.

The military question is as complex as it is acute. On the one hand, the Contras' relations with the Chamorro group were uneasy, combining Somocista disdain for those who had acquiesced in the overthrow of the dictatorship with the profound suspicion that the FSLN had once again contrived to dupe the politicians. At the same time, of course, the counter-revolutionary troops had been subjected to unalloyed anti-communist propaganda, and had visited exceptionally vicious attrition on many rural communities. It is unsurprising that they could not readily accept that the Bolshevik ogre might graciously accede to the decision of a ballot; to believe this was to cast doubt on much of the rationale for the hardships they had imposed and suffered. These troops were largely *campesinos* whose indoctrination naturally omitted the finer points of the 'strategy of tension' or 'low-intensity warfare' that scarcely offer even the most humble cannon fodder a compelling cause for which to lay down their lives. Moreover, the Contras had just cause to fear retribution for their barbarism. If the gringos attached to their field commanders urged mendacity and manoeuvre, their political masters in Washington had cut back funds and seemed to acquiesce in an accord with an enemy who remained fully armed and mobilized.

On the other hand, both Washington and UNO had concentrated their energies on demanding both a change in the nature of the Ejército Popular Sandinista (EPS) from an 'arm of the party' to a 'neutral national force', and a substantial reduction in its numbers. In its most extreme variant such a proposal signified the complete dismantling of the principal agent and ultimate guarantor of the revolution, opening the distinct possibility of white terror. Yet the political conditions did not permit such a maximum programme. First, the army remained undefeated and had effectively reduced the Contras to tactical skirmishing and sabotage. Second, despite its title and the dominance of the FSLN in the high command, it was far from a purely sectarian force and was widely accepted – albeit often grudgingly – as a national organization integral to the revolutionary experience as well as to its state. Many young men had died in its service, and it is a reasonable bet that many who voted against the FSLN were proud of its achievements in much the same way as Cuban citizens who would never join the CP could honour the valour of their troops in Angola. The widespread dislike of the draft reflected a natural desire for peace and aversion to the exigencies and dangers of military life, but it had never mutated into a popular campaign against Sandinista militarism. Third, the FSLN had made it very clear that it would only contemplate limited negotiations on the issue – as required by the peace treaties and as justified by its support within both the electorate and the officer corps, whose corporate interests could be disaggregated from the party but not from the revolution as a whole.

Guarantees Against Retribution

The demobilization of the Contras was essential to UNO both to confirm its acceptance of the international treaties that underwrote its existence and to consolidate the legitimacy of its political enterprise. Yet the continuation of Sandinista forces not only harboured the threat of a coup but also implied acceptance of the revolutionary state. The dilemma was sharper than in any other Latin American transition, and the abundance of weapons held by the citizenry made its resolution essential if the electoral challenge made by the FSLN was not to collapse in renewed chaos and civil war. However, the international scenario could only have encouraged those elements in UNO that had not been die-hard Somocistas to accept what was, in effect, a reversion to the cohabitation with a Bonapartist force that had been the lot of the Nicaraguan bourgeoisie since the establishment of the National Guard in the late 1920s. The conduct of the EPS was infinitely more dependable and civilized than that of the Contras, and the combination of reshuffled senior appointments and formal resignations from the party leadership permitted those Sandinistas whose primary vocation had become institutional to hold their positions and safeguard the revolutionary inheritance.

Again, a little history. In May 1927 Sandino alone refused to sign the Pact of Espino Negro, organized by Washington to terminate the civil war between the Liberals and Conservatives. His reason was the continued presence of US troops on Nicaraguan soil. In August 1987 the FSLN agreed to the Esquipulas accord principally on the grounds that it provided for the elimination of Washington's mercenaries from the national politico-military conflict. In 1933 the withdrawal of the US marines prompted Sandino to accept a cessation of hostilities, to disarm and acquiesce in the resumption of traditional political competition. Within months, he and many of his troops, who had set up a cooperative agricultural community in the interior, were murdered by Somoza's National Guard. Washington was dismayed but did nothing. In 1990 the Sandinistas, keenly sensitive to the lessons of the past, will not tolerate the slightest risk of repeating the fateful mistake made by their forebear. If the old parties are to return, there must be optimal guarantees against retribution, and the constitution of a new militarist sultanate under their wing. Now it is the Contras who are to become pioneer farmers, protected by smooth Spanish generals and indulgent Venezuelan paratroopers against any settling of scores.

At the distance of a few weeks it would be foolhardy in the extreme to aver that this apparently diligent compromise will hold. The citizen army of the revolution's early years has been greatly transformed, but enough of its ethos persists to qualify the non-partisan pretensions of professionalism. It will be exceptionally difficult to conduct deals with Contra warlords such as Israel Galeano, a bloated brute who relishes his record of butchery and yet, along with similar specimens, must now be treated with equanimity as a respected political interlocutor rather than as a common murderer. This, the message echoes from all quarters, is the price of peace. But it is less than a poor guarantee, and we may expect the disarmament agreement to be sharply tested in the coming months on these grounds alone.

Two other possibilities also deserve mention. The first is that the USA will attempt to transform the original compromise into a much more substantial restructuring of the armed forces with the aim of eradicating all but the vestiges of Sandinismo, as vociferously demanded by the ultramontane parties in UNO. This is a logical and beguiling option for those who have been treated to so many beatings at the hands of the EPS. Yet Washington's loathing is sensibly curbed by fear; and if it desisted from a thorough purge of Noriega's PDF, which it trounced in a direct fight, on the grounds that such a move would create more problems than it would solve, this rationale is far more justified in the case of an unvanquished soldiery characterized by a strong sense of mission and years of experience in guerrilla warfare. Secondly, one cannot ignore the possibility that – as hinted above – the new conditions will encourage an institutionalized deepening of those Bonapartist features inherent in Sandinismo but hitherto checked by both the tenure of political power and widespread popular support. Again, the prospects of this are slight, if only because the experience of recent months has underscored the FSLN's need to reinvigorate those critical and receptive aspects of its politics that had become numbed by the demands of holding state power for a prolonged period in conditions of virtual civil war.

In this regard, the decision to hold a party congress and elections is likely to produce debate of an intensity not witnessed since 1975–77, when the three tendencies of the FSLN engaged in a bitter dispute over strategy. In the immediate aftermath of the election, there was talk of a current of *enragés*, principally amongst the party's youth, breaking free from what could be presented as an organization that had lost its radical vocation and capitulated to the familiar sirens of reconciliation. Although such a response must be understood in terms of the bitter mood of the moment, it should not be forgotten that the mantle of anti-imperialism has long veiled an appreciable diversity of views within the FSLN. In 1978–79 the Tercerista faction headed by the Ortega brothers was able to impose its strategy of combining flexibility over political alliances with aggressive determination in military matters. In the process, the more cautious and class-based approaches of the Proletario (Wheelock) and Guerra Popular Prolongada (Borge) tendencies were suspended but never fully discarded. In opposition and with the direct US military threat converted into a more insidious political influence, there may well be some disaggregation of the Sandinismo that was born of an insurrectionary concordat and sustained by the Yanqui siege. At the very least, its terms will have to be reappraised.

External Reaction: The Right

The strength of the international response to the UNO victory is unremarkable. Although global political attention was concentrated at the time on events in Eastern Europe, the fact that the Nicaraguan revolution had been denounced and celebrated with such energy, particularly in the USA, for more than a decade, meant that the poll was bound to attract considerable attention, and its result certain to be accorded critical significance. Naturally, conservative opinion proclaimed this to be a further resounding death knell for socialism, all the more sweet to the ear for occurring in the Western hemisphere. The domino theory that had become unfashionable as a device for propagating anti-communism now appeared to have gone gloriously into reverse, albeit with minimal enterprise on the part of its most devout adepts. For the first time in twenty years, serious thought might be given to the question of counter-revolution in Cuba, which presented certain logistical difficulties because it was an island, but which could not hope to resist for long the cause of freedom coursing through the ether (helped a touch by the broadcasts of Radio and Television Martí from Florida).

Such ebullience was predictable and directly affected the outlook of the left, whose nervousness had already been sharpened by the invasion of Panama – the fate long feared for Nicaragua itself. In tactical terms it seemed as if the USA would now reserve direct use of military force for its anti-narcotics campaign, the righteousness of which could sustain the attendant political and diplomatic risks, whilst anti-communism could be left to the indisputably reasonable requirement of free and fair elections. This is relevant because all the evidence indicates that Washington was preparing to accept the holding of a poll in Nicaragua as justification in itself for some subsequent modest rapprochement with the FSLN, and that it was no less surprised than the left by the final result – a happy bonus for which it was ill prepared.

Two broad factors are at work in this respect. The first, and more contingent, is the experience of Eastern Europe since mid 1989. This produced a close association of the formal convocation of elections by radical regimes with dissident popular pressure. Despite the unacceptably high level of support for the ex-CPs in later polls (particularly Bulgaria and Romania), the whole thrust of the new wave of elections was decidedly anti-communist and could be championed as an intrinsic feature of burgeoning liberal capitalism. If regimes that for decades had been classed as dictatorships now called polls, they did not do so voluntarily, and were unable to derive any credit from this correct administration of the last rites. To be sure, the defeat of the regime was not anticipated in the case of Nicaragua, but the global conditions prevailing early in 1990 greatly reduced potential US embarrassment at a FSLN success, which would be rendered tolerable – if scarcely palatable – by the fact that Sandinista claims to an unassailable democratic mandate would be dimmed by the global surge in the opposite ideological direction. This also, of course, provided a veneer of plausibility to accepting the FSLN's calling of the USA's bluff over demands for a poll that few in Washington had seriously intended to be the final objective of the formidable aggression they had unleashed against Managua.

The unexpected turn of events in Europe complemented the US electoralist strategy for Latin America in that it could now safely be extended to include radical sponsorship of liberal-democratic procedure without causing undue damage to US hegemony (understood as distinct from direct power). Hitherto, acceptance of electoral transitions from dictatorship in South America and the sponsorship of 'demonstration elections' in Central America, where the killing continued and the fraud became more sophisticated and consequential, had not involved serious ideological risk. Although the abandonment of the desultory 'lesser evil' rationale for supporting murderous autocracy had entailed acceptance of communist ministers in Bolivia (during the UDP regime of 1982–85), a quite truculent APRA administration in Peru (1985–90), and the embarrassment of success for straight-talking psychopaths in El Salvador, it had not disturbed Washington's projection of the left as residually incapable of taking the democratic initiative, rather than participating as a subordinate current whose mendacity and instrumentalism might safely be indulged. Now the FSLN's thunder in upsetting this comfortable pattern was stolen by the European wind. This is also important in so far as the only response previously available to Washington was to proclaim democracy in Nicaragua to be the product of its own profoundly undemocratic pressure, the results of which were gratifyingly successful in terms of realpolitik but could barely be trumpeted to the world with any expectation of the USA being seen as the virtuous party. In the event, of course, Chamorro's victory made reliance upon this justification unnecessary, even if the diehards trundled it out anyway.

Inside Latin America, conservative celebration of the election result reflected relief that the developments in Europe were not continentally bound and had encouraged the ascendance of a neo-conservative *Weltanschauung* in those parts of the world that – perhaps 'through their own irresponsibility' – had hitherto resisted its lures. While varieties of conservatism have had considerable strength in Latin America, a protean corporatism has continually disturbed the optimum operation of market forces. No doubt the Mexican constitution was a paltry counterpart to Bolshevism, and a Betancourt or Arévalo proved to be little match for the likes of Mao, Rákosi or Novotny (only Péron was a truly valid contender), but escape from the alien infections of 1917 and 1945–49 had only produced a local radicalism all the more alarming for its modernity. With adjectival economy, the term *comunismo criollo* encapsulates the conservative perception. The disparaged home-grown variant was especially pernicious in that it was precisely its disguise that had nurtured success. Neither Castro nor the Sandinista *Comandantes* had seized power 'fairly and squarely' in the name of socialism. Whether by design ('Leninism through stealth') or default ('purblind Yanqui overreaction to nationalism') they had hustled history. Yet the initial ideological camouflage was soon stripped away to reveal a dependency on Soviet communism that was as dull as it was dangerous. Where, for simple as well as complicated reasons, this had not occurred – Bolivia in 1952–64, Guatemala in 1944–54, Dominican Republic in 1963–65, Chile in 1970–73 – the radical challenge was either suffocated slowly or shot to pieces. Now that official communism was mortally wounded 'at home', regional socialism lacked the only endgame that had yielded success.

The regional political panorama early in 1990 was not one of unambiguous success for the right. Vargas Llosa's resounding defeat in Peru had sharply deflated reactionary arrogance, and Aylwin's comfortable victory in Chile required readjustment to the fairweather friendship of Christian Democracy, which conservatives view with significant suspicion – a fact often ignored by the left. Equally, if Collor in Brazil, Menem in Argentina, Pérez in Venezuela, and Salinas in Mexico were all endeavouring to impose deflationary policies, and appeared to be wrestling free of the statism that they had initially advocated, or to which they had seemed to be shackled, this process was erratic – engendering sharp social discontent, and promising some populist surprises. Even in Panama the euphoria over the US invasion had rapidly been replaced by dismay at the ineptitude of the Endara regime and the bickering amongst an unpopular comprador clique of oligarchic pretensions. The zero-sum view of politics was temporarily boosted by the fact that in 1989 and 1990 there had been an election in every Latin American country except Cuba, Mexico (1988) and

Guatemala (due in late 1990), and that in each the left had been beaten, in many cases very soundly indeed. Yet in Mexico and Brazil the extent of support for the candidates of the left is reaching impressive levels. More generally, neither the reversion to constitutional government, nor the failure of orthodox stabilization to provoke popular revolt, provide a firm basis for conservative hegemony. The former was very largely the product of mass pressure, and the latter owed more to apprehension and exhaustion than to positive acquiescence. In such a context, reactionary celebration of the travails of the left signalled relief at the diminution of its worst fears, but it was not a triumphalism that could be expected long to outlive the impulse of successive election victories.

Within Central America, the right had more pressing cause to express relief, although this was principally in terms of the propagandistic benefits of the defeat of Sandinismo rather than at the removal of a concrete threat to the status quo. In the cases of Guatemala and El Salvador the expectation was that the change of regime in Managua would accelerate negotiations already begun with the insurgent forces, and that it would reduce the intransigence of the radicals. Here, though, it is worth noting that such a possibility had existed well before the 1987 peace agreement, being determined by the national balance of forces before all else. Moreover, as the right in both Guatemala and El Salvador was quick to discover, success in Nicaragua was a two-edged sword, since it removed the principal North American rationale for the indulgence and munificent funding of their own barbarism. As Washington cut back military aid, raised questions about links with the cocaine trade, and began to complain about the violation of human rights, the Janus-like qualities of reactionary nationalism became more evident, and the ruling bloc started to manifest signs of indecision and factionalism.

The FMLN's offensive of November 1989, extensive popular mobilization in Guatemala City over bus-fare rises, and a fierce public-sector strike in Honduras during the spring of 1990, all underlined the extent to which the ruling class in these countries could ill afford to rest on its laurels either as *victor ludorum* in counterfeit polls or as overseer of military conquest. They knew better than Washington that the poor of their countries had long since ceased to be mesmerized by the FSLN's 'good example', because of the hammering Nicaraguans had taken as a result. They also knew that Sandinista logistical aid to the left elsewhere in the isthmus was absolutely minimal, and that US claims over this were risible except for the purposes of propaganda.

The regional accord of August 1987 signalled grudging conservative acceptance of cohabitation with the FSLN. It offered Honduras relief from the marauding Contras camped on its territory; El Salvador some modest extra purchase in dealing with the redoubtable FMLN; Costa Rica a chance to safeguard its borders and liberal-democratic traditions; and Guatemala an improved climate in which to press its claims to democratic status. All governments sought a modicum of autonomy from the USA and the conditions under which interregional trade might assist recovery from acute economic depression. These factors remain dominant, and, with the exception of the demobilization of the Contras, are little altered by the change of government in Nicaragua. Chamorro can offer little new of substance to her regional peers. Her arrival has lifted their spirits but also complicated their lives.

External Reaction: The Left

Although there were some supporters of the revolution who obviously believed that the Sandinistas simply could not lose the poll, and others who would only have countenanced such a possibility if the FSLN itself had signalled it, virtually nobody – even amongst those who were highly critical of FSLN insufficiencies – had given serious attention to the possible ramifications of defeat. Subsequent reactions must, therefore, be treated with proper recognition of the fact that these stemmed from immediate trauma and were largely directed at recovery from an entirely unexpected shock. Hence the energy with which virtue was extracted out of necessity, particularly in terms of the FSLN's democratic vocation, which had been a major feature of North American opposition to Washington's aggression. For that appreciable constituency – especially in the USA but also in Western Europe – for whom Sandinista defiance of imperial arrogance had largely been free of the traditional ideological polarities and their attendant embarrassments, there was a peculiarly cruel irony in the vindication of their beliefs through the collapse of their cause. Yet it was in the nature of their support that they did not feel betrayed.

The reasons for the emergence of such a constituency are as interesting as they are complex, and it is evident that it cannot simply be dismissed as a chronologically convenient outburst of 'Third Worldism' or modish fellow-travelling. Some on the left – myself included – have taken a far too lofty view of this phenomenon, tending to see its singular energy as little more than emotional displacement, and its advocacy as either disingenuous or too bravely innocent to comprehend that unreserved solidarity not only surrenders hostages to fortune but also unerringly mistakes conformity for unity, and independent thought for sectarianism. Perhaps this view stems from excessive caution about support for any party that holds state power. It is also possibly rooted in the too cynical view that the FSLN was idolized because it was 'my enemy's enemy' or simply because it was successful. Losing an election is not heroic, and will test the resilience of the Sandinistas' international following, albeit in a manner quite distinct from that after the defeats of the Spanish Republic and Unidad Popular in Chile. Yet those whose internationalism understood Nicaragua as less than sublimely sui generis, and which also incorporated knowledge and experience of sundry causes either lost or seemingly doomed to perpetual adversity, should remind themselves that a revolution is nothing if it cannot be celebrated.

The consequences of the election defeat within the more orthodox confines of the left are no less acute, particularly in Latin America. There has been some predictable and necessary criticism of Sandinista errors in the campaign itself as well as of the party's economic policy over recent years. However, what is notable about the reaction, at least amongst those currents not dedicated to plying arid doctrinal certainties, is the general absence of recrimination, support for a retreat to the hills, or serious dispute over the fact that the relation between 'armed struggle' and the 'peaceful road to socialism' is more complex when the left holds state power than when it is assailed by it. The principal strategic debates derived from the experiences of Cuba and Chile have lost their sectarian impetus almost everywhere. Nonetheless, it may be expected that some of their constituent features will now be revived and will very possibly exercise more influence over the Latin American left than have events in Europe. In this respect it strikes me as highly likely that northern socialists will undervalue – by reason of both their history and the current focus on Europe – the continuing importance placed by Latin American radicals on the power of counter-revolution. However valid the perceptions of 'imperial overreach', the unsavoury singularity of the conditions in Panama that prompted the US invasion, and the shift by both Washington and national dominant blocs towards constitutionalism, neither domestic US concerns nor conditions in Latin America itself justify claims to a regional 'end of history' eradicating regular cycles of barbarism and doleful impositions of North American 'manifest destiny'. This is not to say that 'redemocratization' is merely ephemeral or that US intromission is incapable of major mutations of both form and degree, but it is to signal that there is palpable reason in daily life from Tijuana to Tierra del Fuego to harbour sharp reservations about the opening of new eras.

It is probably this factor above any other that underpins the continuing respect in which the Cuban government continues to be held, even by those who have long attacked it as a Stalinist *apparat*, and notwithstanding the recent chilling recourse to show trials and executions. In the wake of the Nicaraguan reverse it is surely as true as it is sentimental to see Cuba as the last bastion against the empire. If Castro's politics make this and his expectations of historical absolution increasingly tenuous, it should at least be recognized that the circumstances prevailing in mid 1990 also enhance the symbolic strength of his regime as a bulwark against the gringo, who, together with his eager accomplices, promises far worse villainy. Many of the parallels with Europe being drawn by the pundits are highly inexact in both geopolitical and emotional terms.

Apprehension about heightened US ambitions on Cuba is not misplaced because of the electoral form taken by imperial success in Nicaragua. Superficially this would seem precisely to reverse the trajectory of the Chilean experience, which provided many lessons for the FSLN leadership and which has renewed resonance in the present reversion to the division of powers. Yet if the differences between Chile and Nicaragua are legion, they do not include the role played by the USA, which imposed an economic siege and sponsored terror in both cases. In the first, Allende's longstanding attempt to assert a socialist hegemony through the institutions of bourgeois liberalism was finally terminated by the coup – a risk accepted as integral to the enterprise. In the second, the insurrectionary conquest of power, and establishment of a popular army in its wake, effectively precluded the threat of a military coup but still could not forestall vicious military pressure from outside. The conditions for resisting defeat by force directly enhanced the conditions for defeat through election, the risks of which were certainly not so integral to the revolutionary project but could only be dismissed at exceptionally high cost. Thus, even in the post-dictatorial era, there is a plausible argument that these two signally innovative radical experiments fell foul of the trap of liberal constitutionalism, as well as North American aggression. If the Sandinistas left office with their lives and considerable opportunities to fight another day, many more Nicaraguans than Chileans had died at the hands of the counter-revolution. Seen in this pessimistic light, the Sandinistas may well have had no option, but they ended up moving from the frying-pan to the fire.

The Challenge Ahead

However narrow and wilful such an interpretation might be, it stands close enough to the facts to put us on our guard against single-minded dedication to ideological struggle when the enemy remains fully possessed of naked power and is readily prepared to deploy it. Equally, as the FSLN has long recognized, it underlines the danger of making a complete identification between the protocols of liberal constitution-alism and the respect and practice of civil liberties. The general argu-ment is far too familiar to merit further elaboration in this context. Of greater immediate relevance is the manner in which it will be taken forward in conditions where the right has in most countries dominated a transition to civilian government after prolonged dictatorship and with increasing immiseration of the masses. Here the impact of Nicar-agua is most likely to be felt in the sense that the revolution provided a vital instance of radical initiative for a continental movement largely forced to depend upon a denunciatory discourse set by the logic of opposition and minimally enlivened by the image of 'actually existing socialism'. Sandinismo not only posed the 'threat of a good example' to Washington, it also provided positive sustenance to radicals driven from the adversities of dictatorship to those of constitutionalism – a shift that presents its own difficulties, as well as harbouring those peculiar to the two poles between which it takes place. Thus, it was not just the FSLN's anti-imperialism and the prestige of its victory that was of consequence to the continental movement. Its commitment to an unsubmissive pluralism – much criticized by unreconstructed advo-cates of the dictatorship of the proletariat and by those who simply saw this as the thin end of the wedge – provided a strategic blueprint that both bisected the extremes witnessed in Cuba and Chile, and could be seen as more broadly applicable than the other experiences, despite the widely recognized peculiarities of the revolution. Put bluntly, although the manner of Somoza's overthrow and the ideological fabric of Sandinismo were without a shadow of doubt sui generis, the subsequent political development of the revolution proffered ideas and models that were not – need not be – tied to their historical origins, and that more adequately addressed strategic preoccupations elsewhere than, in their time, had Cuba and Chile.

If such observations have any value, it could be said that the FSLN's defeat at the polls is likely to be both more and less consequential in its ramifications for regional radicalism than the Chilean coup and the bureaucratic ossification in Cuba. In contrast to the former, it has the advantage of permitting the left to fight another day, but also the disadvantage that this eventuality was allowed for when full power was held and so incubates a fundamental pessimism. In contrast to the latter, it has the advantage of allowing a genuine ideological context and thereby subjecting the left to a continuous and enriching challenge; but also, quite obviously, the disadvantage of surrendering the gains made at high cost over many years to electoral decision in highly inequitable conditions. This latter contrast implies a profound optimism. The fact that nowhere else in Central America are these major dilemmas present in advanced form does not mean that they are ignored by a left-wing movement that has been quite exceptionally embattled. The lessons were, indeed, anticipated in the Salvadorean guerrillas' acceptance of a variegated strategy for a ceasefire from early 1984, as well as in the severe setbacks suffered by the Guatemalan rebels in 1981–82, when the militarist logic of their offensive blinded them to the terrible consequences for an unconsulted population. In these countries it has become an iron rule for the left that it cannot act with authority unless it can shoot straight and listen quietly. This axiom is likely to hold for some time to come in Nicaragua too.

Notes

1. *La Jornada*, Mexico City, 28 February 1990.
2. E.J. Hobsbawm, *Nations and Nationalism since 1780*, Cambridge 1990.
3. James Ferguson, *Grenada: Revolution in Reverse*, London 1990.

5

Mario Vargas Llosa:
Parables and Deceits

Some time ago I urged a friend from Lima to read Vargas Llosa's *Historia de Mayta* – clumsily entitled *The Real Life of Alejandro Mayta* in the English edition – so that he might give me an insider's opinion of the book's treatment of the Peruvian revolutionary left over the last thirty years and decode some of the specific events and personalities.[1] This friend, who is not only a socialist but also a gay activist and adviser to the Sandinista government in Nicaragua, understandably shied away from a novel whose author is opposed to almost everything he holds dear. Eventually I thrust a copy of the book into his hands with the rather weak excuse that one might best understand one's enemies when they are trying to do the same. Some weeks later I received a letter succinctly expressing what has subsequently become a general response to the novel within left circles: 'This little monster has a knack for saying the most reactionary things in the most brilliant way.' Such an appraisal could easily be hedged around with nuanced qualifications or rendered into more modulated prose but it is, I believe, entirely accurate. *Mayta* is a very fine novel built around some compelling – if not completely felicitious – literary devices and imagery that is both rich and subtle. Yet, just as one might anticipate little less from such a reputable author, so also is the expectation of a profoundly conservative perspective fully justified and even surpassed. In this text Vargas Llosa directly addresses matters of great importance to him as a political animal as well as a novelist – the shade of Sendero Luminoso is here in all but name.

The book is markedly devoid of the fiercely polemical tone adopted by the author in his public statements and increasingly frequent excursions into journalism, but it provides an extensive display of the assumptions and convictions that underpin Vargas Llosa's more trenchant extramural invectives. One of the novel's principal resources lies in the sympathy with which the central radical protagonist is drawn as an individual, yet its essential character is established by the only constant feature of the text: the understanding that the being of the left is singularly self-determined and, even more importantly, that the catastrophe that is contemporary Peru is centrally attributable to the agency of this left. The notable lack of attention to the wider context within which the ideology and organization of radicalism are engendered is no mundane omission. For whilst all histories, 'imagined' or otherwise, are necessarily partial and Vargas Llosa is justifiably preoccupied with an internal discourse, the core of the book is constituted by the presumption that the semi-fictional Mayta and the entirely real Sendero can only be comprehended through their own vision of the world and esoteric protocols.

Despite its title, the novel has two protagonists – the restless Alejandro Mayta, an obscure Trotskyist attempting to stage an insurrection in the Andes in 1958, and an anonymous narrator endeavouring to reconstruct the story of this abortive revolt in the Peru of a near future when the state of strife that prevails today has escalated to open civil war, invasion by a Cuban–Bolivian revolutionary force and intervention by the US marines. This time gap allows Vargas Llosa to establish, but never explain, a linkage between Mayta's not completely dishonourable failure in the past and the horrendous successes of the faceless subversives of today and tomorrow. The 'plot' of the 1958 rising is subordinate but far from marginal since its unremitting advance towards the disaster we know it will become contains all the elements of detective fiction, to which Vargas Llosa has long been attached. However, the author bobs and weaves around this basic narrative line with a series of literary devices that increasingly dominate the text. The most obvious of these is the constant exchange – most often between paragraphs but sometimes within lines – of the point of narration between the researcher, interviewing Mayta's erstwhile comrades in the first person, and Mayta himself, struggling towards his half-baked destiny in the third. The literary success of this mechanism has been the subject of some discussion.[2] It is, though, of secondary importance within the more general 'relativizing' of the text whereby one revelation after another is subverted through a change of voice as well as developments in the story, continuing Vargas Llosa's established affinity for the artifice of the 'Chinese box'.[3]

Through all but one chapter the precarious nature of the 'truth' of Mayta's escapade is engagingly demonstrated by the contrast between a narrative of 1958 invested with the authority of the third person and the versions of that same past recounted to the narrator by those who have survived it. Although these interlocutors are told that their confidences will be respected and that their account will be used only as a basis for a fiction and not as 'history', they are requested to provide a detailed concrete version of what occurred. Their reminiscences are then shown to be highly varied and fraught with all manner of insufficiency, the lapses and adjustments of memory generally being openly self-serving, although Vargas Llosa is not so banal as to exclude the more extensive and profound difficulties and richness of oral history. The book could easily rest on this basis, but even before the last chapter it is evident that our writer will play his trump card on the decreasingly credulous reader. In the final pages the novel reaches its dénouement in a meeting between the narrator and Mayta himself, which encounter provides both a resolution to the story of the aged agitator and a final subversion when the narrator reveals his own lies and concoctions within the text hitherto, and directly signals the ultimate deceit encompassing all of these – that invented by Mario Vargas Llosa, novelist in the quick.

As Salman Rushdie has commented, this contrived ending lacks conviction, not least because it extinguishes a doubt as to authorship that resists neat consummation after such diligent seduction. One suspects that Don Mario's self-proclaimed extremism of the imagination yields to feigned rapture because it is in embrace with political conservatism: Mayta's embattled trajectory terminates in careworn common-sense and apolitical sobriety yet cannot convincingly be dragged over this final mile unless we are assured that such an account belongs to the man on the dust-jacket and is 'the real story'. The portrait of an exhausted revolutionary is neither unpersuasive nor markedly indulgent, but it is only achieved by the liquidation of literary as well as political subversion, and in this respect the importance of *Mayta* lies far more in its substantive treatment of Vargas Llosa's preferred themes of obsession and ideology than as an exploration of literary form.

The quite widespread identification of this book as more reactionary than its immediate predecessors has undoubtedly been encouraged by its political subject-matter – perhaps also by greater exposure of the thoughts of Vargas Llosa in the English-speaking world following the acclaim and mass sales of *Aunt Julia and the Scriptwriter* (1977) and *War of the End of the World* (1984). However, *Mayta* represents a continuation and distillation of the essential motifs of both novels, fusing the treatment of personal obsession at the heart of *Aunt Julia*, a hilarious semi-autobiographical excursus, with reflection upon the susceptibility of the masses to an apocalyptic vision which courses through *War of the End of the World*, an unqualified tragedy based upon the experience of millenarianism in late nineteenth-century Brazil.[4] *Mayta* does not possess the clarity of genre of either of its antecedents and attempts a much more synthetic vision of the personal and political, being correspondingly less anarchic and grandiose. Its realism is decidedly not of the 'magic' variety that is generally associated with the Latin American literary 'boom' opened in the metropolis by García Márquez's *One Hundred Years of Solitude* and which has, in fact, never been a prominent characteristic of Vargas Llosa's work. The novel relates in tone as well as subject matter those distinctly Peruvian qualities of the author's work which, as Gerry Martin persuasively suggests, set him apart from his peers no less than do his political convictions.[5]

Such a suggestion is undoubtedly hard to substantiate short of evocative disquisitions with regard to national cultures – although the woeful ignorance of the metropolitan audience would in itself perhaps justify any interpretative strategy that brought to the fore the enormous diversity of the subcontinent. It is easy to find in Vargas Llosa's work both the luxuriant hallucinations of García Márquez's Macondo and the hazy streetlife existentialism of Cortazar and Cabrera Infante. Peru is a semi-tropical country and Vargas Llosa's work has shifted with great ease from jungle to sierra to sleepy provincial town to the bawling misty excrescence of the city that is Lima. Indeed *The Green House* (1966), which is perhaps his greatest novel, certainly his most radical and possibly the least popular with metropolitan readers, displays a verdant tropicality of vision every bit the equal of that purveyed by his erstwhile friend García Márquez. Yet its Amazonianism is decisively mediated by the dry sand-storms of Piura and the dour desert spirits who endure them with a lugubrious sensuality that bemuses the reader fitted up by exuberant mirages and the antics of dusky adventurers.

Born in 1936, Vargas Llosa clearly belongs to the generation of 'the boom', flowering during the 1960s in the wake of the Cuban revolution and the end of the recession in Latin American politics and culture that may be traced back beyond the Cold War to the dictatorial epoch of the post-slump 1930s. Equally, he has shared with many of his peers the experience of prolonged sojourn in Europe (Paris, as a student, and London, where he now keeps house in fashionable Knightsbridge). In these sabbaticals he has had ample scope to ruminate upon the exaggerated experience of Latin America, although public renditions of this have increasingly taken the form of bilious denunciation of the vicarious 'Third Worldism' embraced by those borrowing a politics to escape the monotony of their metropolitan comforts. In fact, it was the 1971 'Padilla affair' that prompted his rapid shift away from radical causes and was possibly decisive in softening the impact of the 1973 Chilean coup, so central for the progressive convictions of most of his colleagues. In this differentiation, however, one also has a strong sense of that cynical *hauteur* which is the peculiar property of the middle-class Andean *mestizo*, constantly foraging for material and social acceptance within a still buoyant Hispanic milieu and yet unable fully to turn from the harsh realities of Quechua Indian society embedded in the mountain fastnesses. It is far easier to interpret the dualist relationship between these circuits in socio-cultural terms than in those of political economy, the explanatory excesses of first developmentalist and then dependency theories quickly foundering on the complexities of mixed agrarian systems and the parallax modes of production engendered by mining enclaves. Vargas Llosa grew up in such a Manichaean world and, despite years of sophisticated urban life, still displays some of the bitter ambiguities that comprise its axis and are discernible in the semi-permeable societies of Arequipa (from where his family hails), Piura and the even more remote Cochabamba, where he was raised.

In *Mayta* such a dualism is sharply deployed to supplement the dissection of the internal universe of the left in a remorseless series of impediments to the mission of the sublimely misconceived urban dreamer. There is nothing irreducibly Peruvian about the contradictory logics between urban and rural, Hispanic and indigenous, vanguard and mass, eternal visionary and daily survivalist, but Vargas Llosa can draw on a full local history of such encounters, the geopolitical landscape for which may be said to be particularly distinct in the Andean countries and Guatemala within Latin America as a whole.[6] What, however, is notable about the book is that the author does not exploit the dualism to the full. Even Mayta himself is not completely trounced by the alien environment in which he seeks a secular state of grace. For although he is laid low by *soroche* (mountain sickness) – in itself emblematic but also perhaps an allusion to the asthma which debilitated Ché in his Bolivian campaign -- it is human frailty of an altogether more voluntary nature that scuppers the insurrection. Here Vargas Llosa draws away from the sirens of an alternative romanticism, founded upon an immovable indigenous conservatism, and instead points his pen at the awful opportunism and susceptibility of the provincial petty bourgeoisie. Both the desistance from making the failure of the revolt an absolute *fait accompli* and the identification of its fairweather friends have a logic within the text. But they also correspond to the course of recent Peruvian history. Since 1980 Sendero Luminoso has demonstrated its capacity to overcome many of the impediments that confound Mayta, and for all its extraordinary behaviour this Maoist force has once again disproved the threadbare theory that the highland *campesino* is structurally resistant to insurgent politics; however reluctantly, Vargas Llosa must allow for this. Moreover, despite the excessive importance he attaches to the agency of the middle class in propelling Sendero, he is correct in identifying this stratum as integral to its emergence, and one is not surprised to find such characters presented in less than flattering light in *Mayta*.

One feature of the novel that has not atttracted much critical attention is its development of Vargas Llosa's depiction of the military, always present in his books if only in the shape of Sergeant Lituma. At times the anti-communism of the author's political polemics is so sulphurous that he might be thought to be a closet militarist. It is, of course, true that these days he modulates his attacks on the terrorism of the left with qualitatively less passionate denunciations of that of the armed forces, and it is also the case that the official commission he headed to investigate the death of eight journalists in the village of Uchurracay in January 1983 produced a hotly disputed report that denied military involvement. Yet it would be plain silliness to believe that Vargas Llosa's advocacy of liberal democracy is a mere vanity or simply inconsequential. This is particularly so because he has enjoyed a very much less than friendly relationship with a military that he pilloried mercilessly at the start of his career (*The Time of the Hero*,

1963) and which he opposed politically during the reformist regime of General Velasco (1968–75). Indeed, one should not forget that while the anti-militarism of most Latin American writers was consolidated by the experience of unambiguously right-wing regimes in the 1960s and 1970s, Vargas Llosa was faced in Peru with an authoritarian government of a quite distinct character and enough progressive features to commend it to broad sections of the left. Some facets of this experience can be glimpsed in Mayta's military sponsor, the ebullient Lieutenant Vallejos, who is far more resourceful than the decrepit *político* when it comes to handling firearms or yomping over mountain paths but no less deluded in his conviction that a great social change can be achieved on a purely logistic basis. In this respect Vallejos represents both a reincarnation and a telling extension into the political realm of Captain Pantaleón, that earnest advocate of scientific management in pimping (*Pantaleón and the Lady Visitors*, 1973).

It was perhaps predictable that Vargas Llosa declined to rise to the bait when, at a recent public forum in London, he was politely prompted to comment upon Ronald Reagan's vision of and for Latin America, which in terms of obsession, make-believe and general gobbledegook is hard for even the most ultramontane Maoist zealot to equal and has an enormously greater impact on the human condition of the subcontinent.[7] Although Vargas Llosa has placed on record his opposition to the Contra campaign against Managua and even had the temerity to dissent from Washington's presentation of the Nicaraguan revolution as a product of Muscovite conspiracy, he is not at all concerned to join the chorus of complaint at Washington intervention and sponsorship of terror in the region and is far more interested in signalling the 'dictatorial' character of much of the left engaged in such protest.[8] Apparently still prepared to grant some indulgence to the Sandinistas on the basis of their nationalism and inefficiency – despite the ministerial status of the cleric-poet Ernesto Cardenal, whose committed stanzas he holds in especial disdain – Vargas Llosa is unbridled in his excoration of 'totalitarianism' in Cuba and all those who would offer support to or receive it from the 'dictatorship' of Fidel Castro. Whether it be on the platform of the Pen Club Congress along with Mailer and Shultz or in his column in Madrid's *El País*, he has pursued a boisterous campaign against all those 'politically irresponsible' writers who express some sympathy, however guarded, for the regime in Havana.[9] The most he was prepared to concede in a bitter exchange with the somewhat less than insurrectionary Günter Grass was a bashful retraction of the absurd and abusive division of writers in communist societies into 'courtesans' and 'dissidents'.[10] Grass's measured comments prompted our fiery iconoclast into an unusual reconsideration of his vocabulary; no such minimalist amendments were offered to Benedetti, García Márquez, Cortazar (both before and after his death) or Galeano, castigated in like manner as disciples of the forces of darkness. Much less publicized but in many ways more doleful is the vendetta pursued against Colin Harding, a specialist in Peru then working on *The Times*, who meticulously questioned some of the findings of Vargas Llosa's report on the Uchurracay murders and was for his pains chosen to personify the malevolent European meddler. Vargas Llosa has denounced him as a liar and relentlessly vilified him not only in a stream of Latin American papers but also at a televised public meeting arranged by the Moonies at which Vargas Llosa had the honour of sharing the dais with the infamous Colonel Bo Hi Pak, patron of anti-constitutional coups, sponsor of dictators and paymaster of assassins.[11]

Little wonder, then, that Vargas Llosa does not pause for long over the murderous autocracy in Chile and Paraguay or the decades of genocide in Guatemala. Indeed, it is possibly unsurprising that he has also not chosen to concentrate his literary talents on two key episodes in Peruvian history – the mass uprising led by Tupac Amaru in 1781 and the establishment of the republic by San Martín, Sucre and others in the 1820s. These events positively gush with instances of personal obsession, the entrancement and mobilization of the masses, and the application of both dissident and military minds to the conquest of enormous space and opponents who are fickle and resolute in equal number. Yet one suspects that they have not emerged as themes precisely because, however partially and temporarily, they transcended the limits that Vargas Llosa would have as the incarnation of order, successfully transforming history. The obvious irony is that both Indian rebellion and militarism established the republic of Peru and are integral features of a nationalist ideology upheld by liberal democrats today battling against the former and seeking desperately to avoid the latter. Perhaps Vargas Llosa is rather more nervous about such a history than his bullying polemics suggest.

There are many, particularly in Peru, who would argue that the author of *Mayta* does not want for nerve since his novel takes considerable liberties with the history of the Trotskyist movement in its 'imaginary' tale vacuum-packed against empirical objection by shifting voices. Many of the allusions will be lost on a foreign audience probably content not to ferret around in the by-ways of local radicalism, but it is of some consequence that in playing fast and loose with recognizable personalities and events the book provides a Peruvian reader with a far sharper set of judgements than is readily grasped by a foreigner. Little can be gained from a pedestrian dissection of this 'faction', yet it is worth noting that translation of its acronym hides from the English reader the fact that the garage-based septet that is our hero's vanguard party is the POR, a genuine Trotskyist organization established in the late 1940s. Equally, in May 1962 a sub-lieutenant by the name of Vallejos and a *campesino* leader called Mayta did indeed stage an attack on the prison at Jauja in the company of a POR militant. Both Vallejos and Mayta were killed shortly after the incident.[12] Moreover, in November 1962 Hugo Blanco, Peru's most renowned Trotskyist militant and then a member of the POR, led an armed attack on a Guardia Civil post at the village of Pucyura and was arrested some months later; in the book even Mayta's gait would seem to resemble Blanco's. But Blanco is most decidedly not Mayta. A native of highland Cusco, his inept engagement in armed struggle followed a period of unprecedented success in mobilizing the *campesinado* of the valley of La Convención, where his leadership of the new union led to a series of land occupations that had within a few years prompted not only an enormous growth in peasant organization but also the introduction of an agrarian reform by the Velasco regime.[13] Furthermore, whether in jail or not, Blanco never receded into obscurity – in 1978 more than a quarter of a million Peruvians voted for his ticket in the constituent assembly elections boycotted by Sendero Luminoso.[14] Cognoscenti may find in the resurrected composite Mayta elements of Felipe Buendía and Ismael Frías, long a leading light of the POR and eventually a renegade adviser to the Bonapartist colonels who came to power in 1968.[15] The game, however, is Vargas Llosa's, not ours. Suffice it to say that, like its counterparts all over the world, Peruvian Trotskyism offers some meat to the student of deprecatory sociology by dint of years of isolation and witless as well as necessary factional strife. Yet over forty years of organized existence it has scored some signal victories in national politics that simply cannot be understood in terms of the pathology of sectarian grouplets.

Nonetheless, anybody who has spent enough time inside a Troskyist organization to hear two consecutive political reports could not plausibly deny that Vargas Llosa's anthropological vision has a certain validity; it would be foolish to follow his example in throwing the baby out with the bathwater. According to the author, the choice of a Trotskyist group derived from his year-long membership of a Communist Party student organization in the early 1950s when the Trotskyists were viewed (much as today) as a noxious breed endowed with almost superhuman powers. In this regard Vargas Llosa implicitly passes comment no less upon the myopia of Stalinism than upon that of its revolutionary critics, but his account lacks the authenticity and authority of a bona fide veteran of the radical movement such as Jorge Semprún.[16] Those familiar with Trotskyist traditions will note the absence of any discussion of international issues – a sine qua non of the movement from Colombo to Caracas – and a failure to introduce figures such as Pablo, Posadas and Bressano (Nahuel Moreno) who were not only at the centre of the debates and divisions of the 1950s and 1960s but also closely involved in the affairs of the POR. They could easily have been inserted into the *dramatis personae* to heighten the quixotic element. Yet such absences are completely marginal compared with that of any direct discussion of Sendero, which, as the force behind the catastrophe contrasted with Mayta's amateur dabbling in revolution, is the most potent – if not the original – villain of this piece.

One can understand such a silence, for even seventeen years after its formation Sendero remains a most opaque and mysterious force, issuing only four brief communiqués in five years following the outbreak of its guerrilla war in 1980.[7] In recent months evidence has grown that it is at least collaborating with other groups, most notably those influenced by the Cuban revolution, but it still retains many of the hallmarks of a singularly unrefined Maoism, a political current rarely witnessed in Latin America and yet entrenched with peculiar strength in the sierra of southern Peru. Peruvian Maoism is by no means limited to Sendero, the national teachers' union SUTEP being heavily influenced by the Bandera Roja group that split from the current Sendero leadership in 1970.[18] However, it is Sendero that has achieved global renown and imposed its stamp upon national political life through its rigid adherence to the original orthodoxies of the Maoist creed and their application in a brutal military campaign that has spread beyond the department of Ayacucho ('Corner of the Dead' in Quechua) to the capital and other areas of the country. What little is known of Sendero's organization indicates an attachment to the logic of cellular existence and the rites of dogma that exceeds even Vargas Llosa's images, nurturing not born-again individualists but thousands of diehard militants and a 'great fear' within the dominant classes and state so profound that the military has resorted to the public slaughter of hundreds of political prisoners in Lima's jails (June 1986) as well as 'disappearing' droves of 'suspects' in the backlands.

Vargas Llosa is deeply embroiled in this conflict as a partisan of President Belaúnde (1980–85), who sanctioned the counter-insurgency campaign against Sendero and consistently defended his generals against a flood of well-documented charges that they perpetrated many massacres under the veil of martial law. No doubt our author, who graciously declined to serve as Belaúnde's prime minister, would fully endorse his patron's denigration of Amnesty International as yet another case of privileged and arrogant idealists deliberately evading the moral dilemmas inherent in the practice of politics in the real world. Yet he, who can best most of his adversaries in privilege or arrogance, displays a despondent failure of both politics and imagination in his reluctance to explain why such a ferocious conflict took hold under his friend's regime. Was it because the impoverished peasantry of Ayacucho perceived in a flash the merits of essays written by Mao and Mariátegui sixty years ago? Was it, perhaps, that the frail provincial expert on Kant, Abimäel Guzmán, experienced a quantum jump in his pedagogical talents, permitting him to persuade thousands of compatriots that they had no option but armed struggle precisely at a time when Peru had elected a constitutional regime for the first time in seventeen years? Or was it because the malicious spirit of the mythical Mayta hovered anew above the cordillera?

The reality is both more prosaic and more desperate. It takes little more than a sense of theatre and moderate stealth to string up dead dogs in the Plaza de Armas, but Sendero is not reducible to perverse rituals nor even its extraordinary imbrication of Maoist doctrine with indigenous messianism. If these have attracted a following far larger than even most on the left care to admit, it is because of a withering crisis in the economy and society of Peru evident for more than a decade but driven to the point of irreconcilable polarization by the bankrupt economic credos of Belaúnde and his team of callow

Friedmanite managers. Heedless of the wretched precedent established across the border in Chile and made giddy by illusions every bit
the match of Sendero's, this crew succeeded in sacrificing virtually all
the conquests of the popular anti-militarist struggle before the altar of
capital, destroying in the process much of the glutin that held Peru in a
state somewhere proximate to that of a manageable civil society. The
gravitas of constitutional government, plus a little on temporary loan
from the IMF, was deployed to uphold policies that escalated the
external debt by 30 per cent in two years, increased inflation by 60 per
cent (to 125 per cent) in one, reversed GDP growth from 3 per cent to
−12 per cent inside twenty-four months, cut real wages in 1983 to half
the level of 1977, and threw so many people out of work that less than a
third of the economically active population received a regular wage.[19]
Belaúnde's response to the battering given Peru by the world market
was dullard adherence to the demands of 'popular sacrifice', imposed
with pitiful efficiency. It is this that lies behind the resurgence of
obscure activists otherwise destined to see out their days submerged in
addled disputes over doctrine. Millions of Peruvians have tramped
down from the Andes to people the mushrooming slums of Lima and
then, very often, back again with the expectations of their survivalist
pilgrimage bitterly broken, only to find themselves no less outcast in
their original communities. Moreover, it is not just those who have
returned with a deeply jaundiced vision of city, state and economic
system who have been cleaved from the logic of cantankerous submission. While one might identify in such a group the initial point of
growth for Sendero's campaign, whether via the route from Ayacucho
University's department of education or in a more general refusal to
accept the scavaging and chicanery necessary for subsistence in
contemporary Peru, it is clear that those who stayed camped in the
towns have increasingly joined their ranks. Sendero may have been
subordinated in its birthplace of Ayacucho by repression and the
limited capacity to sustain inter- and intra-communal conflict, but its
emergence as a force elsewhere and particularly in Lima defies any
easy explanation based on either differentiation within the peasantry or
the mysterious powers of Maoist voluntarism. It has not been daunted
by extensive executions nor dimmed by the advent of a new populist
government pledged to reform. More doses of either are unlikely to
extirpate it for a very long time to come. Even Vargas Llosa's formidable imagination cannot face the enormity of this phenomenon.

Oscillating between fury, incomprehension and resignation, he has penned us a parable of great promise that terminates as a paltry conceit. He hears his enemy clearly but understands only the words.

Notes

1. Faber and Faber, London 1986. It is fitting that this modest essay be dedicated to the memory of Nahuel Moreno (1924–87), leader of a singularly popular Trotskyist movement (MAS).

2. Reviewing the English edition, two novelists disagreed on the success of this mechanism in terms of clarity. Salman Rushdie, writing in *The Guardian,* found it acceptable within the context of more profound literary flaws, whilst Adam Mars-Jones, reporting in *The Independent,* was occasionally confused. Neither, however, passed comment on the mini-ambush laid by Vargas Llosa on page 152 (p. 172 in the Spanish edition).

3. Gerald Martin, 'Mario Vargas Llosa: Errant Knight on the Liberal Imagination', in John King, ed., *Modern Latin American Fiction: A Survey,* London 1989. This acute and economical essay provides an excellent assessment of the novelist's oeuvre.

4. Both novels are much better understood when read together with different versions of the same subject. The author's aunt/wife Julia Urquidi Illanes provides a spirited, if somewhat artisanal, counterblast to Vargas Llosa's version of their shared history in *Lo que Varguitas no dijo,* La Paz 1983, whilst nobody should imagine that *The War of the End of the World* exceeds in grandeur Euclides da Cunha's contemporary study of the prophet Antonio Conselheiro and the Canudos campaign, *Os Sertões* (1902).

5. Martin, 'Vargas Llosa: Knight Errant', and 'Boom, Yes; New Novel, No: Further Reflections on the Optical Illusions of the 1960s in Latin America', *Bulletin of Latin American Research,* vol. 3. no. 2, 1984. Martin's study of the modern Latin American novel, *Journeys through the Labyrinth,* London 1989, provides the wider audience with a series of suggestive and often revisionist perspectives on this genre.

6. For a classic novel of the Peruvian sierra, see Ciro Alegría, *Broad and Alien is the World* (1941). English-language readers are still denied access to the fictions of Manuel Scorza, recently killed in a Spanish air crash: *Redoble por Rancas* (1970) and *Historia de Garabombo, el Invisible* (1972). *Hombres de Maíz* (1949) by the Guatemalan Miguel Angel Asturias depicts a not dissimilar society with no less and possibly greater verve.

7. Vargas Llosa in conversation with Jason Wilson and Tariq Ali, ICA, 30 October 1986.

8. *New York Times,* colour supplement, 28 April 1985; *El País,* 30 June 1986.

9. *El País,* 20 January 1986.

10. Ibid., 30 June 1986.

11. Vargas Llosa's version of the circumstances surrounding the murders appeared in *Granta,* no. 9, Harding's critique in no. 11. The exchange, abetted by editing standards worthy of litigation, continued in the following two numbers. Vargas Llosa's invective against Harding, 'El Periodismo como Contrabando', was syndicated throughout Latin America in August 1983. An abundance of detail on Colonel Bo Hi Pak's support for authoritarian regimes on behalf of the Unification Church as well as on the Moonies' extensive economic interests is given in Jean-François Boyer, *L'Empire Moonie,* Paris 1986.

12. Américo Pomaruna, 'Perú: revolución, insurreción, guerrillas', *Cuadernos de Ruedo Iberico*, no. 6, April–May 1966.

13. Blanco's account of his experience is published in English as *Land or Death. The Peasant Struggle in Peru*, New York 1972. A succinct narrative of his activities together with those of the MIR-ELN *focos* of Luis de la Puente, Javier Heraud and Héctor Bejar is given by Richard Gott, *Rural Guerrillas in Latin America*, London 1970. Bejar's own version is contained in *Perú 1965: Apuntes sobre una Experiencia Guerrillera*, Havana 1969, which demonstrates the differences with the Trotskyists no less than do his interesting reflections upon subsequent collaboration with the Velasco regime: 'Perú ante el nuevo ciclo histórico'. *Cuadernos del Centro Latinoamericano de Economía Humana*, Montevideo, no. 36, May 1986.

14. A brief survey of the major events between 1975 and 1983 is given in Mike Reid, *Peru: Paths to Poverty*, Latin America Bureau, London 1984.

15. A distinctly unsympathetic but useful overview of the POR's development may be found in Robert J. Alexander, *Trotskyism in Latin America*, Stanford 1973.

16. *Communism in Spain in the Franco Era. The Autobiography of Federico Sánchez*, London 1977. It might also be added that the communist movement is capable of lampooning the activities of small activist groups in a style no less crushing than that of the confident bourgeois. In the late 1920s the Cuban communist leader Julio Mella remorselessly mocked Haya de la Torre and his fledging APRA – the party that today rules Peru – in the columns of *Entre la Hoz y el Martillo*, but beneath the sarcasm one catches a prescient preoccupation with the dangers of Haya's populism.

17. Lewis Taylor, 'Maoism in the Andes. Sendero Luminoso and the Contemporary Guerrilla Movement in Peru', Centre for Latin American Studies, University of Liverpool, Working Paper no. 2, 1983; Cynthia McClintock, 'Why Peasants Rebel: The Case of Sendero Luminoso', *World Politics*, vol. XXXVII, no. 1, October 1984; Henri Favre, 'Pérou: Sentier Lumineux et Horizons Obscurs', *Problèmes d'Amérique Latine*, no. 72, 1984.

18. Alan Angell, 'Classroom Maoists: The Politics of Peruvian Schoolteachers under Military Government', *Bulletin of Latin American Research*, vol. 1, no. 2, May 1982.

19. Reid, *Peru: Paths to Poverty*.

6

Reassessing Caudillismo in Bolivia, 1825–79

> ... successive revolutions; revolutions in the south, revolutions in the north; revolutions prepared by my enemies, led by my friends, hatched in my home, breaking out all around me.... Good God – they condemn me to a state of perpetual warfare.... Bolivia has become totally incapable of sustaining any government.
>
> President Manuel Isidoro Belzu, 1855[1]

The turmoil of Bolivian politics in the nineteenth century is notorious. In 1918 Nicanor Aranzaes, one of that rather insubstantial group of literati which thrived on the hegemony of the Liberal Party, translated the events of the period 1826 to 1903 into figures, and discovered 185 'revolutions'.[2] Often these were no more than passing infringements of public order in the provinces but they were, nevertheless, decidedly frequent, and there are few years up to the War of the Pacific that were free of disorder. In the red year of 1848 there were fifteen rebellions, eight of them led by General Belzu himself who, despite claims that he was an avid reader of Proudhon and Saint Simon, was as yet concerned with little more than the stentorian productions of the barracks.[3] The rules of war appeared to be the stuff of politics.

Writing from Chuquisaca in 1843, the perceptive Frederick Masterton, first British chargé d'affaires to Bolivia, offered a synopsis of developments since independence which essentially complements Aranzaes's positivist tabulations: 'nothing has been attended to but a series of perfidious revolutions and usurpations of power, shameless robberies of the publick treasury, exortations of tribute from the indigenous Indians, and constant wars with Peru without a national object. Military force has ruled everything by caprice; and right, though ever pompously and theoretically spoken of, has never been practically acted on by any government'.[4] Six years later Masterton's North American colleague spent over three months finding a government to which he could present himself, there being two armies in the field, both issuing decrees and levying taxes.[5] Of the twenty regimes that had more than a completely spurious claim on authority, only three were led by civilians (two belligerent gentlemen, more than disposed to cast aside frock-coat and take up the sword), only four surrendered power voluntarily, while six presidents were assassinated (two whilst holding office), and four died in exile (See Table 1).[6]

It is evident that the politics of insubordination were contagious, and arguable that within the army they were structurally so: 'Those officers who have reached the rank of Colonel do not simply consider the possibility of becoming president or dictator, but believe that they have a right to these positions.'[7] President José Ballivián gave this sentiment his official imprimatur when he stated, probably to his own detriment, 'The soldiers amongst us, in much the same way as in ancient times, are not simply called to serve in the army but also in the highest office.'[8] There was a wealth of vehement condemnations of this state of affairs, much of it unfortunately couched in the resigned tone adopted by Manuel José Cortés who, writing in 1861, pointed out that while the 'laws of progress' were fulfilled by the actions of men, they were enacted by God alone.[9] The more secular and far from disinterested mineowner Avelino Aramayo, who was to play a major part in securing the conditions that would provide for the eradication of *caudillismo*, denigrated the 'pitiable farce', but was content to explain it away in terms of personal ambition.[10] The Manichaean vision of the epoch was nurtured by a species of amateur psychoanalysis, and various protagonists defended on the most tenuous terms according to a writer's ideological affinities, the most celebrated exponent of this art being Alcides Arguedas.[11] Melgarejo, damned as the epitome of *caudillismo*, is alone denied such exoneration. According to that prolific jacobin Tristán Marof, 'Melgarejo is the history of Bolivia'.[12] On the other hand, Masterton's successor, Bruce, ascribed the lack of order and progress to the absence of a 'middle class', a view unsurprisingly not too distant from that of the MNR ideologues Carlos Montenegro and José Fellmann Velarde, the only difference being that they found that class in the urban artisanate, its champion in Belzu, and its unworkable salvation in protectionism.[13]

There is an undoubted danger of regression to a sanitized version of Whig history in concentrating on the manifestation rather than the framework of this chronic instability. This is not to deny the importance of personalist elements of power, which clearly corresponded closely to social and political conditions. While purely coercive activity does not enjoy explanatory primacy, it is apparent that what might be seen as an exotic subculture needs to be given an anthropology in much the same way as it is today necessary to decode the pernicious gobbledegook emanating from the Casa Rosada, the Moneda or the Palacio Quemado. However, we are not yet in a position to explain the predominance of the *condottieri* of the altiplano in terms of a comprehensive political economy, for the historiography of nineteenth-century Bolivia remains very weak despite the impressive achievements made by the young intellectuals grouped around the journal *Avances*.[14] The purpose of this essay is simply to outline in discursive and suggestive fashion some of the principal features of the process.

For Bolivia, as for most countries in nineteenth-century Latin America (perhaps the only exception would be Francia's Paraguay), one can only talk of 'militarism' in a very specific sense for, as vividly depicted by Belzu, military dominance operated not through monolithic unity but by successive schism. Indeed, it is somewhat misconceived to refer to the army rather than armies. It was more a case of the judiciary and legislature lending ephemeral, but by no means entirely worthless, legitimacy to the passage of victors than a case of the institution underwriting the redundancy of the formal division of powers.

In very broad terms, explanations of this pattern of political power tend to revolve around the following factors: the struggle for land; *empleomanía* (pressure for employment) expressive of a more general tendency for the state to constitute little more than an arena for plunder; the renewed need for social control of the lower classes in the wake of their not insubstantial incorporation in the struggle to overthrow colonial control, which itself had to a high degree integrated its repressive apparatus within the production process and its immediate administrative superstructure (*mita, encomienda, corregimiento*, and so on);[15] the sectoral division of the economically dominant bloc which

Table 1 Principal Administrations 1825–84

Simon Bolívar[†]	11/8/25–1/1/26		
Antonio José Sucre[†]	1/1/26–1/1/28		
José Miguel Velasco[○]	12/8/28–14/12/28	Sucre/Potosí	
Pedro Blanco*	25/12/28–1/1/29	Pro-Peru	Peruvian invasion
J.M. Velasco*	2/1/29–24/5/29	Sucre/Potosí	
Andrés Santa Cruz[†]	24/5/29–20/2/39	La Paz	Debasement of coinage (*peso feble*); Peru–Bolivia Confederation (1835–38)
J.M. Velasco*	22/2/39–27/9/41	Sucre/Potosí	
José Ballivián*	27/9/41–23/12/47	La Paz	Peruvian army defeated at Ingavi (1841)
J.M. Velasco*	18/1/48–6/12/48	Sucre/Potosí	
Manuel Isidoro Belzu*	17/12/48–15/8/55	La Paz	Protectionist high-point; artisanal mobilization
Jorge Córdova[†]	15/8/55–21/10/57	La Paz	
José María Linares*[□]	19/12/57–14/1/61	Sucre/Potosí	*Peso feble* issue halted; tariffs reduced
José María Achá[1]*	6/5/61–29/12/64	Cochabamba	
Mariano Melgarejo*	29/12/64–15/1/71	Cochabamba	Renewed debasement; assault on indigenous communities

		La Paz/Sucre	
Agustín Morales*	15/1/71–27/11/72		
Tomás Frias[2]○□	27/11/72–6/5/73	Sucre/Potosí	Free trade established
Adolfo Ballivián†	6/5/73–31/4/74	Sucre/Potosí	
Tomás Frias[3]†□	14/2/75–4/5/76	Sucre/Potosí	[4]
Hilarión Daza*	4/5/76–27/12/79	Sucre/Potosí	War of the Pacific (1879)
Narciso Campero[5]*	19/1/80–3/9/84	Sucre/Potosí	

† = 'elected'
* = came to power through revolt
○ = vice-president/president of congress/provisional administration
□ = civilian

Notes

[1] Junta of ministers removes Linares, followed by four-month crisis from which Acha emerges the victor.
[2] Following the assassination of Morales.
[3] Following the death of Ballivián from natural causes.
[4] Daza in effective control of the army 1872–79, 'strong man' for Frias and Ballivián.
[5] Campero proclaimed president after two separate revolts remove Daza in midst of the War of the Pacific. The main force behind the throne is Colonel Eliodoro Camacho, a Liberal northerner with whom Campero shared an attachment to continue the war.

rapidly became structured around the conflict between free trade and protection as local economies were drawn into the world market directly rather than through the mediation of the colonial power; and regional antagonisms, resulting from a combination of factors but most immediately influenced by the inheritance of colonial boundaries. These, apart from being negotiable in juridical and spatial terms, effected a substantial dislocation of the unifying features of the imperial economic network. All these features inform and interpenetrate each other but in different cases we can identify priorities; for Bolivia the system had its axis around the bounty offered by control of the state and the pressure for employment.

Empleomanía and its Costs

Fifteen years of intermittent but increasingly extensive and bitterly contested warfare bequeathed to the new republic a glut of soldiers and an empty exchequer. Wars with Chile and Peru during the first decade of independence consolidated this legacy and established the defence of pay and station as a residual feature of military activity. If *empleo-manía* was the bane of society, it was only in the military sphere that it had a real impact on state funds since it was provided with the optimum means of self-perpetuation. Yet this is not immediately apparent from the size of regular forces which, in line with the exigencies of petty skirmishing campaigns, were generally small. In 1828 Sucre maintained a force of 2,700 men, which was considered large by the standards of the day. Although Santa Cruz and Ballivián raised armies of 4,500 and 3,700 for the Confederation and Peruvian wars, these were demobbed as rapidly as possible. Belzu, under constant pressure, rarely kept a force larger than 2,300 while Melgarejo's armies fluctuated wildly from 500 in 1865 to a highly unreliable 3,300 on the eve of his overthrow in 1870. Daza, who more than anyone cultivated 'institutionalism' within the orbit of personalist rule, limited the army to 1,500 men right up to the outbreak of the War of the Pacific.[16] Nevertheless, all these armies were top-heavy with officers. In 1843 Ballivián, attempting to reduce the excess stock accumulated over a decade of almost continuous war, removed a hundred officers, but three years later 650 officers and 36 generals remained on the lists.[17] In 1869 Melgarejo retained seven generals, 119 *jefes* and 345 officers to command 1,996 men, a state of affairs that Daza did nothing to ameliorate, paying 384 officers and 637 NCOs but only 825 troopers in 1876.[18]

Although these figures are not extraordinary for the Latin America of the day, they only reveal part of the story, for constant revolts bred equally persistent transfers of allegiance, and made uninterrupted incorporation in the *escalafón* the exception rather than the rule. Perhaps the most 'institutional' figure of the era was Colonel Juan Sarabia y Espinoza, who was promoted to general in 1886 having managed to serve every government since 1842, loyal service which must have entailed support for seven 'revolutions' at the very least. Of the twenty-one generals who at some time supported Melgarejo, fourteen had previously backed his arch-rival Belzu and six had been out of the army for up to twenty years. Many officers certainly had more at stake or less skill in such manoeuvres to sustain a regular career, and there rapidly accumulated a reserve labour army of warriors who under the rules of the game were hardly dispensable and had to be paid off. Ballivián's 1843 purge cost 50,000 pesos when pensions already stood at 112,145 pesos against serving officers' pay of 100,346.[19] Aramayo claimed that Melgarejo paid out twice as much in pensions as in regular pay – a claim that may well carry weight since in 1869 twenty generals, 358 *jefes* and 204 officers drew a pension.[20] Even after the 1871 revolt that removed Melgarejo, and occasioned extensive attrition inside the officer corps, pensions were 50 per cent above regular pay.

Although Ballivián survived the endeavour of pruning the establishment, neither Velasco (1848) nor Linares (1861) was able to repeat the experiment, even when they had a clear mandate from the civilian elite. Consistent with his policies of relieving the fiscal burden on the slowly expanding mining sector, Linares attempted to cut military spending to below 40 per cent of the national budget. He was summarily removed by his military backers, who announced that their new regime 'will, for its part, fulfil the duty of promoting, paying and increasing the pensions of various veterans as far as possible, making good the injustices inflicted on many soldiers by the previous administration'.[21] Throughout a period when state revenue remained stuck at between two and three million pesos the formal costs of sustaining the military were consistently high: never less than 40 per cent and under Melgarejo as high as 70 per cent. The real economic cost was, of course, much greater, as evidenced by constant extraction of forced loans, the formidable looting of insurgent towns, and the ad hoc requisitions of produce to sustain levies that lacked the slightest vestige of quartermanship and were often only retained by the lure of bounty. Melgarejo's methods of raising revenue were so predictable that news of his impending arrival resulted in the almost complete depopulation of Cochabamba in 1865, and when a five-peso levy was decreed to 'reconfirm citizenship' this rich and populous region yielded only 7,000 pesos, necessitating the immediate withdrawal of the army.[22] In similar fashion, the rebels that finally overthrew him – in the name of fiscal sobriety as well as freedom – unleashed a welter of forced loans, seized 50,000 pesos from the mint at Potosí and an equal amount from the mineowner Alfredo Durells, bestowing upon him the rank of colonel in lieu not only of interest but also of principal.[23] Morales, who had lost considerable property in Cochabamba under Belzu and presided over a very uneasy and temporary popular-free trade alliance in 1871–72, did not break from the practice, attempting to wrest a number of important mines in Aullagas from Luis Arteche for alleged non-payment of taxes, a demand that precipitated an immediate political rupture and may well have been the direct cause of the new president's assassination.[24]

Nevertheless, contingent and directly coercive extraction was neither the mainstay of the *caudillos* nor the principal issue of complaint for the civilian oligarchy. The deadweight of sinecure and the endlessly peripatetic business of maintaining authority were primarily maintained by the tribute paid by the indigenous population (on both private estates and communities) and, a matter of far greater contention, revenues acquired through state control of the silver market, closely combined with debasement of the currency.

The Politics of Silver

The state monopoly of the purchase of silver through the Bancos de Rescate, a central legacy of the colony, and the typical absolutist recourse to reduction of the intrinsic value of specie were the two most important issues of the day for the civilian elite, not only because they fortified protection, fuelled inflation and constituted an undeclared but real tax burden on the mining elite, but also because they enabled the military to play a major role in controlling production and circulation as well as to appropriate a major portion of the surplus through the national mint.[25] Thus, until 1873 a tacit alliance may be said to have existed between the employees of the Casa de Moneda in Potosí and a succession of bankrupt generals and their followers, acting as a brake on the liberation of market forces, and inserting a critical space – 'relative autonomy' – between the dominant class and the direct control of policy. We cannot consider the precise co-ordinates and full implications of this here, but a few brief remarks are necessary.

First, the economic impact and political crises engendered by protection were not consistent. Between the heady and transient boom of commercial activity in the first years of independence and the gradual recovery of silver mining in the mid 1850s (effected by a combination of more favourable external conditions and the concentration of ownership in the hands of a comprador faction of the commercial-landowning class) the issue remained contentious but not acutely critical.[26] Second, while we still need to know much more about the textile interests that provided the main impetus for protection, it is evident that they were on the wane, if not in deep recession, and desperate for resuscitation through colonial safeguards.[27] These they obtained with only minor interruption and without substantial contest until the 1850s when the entire system came under concerted challenge. This stemmed from the deep social conflict during the Belzu and Córdova regimes, which were forced to adopt an unprecedented jacobin stance in order to defend the interests of both the urban artisans and the state employees, civilian and military. Henceforth, the free trade bloc was consistent in its pressure but its consolidation as a coherent political force was only gradual, with the realization of its policies only partial until 1873. While Linares was able to halt the issue of the debased coinage known as *peso feble* and reduce tariffs on cloth and bark in 1859, he was still unable to free silver, the key commodity. This uneven development of social and political weight on the part of the mining interests also goes some way to explaining why Melgarejo, who came to power with the backing of the heirs of Linares's *rojo* group, was able to break loose for a while, imposing debasement in 1866.[28]

Although monopoly and debasement operated in unison, they underwent different developments. The price paid by the Bancos de Rescate for silver increasingly moved towards the world market price, being 26 per cent below it in 1829 and only 2 per cent in 1865. This was a gradual increase, not directly determined by the nature of the regime in power, and may well have corresponded more closely with levels of contraband than shifts in the world price which remained very stable until the early 1870s.[29] On the other hand, the *peso feble*, first issued by Santa Cruz in 1830, increasingly dominated the currency, representing 14 per cent of issue in 1830–34 and a staggering 85 per cent in 1850–59.[30] Antonio Mitre has calculated the combined revenue from these two sources at an average of just under 23 per cent of total government income in the 1860s (it is likely to be much higher for the previous decade), compared with approximately 30 per cent from the indigenous tribute. It is worth bearing in mind that since an increasing proportion of the price paid for silver ore by the Bancos de Rescate was in *febles*, the entire system imposed a tax of perhaps 25 per cent on production until well into the 1860s.[31] Finally, there is the important and provocative point that whereas the mineowners considered silver a commodity, and needed to realize the surplus value from its production on the world market in order to prompt accumulation, the governments of the day almost uniformly saw it as 'money', which may have been a happy elision for the purposes of monopoly but was a disastrous manifestation of backwardness for Bolivia's nascent capitalist class.

The Impact on Labour and Land

The impact of military activity upon the markets in land and labour was of secondary importance compared with this intervention in the silver industry. While we do not yet possess a full picture of conscription, it is clear that it did not amass large numbers of men under the colours at any one time, that it was highly random and, in common with many other Latin American countries, bred an extremely high level of desertion; even in the 1880s regimental turnover of 75 per cent was common in an army that numbered less than 3,000 men.[32] Moreover, it seems that the towns were hardest hit by conscription and the countryside by the direct appropriation of goods.[33] Military service continued to be as much socialized as institutionalized with more or less homogeneous levies being raised by governments and rebels from a hard core of veterans, the shoddy national guard (urban militia) and the not insubstantial vagrant population. Clearly this caused periodic disruption of production but it does not appear to have led to a major drain on the labour force as, for example, in Guatemala.[34] From 1838 conscription of *comunarios* (covering the entire population of the communities, not just the *originarios*) was expressly forbidden, and if it took place it was never on such a scale as to excite major complaint. The sole major mobilization of the indigenous communities in this period was during Melgarejo's rule (principally 1866–71). This was compelled by the attack on the communities and organized independently of the 'constitutionalist' rebels and so was not actively inspired by them. The eventual success in co-opting and subduing this movement did not, however, erase the memory; in the 1890s when there was renewed and extensive *campesino* mobilization, the oligarchy resisted demands from the army to extend recruitment to the communities, and was outraged when Pando organized a number under the federal flag in the civil war of 1898–99).[35]

There were complaints from landlords about lack of labour, principally due to flight in order to evade recruiting sergeants, and particularly common in the 1830s when production in Cochabamba and the Yungas was said to have suffered for this reason.[36] However, it was the mineowners who were most outspoken on this score, and there does appear to have been a proclivity to recruit in Potosí where a relatively large and concentrated population was collected around the mines. Occasionally this burden was recognized and regions given dispensation from providing conscripts.[37] But, as Mitre points out, at least until the 1870s the mineowners were incapable of guaranteeing employment for any length of time and, therefore, unable to attract large numbers of workers from the fields. One by-product no doubt was a residual pool of un- or underemployed men in the mining regions.[38] It is possible that a similar situation existed in the northern mines; in 1859 we find working at Corocoro 300 men who had served in Belzu's army and were ready to take up arms against Linares.[39] By the 1870s mineowners, able to pay better wages and offer secure employment, were actively helping their workers to avoid the draft – a practice that was to endure well into the twentieth century.

The question of land is more complex but cannot be separated from that of labour, for exploitation of one depended on control over the other. The central issue in this respect is whether land was obtained *manu militarii*, with generalship effectively co-substantial with proprietorial status as in the platine states. In general it was not. Of course some political and military leaders – Santa Cruz, Velasco, Ballivián, Achá – were landlords of more than modest standing, and Ballivián, like Campero at the end of the period, had mining interests. But others – Belzu, Córdova, Melgarejo, Morales, Daza – made their way up the ranks to supreme power without acquiring important lands. They certainly obtained property, and often at the expense of their adversaries, but they never transformed themselves into leading *hacendados*, and *caudillismo* as a system was not structured around the battle for land. For this to be the case there would have to have been a far greater shift in the pattern of ownership than actually took place within both the private domain and in terms of expropriation of community lands. In the latter case there was indeed constant pressure but it does not appear to have been markedly more acute than that under the colony until the war of the Pacific.[40] This issue has traditionally been centred on Melgarejo's untempered offensive of 1866–70 which carried most weight in the provinces of the altiplano, especially La Paz, and may be seen as the endeavour of a coalition of a faction of the landed oligarchy, state employees, and the encumbent military apparat to generate funds rapidly and secure a basis as rentiers on the richest community holdings.[41] Erwin Grieshaber has produced evidence from tax returns to refute the standard thesis that this offensive was both successful and symptomatic, showing that it was convincingly resisted with a quite impressive degree of repossession taking place, at least in the short term.[42] We still need to know a lot more about this process but it should be stressed that the landowning class was deeply divided over the issue of community lands with an important sector, which included mineowners such as Aramayo, arguing that communal production was high, its produce cheap, and agriculture as a whole of marginal interest to capital.[43] Moreover, the standard liberal-positivist thesis was greatly debilitated insofar as its optimistic proposals were seen as certain to generate rural unrest on a massive scale, prejudicing the collection of the tribute, which was still the largest single item of national revenue. Thus, in 1838 Santa Cruz reversed his earlier measures designed to implement Bolívar's Cuzco and Trujillo decrees. Ballivián also failed to take to its logical conclusion his 1842 declaration that communal lands were held in enfiteusis, and when Achá tried so to do in 1863 he was promptly stalled by a highly vocal Congress. One subsidiary point that may be drawn from this picture is that it further qualifies the image of the military as existing principally to repress, or indeed being consistently capable of repressing, the 'lower orders' in the interests of the oligarchy, a function that was generally secondary to that of mediating relations within the dominant bloc.

The other major factor in this connection, that of spatial expansion and the institution of an economic sub-system that is often rather unhelpfully denominated 'the frontier', was noticeably lacking throughout this period. The various isolated military colonization schemes were never transformed into a dynamo for the conquest of the interior and the operation at a structural level of differential rent. This was, no doubt, largely because of physical conditions but it may also be explained in part by the fact that Bolivia's frontier, in the expanded sense of the term, was internal and rapidly becoming centred on the mining regions of Potosí and southern Oruro.[44]

Regionalism

The final question that ought to be considered at least in outline is whether regional antagonisms were the main propellant for political conflict, a case made forcefully in a recent study by José Luis Roca.[45] It would seem more accurate to describe the process of the transformation of the Audencia de Charcas into Bolivia as one fraught with internal imbalances, which at determinate moments prejudiced the coherence of the territorial unit, rather than as one embodying persistent centrifugal tendencies. Some regions – present-day Beni and Pando – remained cloistered in virtual autarky, and even Santa Cruz was marginalized for much of this period.[46] The principal focus of tension was between the northern entrepot of La Paz, closely integrated in an economic sub-system with Tacna and Arequipa, and the southern axis of Sucre-Potosí, the interests of which lay in maintaining its trade links to the north as well as to the Plate.[47] The most acute manifestation of this rivalry was the threat of annexation of La Paz by Peru, a threat that was not subdued until after the battle of Ingavi in the wake of the failure of that grandoise variant of lower Peruvian hegemony, the Confederation. In the first decades this question undoubtedly had a deep and direct impact upon military activity and organization for the caucus of the Bolivian soldiery was drawn not only from Sucre's Liberation Army (which contained a large number of Peruvians) but also the expeditionary forces from Buenos Aires, the armies of the crown (which had split in the final year of the war along lines that were by no means wholly foreign to localist sentiment), and the indigenous guerrilla groups of Padilla, Lanza, Warnes and others, pledged to an often radical localism.[48] This led to a series of highly fluid alliances in the early years, reaching a peak of confusion in 1828–29 but, largely as a result of Santa Cruz's achievement of internal order at the same time as he attempted a quasi-Bolivarian enterprise in the Confederation, they came to be more firmly structured from the 1830s onwards. The clearest signpost can be found in the persistent but usually short-lived incursions of the southern *caudillo* Velasco, whose challenges for power generally coincided with an escalation of Peruvian ambitions. This proved to be an adequate rectifying balance until the 1850s when the question of regionalist sentiment increasingly became bound up with that of free trade, a point unwittingly signalled by Julio Méndez when he remarked that the practice of horsemanship must be inherently conducive to liberal thought since liberal armies were largely composed of cavalry – almost exclusively raised in the southern pastures of Tarija and Chuquisaca.[49] Yet even Linares, a *potosino*, civilian and ardent free-trader, was neither able nor apparently willing to preside over a wholesale shift of political power to the south once he had removed Belzu's acolyte Córdova. The undeniable importance of La Paz as the nation's largest city and trading centre meant that once the Linares regime fell, something of a stalemate was reached, necessitating the temporary arbitration of two regimes that had their base in Cochabamba while the two main epicentres undertook negotiation and internal realignment of their forces. Significantly, it is only at this point that the advocates of federalism really make themselves heard. We do not hear of federalism again until the end of the century with the breaking of the dominance of silver and the hegemony of Sucre, and then too it was quickly and efficiently suppressed by the unitarians inside the Liberal Party. The 1876 rebellion in Santa Cruz led by Ibañez, while certainly no mere aberration, conformed more closely to the lack of centralized control and the wave of populist and egalitarian mobilization sweeping the country in the 1870s than to a major secessionist drift.[50]

Conclusions

The epoch of *caudillismo* has almost without exception been held to end in 1879 when the ostensible axis of conflict moved from north–south to east–west. The War of the Pacific was the cause of the final collapse of the system, if indeed it merits such a term. Although there were survivals in terms of military organization and political style, there can be no doubt that the war acted as a major watershed. Yet a more incisive periodization must give weight to the partial but qualificative advance of liberalism under Linares. From 1857 onwards no military regime was able fully to turn the clock back. This is true even for Melgarejo who, although he transgressed even the very generous contemporary norms for malfeasance, posed less problems for the dominant bloc than Belzu would have done; it is telling in this regard that Belzu's final attempt to regain power by overthrowing Melgarejo in 1865 was defeated with the assistance of the new southern military strongman, Narciso Campero. The post-Linares military regimes proved costly and unpleasant but they provided necessary barriers against a restless artisanate, and neither Morales nor Daza attempted to redress the balance in favour of protection. In the decade before the war the political challenge to the power of the *chuquisaqueño* elite was identified as emanating less from the army than from a reformulated, fundamentally confused, yet far from impotent *belcista* populism. Its leaders, such men as Méndez and Casimiro Corral, were still obliged to cling to the coat-tails of such dispossessed generals as the veteran *melgarejista* Quintin Quevedo but they also provided the germs of post-bellum liberalism, and in their challenge to the *rojo/constitucionalista* current heralded the arrival of a form of party politics.

While the conflict between free trade and protection is now granted importance in the structuring of political power in nineteenth-century Bolivia, this has largely been as a result of the interpretative work of Guillermo Lora (who has been a Trotskyist militant for thirty-five years and a university professor for only nine months). Lora's work has certainly had the effect of stalling the momentum of epic studies – a veritable discipline in its own right – but it remains to be consolidated and expanded in terms of primary research. What we have suggested here is that the mechanism of the state monopoly over the purchase of silver, the keystone of protection, is critical to the understanding of the rapid, internal schisms of the military as well as of the broad development of social classes; that control over bullion goes a long way to explain the more precise character of political conflict in addition to determining the longer-term formation of regional armies and power blocs. This is not to dismiss the importance of land at all but, rather, to qualify the centrality it is generally supposed to have had in determining the phenomenon of *caudillismo*, and to revise the notion that, in Bolivia at least, the early republican period was characterized principally by spatial dispersal of power with the system as a whole representative of an amalgam of essentially regional authorities, for which there was no organizing principle of consistent importance beyond the maintenance of competition between landed capitals and their internal relations of production. By recognizing that this system interacted, albeit in an uneven and intermittent manner, with one in which control of bullion, and thereby both local accumulation and access to the world market, was contested we can appreciate that while the modern state may have progressively come into being from 1880 onwards, the state itself was not previously absent, or some kind of second-hand sham, but a real power base, weak in that it was constantly 'invaded' but strong inasmuch as it was in many respects the commanding citadel. This is less a paradox than the starting point for a model.

Notes

1. *Mensaje del Presidente Constitucional . . . 1855* (unpaginated).
2. Nicanor Aranzáes, *Las Revoluciones de Bolivia*, La Paz 1918.
3. M. Rigoberto Paredes, *Melgarejo y su tiempo*, La Paz 1962, p. 45.
4. FO 11/1, 30 January 1843.
5. John Appleton to Washington, No. 3, 13 December 1848.
6. N. Andrew N. Cleven, *The Political Organization of Bolivia*, Washington 1940, p. 120.
7. Tomás Caivano, *Historia de la Guerra de América entre Chile, Peru y Bolivia*, Iquique 1904, I, p. 321.
8. *Gaceta del Gobierno*, I, No. 7, 18 January 1843.
9. Manuel José Cortés, *Ensayo sobre la Historia de Bolivia*, Sucre 1861, p. 94.
10. Avelino Aramayo, *Apuntes sobre el Congreso de 1870*, Sucre 1871, p. 4. See also his *Apuntes sobre el Estado Industrial, Económico y Político de Bolivia*, Sucre 1871. A more perceptive viewpoint, but doomed for the purposes of political programme, is to be found in Julio Méndez, *Bolivia antes del 30 de Noviembre de 1874*, Tacna 1875.
11. A. Arguedas, *Los Caudillos Bárbaros: La Plebe en Acción; La Dictadura y la Anarquía; Los Caudillos Letrados*, in *Obras Completas*, Mexico 1959.
12. *Ensayos y Crítica*, La Paz 1961, p. 73.

13. FO 11/8, No. 4, 16 July 1850; Carlos Montenegro, *Nacionalismo y Coloniaje*, La Paz 1953; José Fellmann Velarde, *Historia de Bolivia*, II, La Paz 1970.

14. Only two issues of *Avances* were published before the coup of 1980 which resulted in the exile of many of its leading contributors. The second number, November 1978, is entirely given over to the question of *latifundismo* and the oligarchy. Much of the best work may also be found in *Estudios Bolivianos en Homenaje a Gunnar Mendoza L*, La Paz 1978, and the *cuadernos* of the Centro de Investigación y Promoción del Campesinado (CIPCA). See also Brooke Larson, *Economic and Social Change in an Agrarian Hinterland: Cochabamba (Bolivia) in the late Colonial Period*, PhD, Columbia University 1978; Antonio Mitre, *Silver Mining in XIX Century Bolivia*, PhD, Columbia University 1977; Fernando Cajías, *La Provincia de Atacama 1825–42*, La Paz 1976.

15. Gunter Kahle, 'Die Encomienda als militarische Institution im kolonialen Hispanoamerika', *Jahrbuch für Geschichte von Staat, Wirtschaft und Gesellschaft Lateinamerikas*, 2, 1965; Alfonso García Gallo, 'El Servicio militar en Indias' *Anuario de Historia del Derecho Español*, XXVI, 1965; Leon G. Campbell, *The Military and Society in Colonial Peru*, Philadelphia 1978; Enrique Tandeter, *La Rente Comme Rapport de Production et Comme Rapport de Distribution. Le Cas de l'Industrie Minière de Potosí, 1750–1826*, Thèse de 3e Cycle, Ecole des Hautes Etudes en Sciences Sociales, Paris 1980.

16. Cortés, p. 115; Julio Díaz A, *El Gran Mariscal de Montenegro. Otto Felipe Braun*, La Paz 1945, p. 71; José Manuel Aponte, *La Batalla de Ingavi*, La Paz 1911, p. 124; *Memoria del Ministro de Guerra* (MemMG) ... 1843; FO 11/10, No. 12, 7 September 1852; Hall to Washington, No. 49, 24 September 1865; MemMG ... 1870; ibid ... 1877.

17. *Gaceta del Gobierno*, II, No. 58, 23 December 1843; José María Dalence, *Bosquejo Estadístico de Bolivia*, Chuquisaca 1851, p. 351.

18. MemMG ... 1870; ibid ... 1877. According to the army's organic law there should have been one Major General for every 3,000 men and one Brigadier for every 1,000. In 1846, an average year, there was a general for every 106 soldiers and an officer for every six.

19. *Gaceta del Gobierno*, II, No. 11, 22 August 1843; ibid., I, No. 80, 3 May 1843.

20. MemMG ... 1870.

21. Ramón Sotomayor Valdés, *Estudio Histórico de Bolivia bajo la Administración del Jeneral Don José María de Achá*, Santiago 1874, p. 139.

22. Hall to Washington, No. 46, 17 July 1865.

23. Rand to Washington, No. 15, 9 November 1870.

24. Markbreit to Washington, No. 226, 28 November 1872; Federico Lafaye, *Apuntes para la Historia de Bolivia*, Tacna 1873.

25. Aramayo, *Congreso*, pp. 28–43; *Informe sobre los Asuntos de Bolivia en Europa*, Paris 1877, p. 57; Mitre, pp. 55–76.

26. Gustavo Rodríguez, 'Libre Cambio y el Caracter del Capitalismo; el Caso Boliviano' in *Estudios en Homenaje a Gunnar Mendoza*, pp. 231–248; Mitre, pp. 46–50.

27. Rodríguez, pp. 236–7; Guillermo Lora, *Historia del Movimiento Obrero Boliviano* I, La Paz 1967, pp. 73–100. See Larson, pp. 247–71, for *tocuyo* production in Cochabamba at the turn of the century. She contends that 'by 1850, all Bolivians except the highland Indian population clothed themselves in cloth manufactured in England or one of its colonies ...' (p. 269). This is a position commonly held for Peru at this time, but in the case of Bolivia it might be questioned whether imports were so great, not solely on the basis of Dalence's probably inflated figures for 1846 of 3,572 wool workshops (production valued at 36,681 pesos) and 359 cotton workshops (66,584 pesos) but also on the basis of bad communications and the continued high tariffs until 1859.

28. Julio Benavides, *Historia de la Moneda en Bolivia*, La Paz 1972, pp. 58–62. On debasement see Luis Peñaloza, *Historia Económica de Bolivia*, II, La Paz 1947, pp. 7–42; Watt Stewart, *Henry Meiggs; Yankee Pizarro*, Durham N.C. 1946, pp. 232ff. and, especially detailed, the reports of US Consul Rand in La Paz, 1870.

29. Mitre, p. 61.

30. Ibid., p. 282.

31. Ibid., p. 65.

32. In 1896 the Batallón Sucre lost 197 deserters out of an establishment of 254 men, a not unrepresentative example. Archivo Nacional de Bolivia, Ministerio de Guerra, 1896, Regimental Returns.

33. For details see James Dunkerley, *The Politics of the Bolivian Army; Institutional Development 1879–1935*, D. Phil., University of Oxford 1979, Chapter Two.

34. Manuel Rubio Sánchez, 'Breve Historia del cultivo del añil o xiquilite y de la grana o cochinilla' in *Economía de Guatemala en los Siglos XVIII y XIX*, Guatemala n.d.

35. The rebels of 1871 were keen to disown all responsibility for mobilizing the indigenous population. *Memoria del Secretario Jeneral del Estado, Dr Casimiro Corral*, Sucre 1871, p. 2. On the opposition to conscription in the 1890s, *Interpelación del Sr Ministro de Guerra, Dr Luis Paz 1895*, Sucre 1897, and on 1898 Ramiro Condarco Morales, *Zarate. El Temible Willka*, La Paz 1965; Andrew Pearse, *The Latin American Peasant*, London 1975.

36. José Agustín Morales, *Monografía de las Provincias del Nor y Sur Yungas*, La Paz 1929, pp. 191–2; Aramayo, *Estado*, p. 79.

37. For example, Chichas, Omasuyos, Oruro, Tarija, Tarapacá and Poopó for two years in 1842, and Tarija and Chichas for ten years in 1861. There were often political motives behind such measures. *Gaceta del Gobierno*, II, 10 October 1843; José Agustín Morales, *Los Primeros Cien Años de la República de Bolivia*, II, La Paz 1926, p. 32.

38. Mitre, pp. 202–5.

39. John Cotton Smith to Washington, No. 6, 13 March 1859.

40. Erwin P. Grieshaber, *Survival of Peasant Communities in Nineteenth Century Bolivia*, PhD, University of North Carolina at Chapel Hill, 1977, pp. 132ff., 242; Silvia Rivera Cusicanqui, 'La Expansión del Latifundio en el Altiplano Boliviano. Elementos para la Caracterización de una Oligarquía Regional', *Avances*, 2, pp. 95–118.

41. According to the Chilean ambassador, 'a multitude of vagrant soldiers, public employees owed back-pay, relations and retainers of government ministers' were the main beneficiaries, Ramón Sotomayor Valdés, *La Legación de Chile en Bolivia*, Santiago 1912, p. 93. For details of the 1866 and 1868 measures combined with orthodox interpretation, liberal and 'anti-imperialist' alike, see Luis Antezana, *El Feudalismo de Melgarejo y la Reforma Agraria*, La Paz 1970, pp. 19–73; Arturo Urquidi, *Las Comunidades Indígenas en Bolivia*, Cochabamba 1970, pp. 62–4; Peñaloza, I, pp. 252–9; Fellmann Velarde, pp. 179–214, passim; Alfredo Sanjinés, *La Reforma Agraria en Bolivia*, La Paz 1930.

42. Grieshaber, p. 200.

43. Aramayo, *Congreso*, pp. 21–4; José Maria Santivañez, *Reivindicación de los terrenos de comunidad*, Cochabamba 1871. For support for alienation see José Vicente Dorado, *Proyecto de repartición de tierras y venta de ellas entre los indígenas*, Sucre 1864; Juan de Dios Zambrana, *Dos palabras sobre la venta de tierras realengas*, Cochabamba 1871.

44. See, inter alia, José Cardús, *Las Misiones Franciscanas entre los Infieles de Bolivia*, Barcelona 1886; J. Lavadenz, *La Colonización de Bolivia durante la primera Centuria de Independencia*, La Paz 1925; Julio Díaz A., *Expediciones y Exploradores del Suelo Boliviano*, La Paz 1971; Cristián Suárez, *Exploraciones en el Oriente Boliviano*, La Paz 1919.

45. 'The history of Bolivia is not a history of class struggle. It is rather the history of its regional struggles' J.L. Roca, *Fisonomía del Regionalismo Boliviano*, La Paz 1980, p. 9.

46. Matías Carrasco, *Descripción Sinóptica de Mojos*, Chuquisaca 1830; Antonio Carvalho Urey, *Bosquejo Socioeconómico del Beni*, Sucre 1976; Chelio Luna Pizarro, *Ensayo Monográfico del Departamento de Pando*, Sucre. 1976.

47. J. Valerie Fifer, *Bolivia: Land, Location and Politics since 1825*, Cambridge 1972.

48. Charles W. Arnade, *La Dramática Insurgencia de Bolivia*, La Paz 1972; William Lofstrom, *The Promise and Problems of Reform: Attempted Economic and Social Change in the First Years of Bolivian Independence*, PhD, Cornell University, 1972; Tambor Mayor Vargas, *Diario de un soldado de la independencia altoperuana en los valles de Sicasica y Hayopaya*, ed. Gunnar Mendoza, Sucre 1954; Julio Díaz A., *Los Generales de Bolivia*, La Paz. 1929.

49. Mendez, p. 19.

50. Lora, pp. 417 ff.; Roca, p. 378; Hernando Sanabria Fernández, *Bosquejo de la contribución de Santa Cruz a la formación de la nacionalidad*, Santa Cruz 1942, which challenges the separatist theses of Plácido Molina, *Observaciones y rectificaciones a la historia de Santa Cruz de la Sierra*, La Paz 1936.

7

Political Transition and Economic Stabilization: Bolivia, 1982–89

I could picture myself, in the Chamber of Deputies, proclaiming a virile and eloquent speech: my brow lofty, my gaze steadfast, my diction precise and the words flowing with an eloquence worthy of Baptista. The left side, occupied by the opposition, would look on me with fury, while the right would applaud the orotund, logical periods of the Catiline oration with which I was about to flatten my adversaries.

Armando Chirveches, *La Candidatura de Rojas*, 1909

The MNR was a populist party, very much like Peronism. But when it came to power it was able to grasp what had to be done.

Gonzalo Sánchez de Lozada, Buenos Aires, July 1989.

For many Bolivians there was more than a touch of irony in the fact that at the inauguration of Carlos Saúl Menem as President of Argentina in July 1989 so much attention – for once respectful and inquiring – should be paid to one of their number, present as a guest of honour. The man in question, Gonzalo Sánchez de Lozada, was treated as little less than a Delphic oracle by Julio Alsogaray, Menem's economic adviser, Nicaraguan President Daniel Ortega and the local media, all anxious to learn how this ex-minister of planning and prospective president had contrived to cut Bolivia's inflation rate from 15,000 per cent to 16 per cent in the space of two years without provoking food riots or a widespread collapse of social order. Many in La Paz had good cause to wince at 'Goni's' casual injunction – rendered in a thick accent bred of a youth spent in North America –

that the only stabilization plan worth its salt was one accompanied by a state of siege, under which recalcitrant trade unionists could be packed off to Patagonia for a while. Although this observation derived directly from the Bolivian experience, it scarcely modulated with the discourse of democracy accompanying the first handover between elected presidents in Argentina in more than sixty years. Nonetheless, whatever their political colours, those Bolivians who had witnessed the role of the Argentine military advisers in the coup of July 1980 and knew of the failure of their rich neighbour to pay the millions of dollars it owed for imports of natural gas were inclined to indulge the sly rumours that Menem had asked Sánchez de Lozada to be his economy minister and another Bolivian guest, Hugo Banzer Suárez – ex-dictator and also challenger for the presidency – to be chief of police.

The cultural aspects of such badinage should not be disregarded, but beneath it lies the important fact that the political economy of Bolivia was no longer being treated abroad as a hopeless 'basket case' administered through corporatist politics that shifted between military authoritarianism and a syndicalist-led 'populism'.[1] In fact, many of the features that underpinned this perception remained intact after both the return to constitutional government in October 1982 and the election of the Movimiento Nacionalista Revolucionario (MNR) in July 1985. Equally, it should be said that recent foreign attention to the Bolivian economy has not been matched by an interest in the country's politics.[2] Indeed, longstanding presumptions have been only partially dislocated since in both economic and political fields Bolivia has continued to manifest extreme experiences since 1982.

Apart from the fact that the country remains the poorest in mainland America, it has suffered from both the greatest inflation and the most severe deflationary policies witnessed in the continent since the early 1970s. At the same time, the first two civilian governments since the collapse of dictatorship served in their own ways to uphold – and even encourage – the image of a bi-polar model of politics, albeit within the broad parameters of the rule of law. (The first time, it might be added, since the mid-1940s, when the last stage of the government of Gualberto Villarroel (1943–46) and the first of that led by Enrique Hertzog (1947–49) witnessed respectively 'populist' and 'authoritarian' policies applied under fragile but discernible constitutional conditions.)

In many respects, 'redemocratization' in Bolivia has been associated less with the institutional tasks of establishing a constitutional polity than with the expression of starkly contrasting social and economic policies. On the one hand, the coalition government of the Unión Democrática y Popular (UDP; 1982–85) led by Hernán Siles Zuazo may be viewed as typically 'populist' in that its essential thrust was towards deficit financing, acquiescence in labour demands, radical rhetoric, and a notable respect for human rights. On the other, the MNR government led by Víctor Paz Estenssoro (1985–89) responded to an extraordinary economic crisis exacerbated – but by no means generated – by the UDP with an exceptionally severe and orthodox adjustment programme, alliance with Banzer's right-wing Acción Democrática Nacionalista (ADN), disregard for the *fuero sindical,* and a clear disposition to reduce the state, encourage private capital, and collaborate with the international status quo on issues such as the debt (in a formally heterodox but practically conformist manner) and the cocaine trade, or *narcotráfico* (on a formally conformist but practically heterodox basis).

The sense of an essential modal continuity with the pre-dictatorial era was sustained by the enduring dominance of political life by an 'historical' party – the right (Paz) and left (Siles) wings of the MNR – although such a pattern is also visible elsewhere, with the partial and complicated exceptions of Brazil and Ecuador. However, in the Bolivian case this sense was peculiarly enhanced by the fact that the two post-dictatorial presidents were themselves the principal architects of the state born of the 1952 revolution (Paz being president in 1952–56 and 1960–64, Siles in 1956–60). Indeed, although the passage of time and changing circumstances determined that they could no longer conduct themselves as twenty or thirty years earlier – a fact most evident in the need to form coalitions and leave the more energetic aspects of *caudillismo* to subalterns of a younger generation – the cyclical features of political life were underscored in a profoundly paradoxical fashion in that Paz, who had nationalized the tin mines, introduced an agrarian reform, and applied highly inflationary policies in the first years of the revolution, now sought to dismember the state mining corporation (Comibol), announced a substantial adjustment to the agrarian reform, and conducted a rigorously deflationary economic policy. Siles, by contrast, had initially been associated with the MNR's conservative wing, and in 1956–57 entered into a decisive conflict with the trade unions grouped in the Central Obrera Boliviana (COB)

175

precisely by applying an orthodox stabilization plan that cut real wages, increased unemployment and reduced state expenditure to the requirements of the IMF and Washington. The fact that he strenuously resisted taking such a course in the early 1980s was widely perceived as emanating not just from a commitment to 'populism' but also from a personal refusal to relive the extreme bitterness of the mid 1950s. These reversals of prior practice were not, in fact, as simple as depicted, but they did throw into such sharp relief the trajectory of individual personalities that even in the 1989 election dominated by figures of the 1970s (Banzer and Jaime Paz Zamora of the Movimiento de la Izquierda Revolucionaria [MIR]), and the 1980s (Sánchez de Lozada and Carlos Palenque of Conciencia de Patria [CONDEPA]), it was easy to underestimate the degree to which Bolivian politics had changed.

The general lack of interest in discovering the degree of balance between, on the one hand, Bolivia as *part of* the regional experience of redemocratization and a manifestation of that experience in extremis (the relationship unity/diversity), and, on the other, the persistence of the old/'traditional' and the emergence of the new/'modern' (the relationship continuity/rupture) cannot be properly rectified here. However, it should be noted at the outset that while this essay does not pretend to deal in detail with economic management,[3] the coca and cocaine economies,[4] or the travails of the left[5] – all critical issues in the post-dictatorial era – none of these phenomena lacks features that run counter to received beliefs and that confuse easy paradigms.

With respect to the economy, it is evident that, in addition to notable failures to spur growth under both administrations, after 1985 the state sector was simply diminished rather than overhauled, agriculture was largely ignored and excluded from fiscal reform for purely political reasons (the 'traditional' *movimientistas* over-ruling the 'modern' technocrats), and with the exception of a few instances of co-operativization (most notably municipal telephone systems) and asset-stripping (the sale of Comibol's reserves of unprocessed ore), privatization remained a pious hope. Similarly, following a constant pattern since 1952, efforts to encourage new private investment produced insignificant results beyond recycling an increased proportion of narcodollars through formal channels. The social cost of both hyperinflation under the UDP and stabilization under the MNR was exceptionally high; the latter altered its form but certainly did not reduce its impact.

In terms of coca and cocaine the record of the last decade is similarly mixed. Whilst there have been indisputably major shifts in the patterns of production, population and labour in certain regions (Cochabamba, Santa Cruz and the Beni), and the officially sanctioned circulation of narcodollars has contributed significantly to mitigating the effects of the depression, there was no escalation of mafia-led violence on the scale witnessed in Colombia or, under rather different political and productive conditions, Peru. Equally, *narcotráfico* is not only based on legal cultivation of coca (in all areas until late July 1989; legally, only in the Yungas of La Paz thereafter), but it has also failed to produce distinct cartels. Rather, insofar as the capital flight of the 1970s and early 1980s has been reversed, its assets have been recirculated through established structures and activities. In the same vein, it has deepened rather than extended previous systems of kinship patronage and corruption, building on existing modes of illegal practice in the armed forces, police and leading political parties in a relatively 'unpartisan' fashion. The legacy of the open association of the military regime of 1980–82 with the cocaine trade has been a pattern of discreet infiltration – not the much-vaunted 'takeover' – and, with several honourable exceptions, a response to US pressure that follows the logic of '*obedezco pero no cumplo*' rather than decisive action. Although between 1984 and 1987 the US changed the emphasis of its policy from halting trade in cocaine to reducing production of coca, the terms it demanded of La Paz on both counts could not possibly have been met without destroying both the constitutional order and the economy – a fact clearly understood, if never admitted, in the US embassy.

Finally, debate over the defeat of the left has frequently suffered from the *schadenfreude* of disillusioned fellow-travellers and closet reactionaries. Both they and the honest celebrants of the collapse of radicalism may properly identify this in the left's own terms – the structures and discourses derived from 1917 and 1952 – yet these must also be assessed in the light of the weaknesses of the right and those features of the new conservative order that have preserved the need for (and incidence of) popular mobilization at the same time as they have altered its forms. Although the defeat of traditional radicalism was given a definitive character first by the association of *both* the COB and the parties of the left with the chaos of the UDP period, and then by the effective dismemberment of the miners' union (FSTMB) following the 1985 tin crash, the moral authority of the left has been far less damaged than has its social project. An apparently minor compensation that might be deemed intrinsic to such a decisive setback in terms of power politics, this is, in fact, a matter of considerable consequence in a country where the state imbricates closely with civil society, where the left has a minimal tradition of violence, and where the left's failings were seen (with some justification) to result from it being 'out of date' in its methods rather than wrong in its ideas.

Thus, after 1985 the right exercised the political power given it by the electorate with both flair and decision, but it failed to establish hegemony; at best it won acquiescence, which is a necessary but insufficient condition for hegemony. At the same time, it signally failed to institutionalize either the fragile constitutional order or its own domination. '*Concertación*' proceeded by pacts, yet these pacts depended upon a division of the administrative spoils of the state between parties that had very diverse histories but minimal ideological differences.

The failures of the left between 1982 and 1985 provided the right – including the MIR – with neither the necessity nor the incentive to engage in any compromise beyond cabinet alliances. This certainly enabled the deflationary programme to be imposed without great difficulty, yet by the time of the 1989 election campaign the contradictions of such an unchallenged dominion had been laid fully bare. Not only was the 1985 MNR-ADN 'Pacto por la Democracia' broken on the premise – in the words of MNR Foreign Minister Guillermo Bedregal – that 'pacts are made to be broken', but the right also found itself engaged in a three-way internecine conflict resulting in a so-called '*triple empate*' (very roughly a quarter of the votes for each of the ADN, MNR and MIR) that could only be managed by electoral malpractice and a twelve-week circus of offers and counter-offers over the spoils of state in an effort to secure the presidency through a vote in congress. This process involved a suborning of the judiciary that paralleled the extraordinarily prolonged and inefficient 'trial' of the leading figures of the 1980–82 dictatorship, most particularly General García Mesa, who happily absconded in the middle of deliberations. In short, the final months of the 1985–89 MNR administration witnessed an outbreak of *politiquería* of such proportions that the right came close to losing its already tenuous claim to uphold constitutionalism, whatever its successes on the economic front. The majority of the left stood paralysed before this scenario, but a three-week hunger strike by two young radical leaders – Roger Cortez (Partido Socialist-1; PS-1) and Víctor Hugo Cárdenas (Movimiento Revolucionario Tupaj Katari de Liberación Nacional; MRTKL) – in protest at the fraudulent cancellation of fourteen election results (including their own, but also those of all other parties bar the MIR, which was the principal force 'managing' the 1986 election law it had sponsored in congress) not only drew widespread sympathy but also signalled the potential for a radical renaissance within the constitutionalist framework.

This preliminary qualification to a broadly held view of the primary qualities of the transition to constitutional government highlights the importance of those aspects of politics that are not immediately competitive and relate to what we might call the moral economy of public conduct.[6] On such a non-partisan plane the Bolivian experience of transition proves more complex and fragile than many care to admit. Seven years after it had been installed, the critical issue with regard to the consolidation of parliamentary democracy was whether this could be ensured through the dominance of forces that had little to do with its initial restoration and which were content to maximize the advantages of their economic policies without attending to the institutional and ideological fissures bequeathed by the collapse of the traditions of 1952. The administrations of Siles and Víctor Paz were largely able to camouflage this structural weakness (one of the few characteristics that they shared), but it remained far from certain that a third regime, bereft of a historical discourse and the privilege of catharsis provided by initial bouts of redistribution or deflation, would prove capable of ensuring stability within or without the parameters of the 1967 constitution, which was, after all, the product of a military regime.

Although superstition is by no means the first victim of modernity or a negligible factor in politics, it is perhaps a touch sour to note that when, during the congressional debate of 4 August 1989 to elect the new president, ex-deputy Víctor Hugo Cárdenas sought to support his rejection of the rigged results of the May poll with a quote from the scriptures, it was discovered that the bible upon which the new members of the legislature had sworn their oath was, in fact, a missal in Latin, unintelligible to all. At the time, this incident provoked some levity, but as the notably inferior contributions from the floor dragged on until seven the next morning there was comment in the *barra* that the next four years would be based as much on ignorance as on blind faith.

Table 1   Bolivian Governments, 1952–82

1952–56	Víctor Paz Estenssoro (MNR)	April 1952 National Revolution; popular mobilization; major mines nationalized; agrarian reform; rule by decree; rightist opponents repressed; inflation.
1956–60	Hernán Siles Zuazo (MNR)	'Semi-open' election; deflation; army rebuilt; right and left opposition harassed; centralist control of MNR; COB in retreat.
1960–64	Víctor Paz Estenssoro (MNR)	'Semi-open' election; economic stability; COB subordinate; MNR divisions grow; army role increases; left harassed.
1964	Víctor Paz Estenssoro (MNR)	'Semi-open' election; MNR splits; army becomes main political arbiter.
1964–69	René Barrientos Ortuño (military)	Coup, followed by repression of COB and left; military–*campesino* pact; economic stability with opening to foreign capital; 1967 constitution; controlled congress; short-lived guerrilla action; massacres in mines.
1969	Luis Adolfo Siles Salinas (PDC)	Vice-presidential succession after death of Barrientos; effective military rule.
1969–70	Alfredo Ovando Candia (military)	Coup; 'nationalist' military rule with mixed cabinet; short-lived guerrilla action; left recovers in conditions of semi-legality.
1970–71	Juan José Torres (military)	Coup; 'left nationalist' military rule; COB-dominated *asamblea popular*; political polarization.
1971–78	Hugo Banzer Suárez (military)	Coup; right-wing authoritarianism; military alliance with MNR (Paz) and FSB to 1974; 1974–78 'institutionalist' regime under personalist control; COB and left repressed; collapse of military–*campesino* pact; economic growth; progressive indebtedness.
1978	Juan Pereda Asbún (military)	Fraudulent election followed by coup; weakened dictatorship.
1978–79	David Padilla Arancibia (military)	Coup; 'benign dictatorship' by army constitutionalists.

1979	Walter Guevara Arce (PRA/MNR)	Elected by congress after failure of Siles (31.22%) and Paz (31.13%) to secure victory in poll; weakened executive.
1979	Alberto Natusch Busch (military)	Coup; 16-day dictatorship defeated by worker, congressional and US opposition.
1979–80	Lidia Gueiler Tejada (PRIN/MNR)	Appointed by congress; weakened executive; attempts at deflation.
1980–81	Luis García Mesa (military)	Coup, following UDP victory in elections; left repressed; ADN militants serve rightist dictatorship tarnished by support from *narcotráfico*.
1981	Military Junta	Coup, following US and military opposition to García Mesa and Interior Minister Luis Arce Gómez; left remains repressed; military divided.
1981	Celso Torrelio Villa (military)	Internal coup; army hardliners retain power but adjust policies to US demands.
1982	Guido Vildoso Calderón (military)	Institutional agreement; hardliners lose power to 'transitionalists'; curbs on COB lifted; economic crisis deepens.

Background

Discussion of political transitions – broadly understood here to signify changes of governmental system – cannot be limited to factors of conjuncture and agency, although these are the most apparent constituents of a phenomenon in which elements of rupture are more pronounced than those of continuity. This is especially true of Bolivia, where, as has already been inferred, modern politics can be described as a 'continuity of ruptures'. Some sense of this may be gleaned from Table 1. A number of very broad points signalled by the table and relevant to an understanding of developments after 1982 deserve further emphasis.

(i) Governmental stability was not primarily associated with constitutionalism, still less with the holding of elections.

Insofar as such an association can be stipulated, it applies only to the period 1899–1930 under the *ancien régime* of the Liberal and Republican parties, during the domination of the tin oligarchy, prior to the introduction of universal suffrage and with exceptionally insecure terms of competition.

From 1956 the MNR presided over a full and formal constitutional apparatus. However, this was heavily manipulated, coexisted with important mechanisms of 'popular'/party control (militias; secret police; expanded syndicalist *fueros*), and reflected – even encouraged – political instability from 1960 onwards.

The *banzerato* of 1971–78 was profoundly anti-democratic in character and, in line with similar regimes in the Southern Cone, postulated a direct relationship between stability and the absence of political competition and civil liberties.

(ii) Constitutionalism was broadly viewed as intrinsically weak, highly vulnerable to alternative means of expressing corporate interests, and more of a mechanism of truce/transition than continuity. It was not closely identified with the interests of any social class.

After 1964 the *fuero sindical* had been suppressed under dictatorships but also respected by some military regimes, notably Torres but also Padilla, and was not intimately associated with a full division of powers. The union movement had historically gained most under 'Bonapartist' regimes (Busch, Villarroel, MNR, Torres). Similarly, the right had flourished under authoritarianism (1946–51; 1964–69; 1971–78) and found itself critically divided in 'open' elections (1951; 1960; 1964).

As a result, civilian conservatives were accustomed to 'knock on the barracks door' and service military regimes whilst many on the left continued to place hopes in 'progressive' officers right up to the early 1980s. (Outside of the COB leadership – vulnerable but divided over this issue since 1964 – the Communist Party (PCB) and MIR were the most prone to this option, particularly in 1979–81.)

The first election since 1951 for which the result was not, for various reasons, a foregone conclusion, was that of 1979. In this respect, the most important feature of constitutionalism was greatly diminished in the popular eye.

Such a trajectory meant that it was not just extremist political actors but broad sectors of civil society that harboured substantial doubts as to the value of constitutionalism in modulating antagonistic social programmes for any significant period of time. It was identified with stalemate, not consensus; it lacked hegemony.

(iii) By the late 1970s the political legacy of 1952 had become dissipated to the degree that no single electoral front could secure a victory in terms of its identification with the revolution. At the same time, both the right and the left lacked the ability to break from minority electoral status on their own. As a result, party alignments remained very fluid and dominated by pragmatism.

From 1978 to 1983 this process revolved around three insecure nuclei:

(a) on the right, Banzer's ADN, the most constant formation but still prone to militarist overtures and limited in its popular appeal by both its conservatism and the authoritarian past of its leader;

(b) on the centre-right, Víctor Paz's MNR, bolstered by its association with 1952 (particularly in the *campo*) yet limited by Paz's erstwhile collaboration with Banzer, and a significant right-wing current still amenable to cooperation with the military; alliance with Oscar Zamora's 'Maoist' PCB-ML counteracted these tendencies to a strictly minimal degree and after 1979 was of greater regional than ideological importance (Zamora, like the Paz family, is from Tarija; in 1989 he backed the MIR-NM and became minister of labour);

(c) on the left, Siles's MNRI, which compensated for a lesser inheritance from the revolutionary era with its progressive stance from the early 1970s. However, the party was less disciplined and emphatically led than the MNR and depended heavily upon its alliance with both the 'modern' left (MIR) and that of more orthodox hue (PCB), which alienated other important radical currents (particularly the PS-1) and made the front the least stable of all, reliant on tactical as well as conviction voting by many members of the COB.

It is not until 1982 that these currents are able to operate with significant independence from the officer corps. They failed to establish any viable coalition government before October of that year; and at no stage between 1979 and 1989 did an electoral front win a clear mandate at the polls.

As a consequence, exceptionally fluid terms of competition aggravated ideological differences to spur organizational division, a multiplicity of tactical alliances, and a progressive erosion of political affinities constructed over three decades.

(iv) The military remained critically divided between 1978 and 1982.

A number of factors are evident here: antipathy to Banzer's personalist rule; the endurance of a subordinate 'progressive Bonapartism' (derived not only from the 1930s and 1940s but also from the influence of the MNR and the impact of the Velasco regime in Peru); the competitive influences of, particularly, Argentina (anti-communism) and the US (anti-*narcotráfico*).

(v) Syndicalism continued to exercise considerable popular authority.

Although the COB leadership consistently desisted from pursuing the central objective of its 1970 programme to establish a popular, socialist democracy, the rank and file were centrally responsible for mass opposition to militarism between 1977 and 1982. This not only enhanced the COB's legitimacy but also heightened that of direct action although it was now in significant contradiction with the end – constitutional government – to which it was employed.

The anti-dictatorial struggle was, therefore, not only conducted along traditional corporatist lines, it also enlivened expectations of economic and political reorganization that were singularly at odds with the objectives and capabilities of the major political parties.

(vi) The violation of human rights and culture of violence followed a pattern distinct from that elsewhere in the Southern Cone (except Paraguay).

The left had a very marginal history and culture of violence; guerrillaism was insignificant as a factor either in generating dictatorial government in the first place or in overthrowing it. Whilst appreciable, the level of terror under Banzer was notably lower than that in Chile or Argentina. That under García Mesa was temporarily of a comparable level but occurred after two years of struggle, without US support and amidst extreme military division over paramilitary activity organized by Argentine 'experts' and foreign fascists. Active resistance continued throughout and fear was not systematized.

As a result, constitutionalism was not as closely associated as elsewhere with either a 'settling of scores' or 'peace at any price'. This was a two-edged sword. On the one hand, it facilitated military acquiescence in transition through the scapegoating of very few individuals (excluding Banzer – unsuccessfully charged in congress in 1979 – and García Mesa's associates bar members of the cabinet). On the other, it

reduced the cathartic and consensual qualities of civilian administration in the immediate post-dictatorial period.

(vii) The chronological pattern of 'redemocratization' was at variance
with that elsewhere.

Pressure from Washington and mass mobilization from late 1977
produced what was, in regional terms, an early experience of transition, without a graduated *'apertura'* or support from neighbouring
states (except Peruvian neutrality). Recidivist militarism thereby
gained critical external support, notably from Argentina. The left, by
contrast, was in a position to be spurred by the example of the
Nicaraguan revolution (notably in November 1979).

The eventual inauguration of Siles in October 1982 more closely fits
the regional pattern, but it should be noted that he entered office
having won elections held in 1980 on a platform ill suited to the new
political and economic conditions. Unlike the pattern elsewhere
(except Ecuador), the left took office before the right, which actively
sought such an outcome once militarism was clearly doomed.

(viii) The role of Washington was important but not decisive.

Under Carter, pressure on the military was forthright and spurred
reactionary nationalism. However, conservative expectations of
fulsome support from Reagan were dashed by the cocaine issue, which
obliged continued policies of containment despite the relative strength
of the left.

This combination had the effect of curbing left-wing nationalism
and enabled the US to maintain a relatively low profile, relying less on
'intervention' than on 'benign non-collaboration'. Both before and
after 1982 the effect was eventually decisive but slow to emerge.

(ix) The military regimes did not attempt to introduce a neo-liberal
economic model.

Despite fierce efforts to suppress wage costs, occasional endeavours
at privatization, (unrewarding) concessions to foreign capital and
general adhesion (up to 1978) to IMF directives, the military maintained the MNR's statist approach. Its constituency was upheld
through reapportioning the surpluses, contracts and loans accumulated through the post-1952 public sector exchange rate policies favourable to agri-business, and proscriptions of trade unions.

This pattern was facilitated by the price and loan boom of the mid 1970s, which terminated in the midst of the transition. Restoration of civilian government occurred within weeks of the 1982 debt crisis and after twenty-four months of extensive pillaging of public finances (through both old-fashioned larceny and the raising of dubious loans).

Economic and political 'logics' were, therefore, as elsewhere, 'out of sequence'. Yet Bolivia was partly distinctive in that no major orthodox deflationary offensive had been attempted prior to redemocratization; this option thus remained pending. (A broadly similar position obtained in Peru in 1980, but under much more favourable circumstances; even in 1989 the Paraguayan economy remained singular enough not to admit to ready comparison; one might argue about the degree of 'shock' inflicted by Martínez de Hoz in Argentina, but if it was more modulated than in Chile it was certainly more concerted than any policy hitherto essayed in Bolivia.)

(x) The period of transition itself witnessed no significant 'new social movements' to which its success might be attributed.

It is the case that the *campesino* movement acquired unprecedented weight and independent organizational form in the CSUTCB in 1979, but this development upheld in more radical form many of the 'traditions' of the altiplano, restoring some of the diminished influence of the rural majority. It did not represent a major shift in socio-economic structures, and neither did it produce a decisive realignment of political power or patronage; radical expectations for this were soon dimmed by the MNR's resurgent electoral appeal and the latent anti-communism of *katarismo*.

The issue of formal, national political power was decided between 1977 and 1982 very much in terms of established forces and discourses. It was only after 1983–84 that the parameters of collective identity and organization – in both town and countryside – began to register significant change. However, it should be noted that (a) the growth of the 1970s had expanded the urban middle class, providing Banzer with a constituency, primarily at the expense of the MNR, and (b) the germs of economic change – *narcotráfico* and weakness in the mining sector – were already quite evident in the early 1980s, and both played a part in the transition, even if at that stage through familiar patterns of behaviour and organization.

The Government of the UDP, October 1982 to August 1985

The popular euphoria that greeted the inauguration of Siles in mid October 1982 at the head of the UDP coalition (MNRI; MIR; PCB) was not entirely misplaced. The armed forces were badly divided, demoralized, tarnished by association with *narcotráfico*, and now controlled by a determined group of generals who had taken up arms against the dictatorship in 1981, enjoyed US support and clearly favoured civilian rule (even if they were notably sympathetic to Paz's MNR). The anti-dictatorial mobilizations of September and October indicated a level of support for constitutionalism that cowed the civil police and effectively drove García Mesa's paramilitary apparatus underground (which, in local terms, meant that they stashed their weapons, kept their heads down and started looking for new jobs; whilst they had, occasionally, acted like the Romanian Securitate, they were never treated like them, for good or ill). Although the UDP contained communists, it was soberly welcomed by Reagan's White House, received much more resolute European support (particularly from France and Spain) and a clear signal from the conservative parties that they would respect the 1980 election results. On the international plane, the Malvinas defeat and economic recession had evidently reduced the spoiling capacity of the Argentine junta; Brazil continued to move cautiously towards civilian rule; Peru had already achieved it. Ecuador, Colombia and Venezuela all offered forthright support; the military's previous aggression towards the Andean Pact had bred abnormally warm sympathy for the civilian opposition, of which Siles was the clear figurehead.

Nevertheless, from its first day in office the new government faced considerable problems. Official figures for the third quarter of 1982 indicated a major economic crisis (see Appendix I) while estimates for capital flight in 1980 and 1981 stood at \$370m. and \$347m. respectively – more than a third of legal export earnings.[7] The UDP largely owed its restoration to power to the COB, whose rank and file had borne the brunt of the repression, had been unable to defend their wages against an inflation rate of nigh on 15 per cent per month, and were both well organized and in boisterous mood. Although the PCB was in office (ministries of labour and mines), its capacity to influence the independent majority of the COB leadership and a traditionally suspicious membership was very limited. Equally, control of the executive was qualified by the fact that the UDP lacked control of congress, where the informal MNR-ADN bloc possessed an effective majority in the Senate and was very close to one in the House of Deputies. Fully aware of the pitfalls this threatened, Siles had resisted acceptance of the 1980 poll result and insisted upon new elections that would reflect the state of public opinion after two years of military rule (including the collaboration of senior *adenistas*). In this he was supported by the PCB, which called for fresh elections in December 1982. However, the MIR, whose Jaime Paz Zamora held the vice-presidency, joined the right in demanding an immediate ratification of the 1980 result under the slogan '*el hambre no espera*'. This, together with manifest differences of opinion within the MNRI, signalled important tensions within the alliance even before it had entered office. At the same time *institucionalista* control of the military did not extend to a purge of the officer corps beyond those very few figures publicly associated with *narcotráfico*. If the armed forces were, as a whole, compliant, there were still at large, and in important commands, officers appalled at the sight of the PCB taking cabinet portfolios. Moreover, the cocaine trade had not diminished at all, and the administration faced major – if not insuperable – difficulties in subduing it, with or without US support (which it clearly sought to avoid).

Finally, although Siles's frail appearance and gentle comportment contrasted favourably with the brusque demeanour of the soldiers who had preceded him, providing an avuncular image suited to a new era of consensus, it soon became clear that he lacked resolution and control over his cabinet, party and coalition allies. Despite enjoying broad sympathy, he was scarcely even *primus inter pares* within the government – a position of critical weakness with respect to managing the inevitable rush for the spoils of office (never enjoyed by the MIR and PCB, and not for over a decade by the MNRI) and still more so with regard to upholding executive authority against a congress that was able to mask its ideological enmity with demands for a full division of powers.

Siles saw his political role as one of averting conflict at all costs and maintaining public order without resort to violence. His past clashes with the COB, strong commitment to pacifism, and dedication to consensus politics betokened an outlook that was supremely suited to the tone of civilism and no less ill-suited to giving it substance. However, if the president's disposition aggravated the fissures and confusions within the UDP, these were equally the result of objective circumstances over which even the most determined government would have had little control. It should be noted here that comparisons between the UDP and MNR administrations are invidious insofar as Víctor Paz took office after Siles had endured a swathe of political problems that were intrinsic to any first post-dictatorial administration – a fact that could not have been ignored by the right when it supported the UDP's entry into government. (In this respect, the MIR rapidly learned an invaluable lesson, for which it paid a high price as a party but a rather low one in terms of its most ambitious leaders.) Siles's preferred option was not only at variance with popular sentiment, it also appeared to be sectarian and ran the risk of prolonging the stalemates of 1978–80. The right, by contrast, could maximize the advantages of opposition and what in technical parlance could be described as a 'depressed learning curve'. Although it had good reason to fear a flurry of radical policies, it could also perceive that the UDP was in a poor position to meet the very high expectations of the populace.

In sum, the UDP was faced with an unprecedented economic crisis when it lacked internal cohesion, decisive leadership, full military support and control over both congress and the economy's leading commodity, cocaine. It was not, then, surprising that within a year its popular support was greatly diminished and that in less than three it was comprehensively defeated at the polls. However, the scale of that defeat was by no means a foregone conclusion and reflects multiple errors, the opposition of the COB and the resurgence of the right. The trajectory of this decline into confusion, inaction and then effective abdication and its most pronounced features deserve some further cursory observations.

The Economy

The UDP's economic policies have been characterized – most frequently after Paz's 1985 deflation – as both technically inept and irresponsibly redistributionist. In fact, they were profoundly inconsistent, sometimes attempting stabilization at the expense of capital and in defence of wages (November 1982; May 1985), sometimes seeking an orthodox deflation that clearly prejudiced labour, even if it did not appreciably assist productive capital (April 1984; November 1984; February 1985). Table 2 gives a summary depiction of the principal measures, which may best be understood in conjunction with the appendices. Whilst the abject failure of all these initiatives is indisputable and borne out by the statistics, several less obvious points deserve brief comment.

The first is the least publicized by critics on the right: many entrepreneurs/speculators made fabulous fortunes out of hyperinflation by either acquiring cheap dollars from the Banco Central and selling them on the parallel market (which existed throughout, regardless of periodic proscription) or simply 'informally repatriating' dollar savings to the same end. Equally, the consistently – and massively – over-valued exchange rate encouraged enormous profits through contraband, which was a far more 'socialized' activity but still the means for remarkable concentrations of wealth. (In contrast to the crisis of 1954–57, goods remained available throughout, but only a minuscule percentage could be bought at subsidized rates, and there was no real effort, unlike in the 1950s, to exercise physical control over the black market except occasionally that in dollars.) The restrictions on the formal banking sector were also offset by the fact that it took loans at zero interest and extended them at nominal rates, thereby sharing in the government's short-term 'seigneurage gains' made by printing money.

Second, whilst within months the UDP's management of the economy was badly 'in drift' by seeking simultaneously (and equally fruitlessly) to assuage the IMF and popular pressure, the administration started with a clear strategy that was partly misconceived and partly misapplied. This was the November 1982 'dedollarization', which converted all internal dollar obligations at a rate of Bs 145 and lifted state responsibility for private dollar debts as well as the exchange risk of dollar deposits – realized two days later with a devaluation to Bs 196. The aim here was to secure governmental control of all dollar transactions and fortify the peso; this failed almost at once as foreign banks closed, local institutions shifted their operations to the 'grey market', and private savers conducted their business on the parallel market. Confidence in the peso plummeted and the economy was rapidly 'redollarized' but now on informal terms with the state entirely lacking control.[8] The legality of this excessively aggressive measure was rejected by the courts in 1984, by which time its failure was apparent to

Table 2   Major UDP Economic 'Packages'

November 1982	Devaluation: Bs 44.5–200 per US$ (parallel rate: 250); min. wage: Bs 5,990–8,490 (US$42); indexation of wages; private banks excluded from exchange market ('dedollarization').
November 1983	Devaluation: Bs 200–500 per US$ (parallel rate: 1,200); reduced subsidies on foodstuffs; disputed indexation maintained; min. wage at Bs 30,100 (US$33).
April 1984	Devaluation: Bs 500–2,000 per US$ (parallel rate: 3,000); formal indexation halted (av. productive sector wage rise is 13%; 40,000 public sector employees get food bonus at 50% of wage).
July 1984	Basic prices officially controlled; av. 30% wage rise; official limit on debt service repayments at 25% export revenues.
August 1984	Devaluation: Bs 2,000–5,000 per US$ (parallel rate: 6,500); dual exchange rate, treasury subsidizing rate of Bs 2,000 for 'essential imports'; reduced wage rises.
November 1984	Devaluation: Bs 9,000 (single rate) per US$ (parallel rate: 17,000); reduced wage rises; min. wage raised to Bs 407,855 (US$20); general wage rise is by factor of 13.55 relative to Nov. 1983.
February 1985	Devaluation: Bs 9,000–45,000 per US$ (parallel rate: 160,000); reduced wage rise (bonus of Bs 3.1 m).
May 1985	Devaluation: Bs 45,000–67,000 per US$ (parallel rate: 275,000); formal wage indexation restored; min. wage at Bs 6.2m (US$21).

all – the government began issuing gold and dollar bonds in August of that year – even those members of the COB for whom the *escala móvil* (indexation) was the economic defence equivalent to that of holding dollars for savers (of whom there were a great many with modest deposits who also earned wages and initially supported the UDP).

Third, the UDP's much-publicized resort to increasing emission of notes – characteristic of hyperinflation – should not obscure an equally critical factor: the collapse of public revenues, which fell from 9 per cent of GDP in 1980 to 1.3 per cent in the first nine months of 1985. Collection time-lags under conditions of acute inflation, together with the fact that some three-fifths of central government revenues were related to the official exchange rate, meant that income fell faster than expenditure. It has been correctly noted that 'the hyperinflation under

Siles was not so much a result of new spending as the inability to restrain spending in the face of falling foreign loans, falling tax revenues, and higher debt service payments abroad.'[10] The notion that the UDP was 'spendthrift' is not, then, at all true in the popular sense of the term – the COB persistently made this point – but it may be applied insofar as the government was unprepared or unable – the degree varied – fully to pass on the structural and conjunctural costs of the crisis to the popular sector either through its own initiatives or by accepting those demanded by the banks in return for reducing the external pressure. Once the government's effort to control dollar deposits collapsed it simply trod water, trying to mediate internal and external pressures only when they became absolutely intolerable. (By 1984 the internal limits of tolerance corresponded to a general strike of more than a fortnight; the external ones extended to the impounding of Lloyd Aereo Boliviano's aged Boeing 707 at Miami airport.) Reductions in public investment were thus preferred to those of real wages although the effects were barely slower to emerge and would be fully exploited by the MNR after 1985.

The character of the UDP's 'packages' roughly reflects the administration's political fortunes. Between November 1982 and April 1984 it sought to protect real wages although the COB as well as private enterprise (CEPB) criticized all the measures of this period, fiercely disputed official assessments of the retail price index, and staged a number of effective strikes at the slightest hint of backsliding by the ministry. From April 1984 to May 1985 the administration openly rejected indexation but was obliged at the end of May 1984 to acquiesce in the COB's demand for a formal limit on debt service repayments (although inflation was now so great that this was of little real consequence other than to harden the attitude of the banks, already determined in their opposition as a result of 'dedollarization'). This period also witnessed a series of major strikes – particularly the general stoppages of November 1984 and March 1985 – the exceptional duration of which may be partially attributed to the relatively low real cost of lost wages. These destroyed first the UDP's capacity to serve out its term (the agreement of 21 November 1984 to advance elections) and then its hopes for a respectable election result. The May 1985 restoration of indexation (agreed, but reneged upon, in March) was the most palpable indication by the rump of the UDP (now effectively a section of the MNRI and some independent technocrats) that it had lost both the economic and political battles and would 'retreat in glory', complicating life for its successor.

The inconsistency of these policies – both in themselves and as a whole – should not simply be put down to ineptitude or the mesmerism induced by the scale of the crisis. It also reflected political divisions within the UDP, 'dedollarization' being essentially a MIR initiative, the 'heterodoxy' of November 1983 to May 1985 being largely the product of independent technicians who tried to move towards the IMF but were forestalled tactically by the left, and the 'final fling', a traditional populist gesture in which the small clique around Siles, exasperated by rightist criticisms that it had pampered the workers, decided to do just that. Equally, while the IMF consistently refused to issue its imprimatur for any of the measures, it is noteworthy that the November 1982 package – arguably the most coherent and radical of all; certainly the most broadly unpopular – was attacked by Banzer for reducing real wages and exacting an unacceptable sacrifice from the poor.[11] The MNR also criticized it because 'it does not respond to popular interests but, rather, to the requirements of the IMF ... it seeks to reduce the level of internal demand, and in order to do this uses as an instrument a pitiless reduction in the purchasing power of wages'.[12] In the same vein, following the November 1983 measures, the MNR tabled a bill in the lower house to increase wages by 100 per cent, and this was passed in the Senate with ADN support (although the CEPB, now aware of the costs of political spoiling, reacted with disdain).

Thus, although an orthodox deflation would certainly have represented a surrender of the UDP's programme, the opposition was also fearful of this option and was careful not to pronounce it 'the only alternative' until the government's back had been broken in late 1984. This is understandable in political terms, but it should be borne in mind that the right, no less than the UDP, was apprehensive of the high social costs and threat of disorder; it also lacked familiarity with the techniques of managing high inflation (absent from Bolivia for the better part of three decades). Moreover, a significant entrepreneurial sector stood to lose heavily in terms of both reduced speculative opportunities and the inevitable reduction of a public sector upon which it was parasitic. To aver, as has one supposed expert, that Bolivians were either stupid, forgetful or selfish in failing to embrace orthodoxy earlier is to display an unforgivable arrogance.[13] There were plenty of people – inside the UDP and out – who by mid 1983 were making technically and morally informed judgements as to the relative social and performance related costs of inflation and deflation. By the end of that year circumstances beyond the UDP's control determined that either could only prevail in acute and sustained form. Profoundly inequitable though the former was, its relative merit – in political terms – was that it was, at least until late 1984, corrosive rather than explosive. Pathetic and acquiescent though the government's position may appear, it was not simply bred of cowardice, and it upheld a shard of its original mandate not to provoke violence, the potential for which would be far greater through a decisive U-turn than through an entirely new mandate. In this respect, then, electoralism was not simply formally desirable but also – from a managerial perspective – entirely necessary.

In the end, of course, Siles did deploy troops, and this initiative (March 1985) undoubtedly prepared the ground for the MNR, which during the ensuing election campaign kept its policy options very vague indeed, simply repeating the now familiar catechism that an agreement with the IMF was essential and more favourable conditions for private capital were the only means by which to resolve the crisis.[14] Mention should also be made of the fact that despite the effective boycott of the UDP by the international banks and the IMF, the US government was apparently unwilling to force the Siles administration into a corner as resolutely as it had in 1956. This was certainly informed by the prospect of a conservative regime and the need to retain anti-cocaine operations, but increases in economic and military aid – from $19.7 m. in 1982 to $78.1 m. in 1984 – also reflect the perception that if the Siles government presided over a completely chaotic economy, at least it did so through constitutional means and on terms that were in reality barely less distinct from those demanded by the COB than they were from those espoused by Banzer (whom the State Department, at least, did not greatly trust) and eventually implemented by Paz and Sánchez de Lozada. Demonstration of the costs of irresponsibility were best left to the strictly economic domain; any manifestly political retribution carried an unnecessarily high price.

Whether purposefully or perforce heterodox, the UDP's economic policies did not enjoy even a brief flourish of success, as for instance did those of APRA in Peru. Even the diminished rate of contraction in 1984 may be ascribed to the recovery of agriculture after the climatic ravages of the previous year – a critical if conjunctural setback. In effect, by October 1982 the crisis was already too deep-seated and externally determined to allow for remedies that fell short of absolute radicalism. Following the failure of 'dedollarization' – that, in terms of both inflation and exchange rates, took nine months to become fully evident (Appendices II and III) – the UDP was doomed to manage rather than resolve the crisis although it could be argued in more precise terms that it was not until the second half of 1984 that a 'progressive remedy' was completely beyond hope. Certainly, it was between September and November 1984 that both the COB and the right moved into decisive confrontation with the government and each other, provoking a momentary revival of real wages but also the precipitate calling of elections that deprived the regime of any incentive to engage in structural remedies. At most, therefore, the UDP's political authority to deal with the economy lasted barely twenty-four months, and it was evident well before November 1984 that such authority would not resist a major challenge.

Politics

The UDP years are widely viewed as a failure of the left both in government and outside it. However, as with the economy, the UDP's social policies were scarcely radical. Indeed, within three months of coming to power it could be said that only the presence of the PCB in the regime upheld any pretence of radicalism, sustained more by rhetoric and opposition attacks than by substantive policy. Nevertheless, when, in November 1984, the communist leader Marcos Domic defended the alliance in a final, futile effort to avert its collapse, he could legitimately point to a number of identifiably 'progressive' measures.

In foreign affairs, relations were established with Sandinista Nicaragua and re-established with Cuba – a matter of anxiety to the high command, which was quick to inspect medical equipment donated by Havana to La Paz's Hospital del Niño on the grounds that it might be used for spying on the Estado Mayor General next door. Relations with the Soviet Union also improved (although, to the PCB's chagrin, the government condemned the occupation of Afghanistan), yet Siles took a very low profile on Central America as a whole. By contrast, an early and unique success was scored with the detention and extradition to

France of Klaus Barbie by an interior ministry that promised to be just as competent at such operations as it had been under the military. Although at home the government was soon and justifiably seen to be weak and inactive in dealing with the extreme right, its image abroad was, at least for a while, far more impressive.

Perhaps the most notable and enduring success of the UDP was its health policy, and particularly the establishment of the Comités Populares de Salud, which effectively combined a progressive approach to preventative medicine with popular mobilization in a campaign that eliminated polio and dramatically reduced the incidence of measles within two years through the inoculation of three-quarters of all infants. Indeed, despite the strongly collectivist thrust of this initiative, the right was obliged to recognize its popularity, and promised in the 1985 election campaign to retain the programme. (A promise that was technically honoured although in practice the committees soon became a conduit for clientelism and corruption.)

If it was only in the field of health that the UDP even approximated to what was from its inception (in 1978) an exceptionally vague programme, it should be noted that the alliance itself effectively collapsed within weeks of coming to office. In formal terms the UDP was finally dissolved in December 1984, but it was the departure of the MIR from government in January 1983 that damaged the coalition beyond repair. Although the MIR, and especially Jaime Paz Zamora, staged this exceptionally early rupture primarily for sectarian ends, the plausible ostensible cause was in-fighting within the MNRI and the consequent failure to formulate coherent policy and eradicate the vestiges of the dictatorship's paramilitary apparatus.

The MNRI was indeed badly divided and would remain so to the end, the desertion of one faction led by Samuel Gallardo giving the opposition control of both houses of congress by eleven votes in August 1984. By that stage dissidence was determined principally by the desire to protect political careers, readily achieved by 'rejoining' the MNR, which was ever open to erstwhile renegades and sufficiently lax in its interpretation of 'revolutionary nationalism' not to cause ideological inconvenience for those who had previously cavorted with communists and lambasted Víctor Paz – a man who harboured grudges with exceptional rancour but dissembled with the affability of a political genius. Opportunist though such moves were, they did not in reality break anything but the organizational boundaries of the MNRI's conduct since the party owed its existence less to a clear programmatic distinction from its forebear than a different set of allies at home and, to a lesser extent, abroad. It revindicated the more progressive features of the 'revolutionary era' and took a more principled stance on dictatorship, but its *modus operandi* remained very similar to that of the MNR.[15] Indeed, this shared clientelist inheritance was at the heart of the MNRI's early fissures (December 1982 to July 1983) when, shortly after coming to office, there was a very public and debilitating controversy over ministerial *feudos* and access to the placid Siles, with further personalist subfractions rapidly proliferating around them (Roncal; Velarde; Gallardo). These divisions were not entirely concerned with the spoils of office; they also related to treatment of the left, the COB and *narcotráfico*. However, the issues at stake never merited the degree of conflict and air of crisis that attended them, and the MNRI singularly failed to provide the discipline and sobriety necessary to contain the contagion of *politiquería*. Siles's personal involvement tarnished his reputation, and it is telling that although the MNR later suffered from comparable conflicts in government, Víctor Paz scrupulously kept himself above them, limiting public pronouncements to the absolute minimum required by the protocols of office (quite the reverse of his proclivity for personal attacks in previous decades).

Insofar as such disorganization within the coalition's senior partner affected both the internal temper and external image of the government, it damaged the MIR and PCB. Yet the difficulties displayed by these parties were by no means reducible to this issue. The MIR came under pressure across the board, from initial disputes with the MNRI over appointments in the customs service, to limiting the damage caused by 'dedollarization' and assuaging a rank and file that had suffered sharply under the dictatorship and now saw very little effort being made to settle accounts with the paramilitaries. Although very loose, the MIR's rhetoric was notably more buoyant than that of the MNRI and PCB, and the expectations harboured by its generally youthful following, which had waited four years for power, were correspondingly higher. Moreover, as vice president, Jaime Paz Zamora was closely associated with the administration whilst – true to the traditions of his office – lacking even minimal influence over it. For some fifteen months it appeared as if the MIR was reacting as one to its anomalous position of being in the government via Paz Zamora's position and its continuing membership of the UDP yet rejecting places in cabinet and acting – at the very best – as a fairweather friend in congress and the COB. Its attacks on the 'incoherence' of economic policy enabled the MIR to diminish its association with 'dedollarization' but also obscured a growing split between the party's right wing (Paz Zamora; Eid; Capobianco) and the more radical current that was itself divided between 'socialists' leaning towards the PCB (Aranibar; Ferrufino) and 'syndicalists' identified with the anti-PCB factions within the COB (Delgadillo). This process remained unclear for over a year, in part simply because of the very bluntness with which Paz Zamora attacked Siles and the cabinet – even when he himself was acting as president during Siles's trips abroad – and in part because until mid 1984 the vice president found it easier to support anti-government initiatives from the left, notably the FSTMB's unilateral imposition of *cogestión mayoritaria* in Comibol in April 1983, which he had the temerity to welcome as a revival of the true traditions of 1952.[16] (It should be noted that this stance had the added advantage for Paz Zamora of embarrassing the PCB as well as Siles.)

Both the MNRI and the PCB justifiably distrusted the MIR's motives from the moment it quit the cabinet, not least because this seemed to presage a challenge for dominant influence, if not outright power. However, the MNRI was in no position to launch a complete assault on the *miristas*, and the Communists disliked their replacement by Christian Democrats and independent technocrats as well as maintaining a greater commitment to unity than was recognized outside the party at the time. This, together with the fact that the MIR continued to enjoy appreciable popular support, delayed a complete schism within the UDP and permitted the party's return to government in April 1984. Yet the terms of re-entry into the fold rapidly revealed the tensions that had been gestating within the party itself. From Paz Zamora's perspective there was by this stage nothing more to be gained – and indeed quite a bit to be lost – from continuing to act as a 'Trojan horse'. From the viewpoint of the MIR's radical wing there still remained the possibility of rapprochement between the UDP and the COB based on the initial redistributionist policies of the alliance. *Cogestión* had been obtained in Comibol, *cogobierno* was no longer a viable option, the PCB favoured their re-inclusion, and the right's growing challenge might still be resisted.

Nevertheless, the economic policy agreed by the majority of the cabinet following the MIR's return precisely ended indexation and sought to shift back to orthodoxy in controlling inflation – a telling fact in the light of developments in 1989. As a result, Delgadillo immediately quit both the cabinet and the party, establishing MIR-Masas, which would challenge the UDP within the COB as part of the Dirección Revolucionaria Unificada (DRU). The larger radical group led by Antonio Aranibar rejected this line as misguided in its aggression towards the PCB and its excessive economism. However, if the Aranibar faction appeared to be associated with official attacks on 'ultra-leftism', which escalated following the DRU's gaining of control of the COB at its sixth congress in September 1984, a second split was made inevitable by the polarization of the final months of that year, the irreversible collapse of the UDP in December, and Paz Zamora's clear intention to stage an electoral campaign based on personalism and a concerted retreat from the party's radical heritage. This led, in January 1985, to the formation of the MIR-Bolivia Libre (MBL), which contained some of the party's most talented cadre and sought to restore the unity of the left under conditions of headlong retreat. The basis for such a recomposition was entirely absent prior to the election, the prolonged general strike of March 1985 exacerbating expectations of dual power through the COB and generating a fierce debate within the left over the viability of constitutionalism per se.

As befits its traditions, the internal response of the PCB to its participation in a chaotic and unpopular coalition was more modulated and less public. In terms of collective temperament and ideology the party was better adjusted to the vagaries of 'popular frontism'. However, it suffered the consequences to an unprecedentedly high degree despite the fact that Bolivian communism had since its inception been obliged to contend with powerful forces to its left. Historically, these had been represented in the syndicalist sphere by Juan Lechín Oquendo, whose careering pragmatism easily embraced calls for armed struggle and workers' power, and in the political realm by Trotskyism; the two had often entered into short but effective 'anti-Stalinist' alliances. Under the UDP the Trotskyist threat was in itself of little consequence. Beyond the university, the Partido Obrero Revolucionario (POR) signally failed to capitalize on popular disenchantment; its clear-headedness with regard to the debilities of the local capitalist economy was accompanied by a remarkable misconception that the radical form of popular mobilization reflected an equally strong commitment to political revolution. This cardinal error of failing to distinguish between appearances and reality was insufficiently mitigated by explaining several unrealized 'revolutionary situations' in terms of the 'absence of leadership' (either a truism or a damning self-indictment).[17] Nonetheless, if the POR had become petrified by sectarian propagation, the longstanding Trotskyist heritage had left its mark on a large number of activists for whom there appeared to be no alternative other than the COB to counteract the PCB's 'collaborationism' and consolidate a defence of the working class. Thus, the communists' problems in controlling the ministries of mines and labour throughout this period extended beyond a loss in rank and file support in the unions to confronting a radical critique of the contradictions of managing a capitalist slump under a proletarian banner.

In the first instance conflict took a familiar form through the FSTMB's occupation of Comibol (April 1983), which the party leadership first tried to avert, then mediate, and finally had shamefacedly to accept and join. After all, *cogestión* had been a leitmotif of the 1952 revolution, was part of the PCB's programme, and enjoyed broad support within its principal union constituency. Moreover, Simón Reyes, one of the party's most prominent leaders, headed the new management structure, which did not in itself damage the popular front strategy and owed more to the *autogestionario* current in the COB than to the party's major political enemies rapidly grouping around Lechín. However, it was not long before what was a containable instance of 'workerism' was exacerbated by economic conditions into an irresistible militancy over wages. Here the PCB was comprehensively defeated by both policy and circumstances. It could not fail to be seen to be defending real wages and yet this entailed strike action against a government in which it was participating. Moreover, by mid 1984 such strikes were patently taking on a politically critical character, incorporating legitimate expectations as well as the 'demagogy' assailed by the party. It is, however, notable that it was only at the PCB's fifth congress in February 1985 – after the UDP had split and the party had left government – that dissidence took open form with a group led by Ramiro Barrenechea and based largely on the youth movement eventually breaking away in August.[18]

The role of the COB under the UDP naturally combined popular discontent over the economy with more politically motivated initiatives by factions of the left for which the organization has traditionally been the premier site of competition. As noted above, one major axis of this conflict was between the PCB and Juan Lechín, who struck increasingly radical poses as the rank and file lost patience with the government. Although relations between the regime and a COB leadership dominated by forces unsympathetic to the UDP were fraught throughout and never escaped the cycle of devaluation and strike action, they deteriorated beyond repair in September 1984 when the sixth congress of the COB produced a clear polarization between the PCB and the DRU, which went out of its way to distance formal support for constitutionalism from backing for the UDP (a 'bourgeois government') and continued to insist upon implementation of the COB's emergency plan – complete default on the external debt, full indexation, curbs on capital, and workers' control.[19] The ensuing twenty-day general strike in November produced Siles's effective abdication in the Church-sponsored agreement to advance elections.

It was, though, the strike of March 1985 that more profoundly determined subsequent developments, since the week-long occupation of La Paz by miners was unparalleled in its scale and appeared to promise a decisive settling of accounts amidst incessant discharges of dynamite that traumatized the middle class. For several days it appeared that a 'gentlemen's agreement' over elections would be swept away by proletarian activism, redolent of 1952 in its appeal to communitarianism. Whether by design or default, Siles let this wave roll unimpeded until it began to lose impetus. The COB leadership failed to present any new political proposal and, having already rejected the offer of *cogobierno* as a reheated trick of the 1950s, resolutely resisted any more radical option, for which it was even less prepared. Thus, although a state of virtual dual power prevailed for nigh on two weeks, this corresponded almost entirely to the stamina of the rank and file, prepared to face down the government for pay and denounce elections as useless but not to take state power. When the troops were deployed without major conflict the true limits of syndicalism were exposed. The end of the '*jornadas de marzo*' produced the single most emphatic deflation of the popular movement and the left. Mass mobilization had not so much failed as demonstrated its essentially conservative character and thus a vulnerability which the right henceforth felt able to exploit by challenging the COB to 'showdowns' where the unions lacked an endgame.

In political terms the intransigence of the COB leadership stemmed from an acute anxiety to avert the compromises sprung on it by the MNR in the 1950s. This had instilled such a dedication to organizational independence that the syndicalist vanguard not only held to devices – *escala móvil* and *cogestión mayoritaria* – that optimized its distance from the regime but also preferred the risks of constant conflict to those of a social pact. These instincts were further deepened by prolonged experience of resistance to dictatorship that had enlivened skills of agitation but dulled those of negotiation needed to realize gains from it. Such proclivities had become ideologized less into a discourse of anarcho-syndicalism – although this lay close to the surface – than into a simultaneous celebration and denial of the limits of economism. The political forces seeking control of the COB fell prey to the slogans of its 'apolitical maximalism', either by stoking up expectations they could not meet (DRU) or by seeking to fulfil them at a 'capitulationist level' (PCB/Escobar). This, of course, is a general pattern, but the political and economic circumstances prevailing in Bolivia between 1982 and 1985 gave it decisive importance within national political life.

The impasse reached in March 1985 was broken in the elections of July, and converted into defeat by Decree 21060, driving the left from the centre of politics and transforming what had hitherto been consequential debates over strategy into esoteric theoretical disputes. However, the objective dilemmas and difficulties encountered during the UDP period were clearly immense, and the failure to resolve them outside of slogans reflected the degree of popular pressure on the left no less than it did the political shortcomings of the principal parties. Indeed, in terms of incidence, popular mobilization continued at an equal – and occasionally higher – rate under the MNR, suggesting that the left was responsible less for bringing people on to the streets than for orchestrating them once they were there, which was very often. Such matters are exceptionally hard to quantify, but it is telling that between October 1983 and June 1984 – 'quiet' at a national level by dint of the fact that there was only one 24-hour general strike – there was a total of 554 officially registered industrial or social 'conflicts'.[20]

Urban stoppages and conflicts dominated, but one key feature of this period was increased recourse by *campesinos* to road-blocks (*bloqueos*), which were highly effective, required a relatively slight physical presence, and could not readily be countered except through force, which the UDP only employed with the utmost reluctance. In 1983 and 1984 there were eighteen major *bloqueos*, which, following the example first set in opposition to the 1979 Natusch coup, both strengthened the confidence of the CSUTCB and its allied *katarista* currents and also suggested that the political imbalance between town/ mine and countryside was being rectified.[21] In some sense this was true. Even after three decades of urbanization the rural population remained substantial and could swing an election – a matter of unprecedented importance. Equally, the decline – soon to be collapse – of mining and the expansion of cocaine had already begun a process of migration to and within certain rural areas (notably from the alti- plano to the Chapare) and greatly enhanced both the value of coca production and the resolution with which it had to be defended (see below). Moreover, whilst it was to be some time before the experience of Sendero Luminoso in Peru was recognized to be a major pheno- menon, fears of this example imbricating with a resurgent rural radicalism were harboured beyond the ranks of the military.

Yet these factors did not so much underlie a progressive polarization in the *campo* as reflect a reduction in political control. As in the urban sector, mobilization and direct action were aggressive but limited in their objectives; *caudillismo* and localism continued to prevail (one reason for the large number of incidents), and if the parameters of the 'limited good' were palpably being eroded, they were still tighter than the right feared and the left hoped. Although the fact is often greatly exaggerated, inflation did prejudice rural labour less profoundly than urban workers; the drought of 1983 bred more survivalism than subversion; and the UDP's chaotic efforts at co-optation through 'cogestión' (CORACA) increased bureaucratic in-fighting. The end result was sufficient discontent and activism to maintain political uncertainty in the countryside, but not enough for this to alter the balance of power at the national level. The MNR old guard, well aware that a similar situation had obtained prior to the coup of 1964, subsequently took the line of least resistance, excluding the country- side from its initial tax reforms and delaying introduction of modific- ations to the 1953 agrarian reform proposed by their technocrats. They still did not escape trouble, but it is probable that this would have been much more serious if the UDP experience had not clearly signalled a threat that had been obscured for several years by military government.

Conservative victories in the polls of 1985 and 1989 have led many commentators and the right itself to overemphasize the degree to which it altered its *modus operandi* prior to the collapse of the UDP. Whilst it is certainly the case that both the COB and the parties of the radical left underestimated the degree and ramifications of conservative compliance with constitutionalism, their failure either to modulate a Manichaean vision bred of two decades of dictatorship or to move beyond a fundamentally cautious and defensive acceptance of liberal democracy was not solely the result of ingrained custom. Banzer's establishment of the ADN and acceptance of defeat in the polls of 1979 and 1980 signalled an important shift, but this had not forestalled the coups of Natusch and García Mesa, and leading *adenistas* served these military regimes. Equally, although the US response to militarism after 1979 was more aggressive than in any other South American country, Washington's influence was far from decisive, and recidivist *golpistas* continued to agitate throughout the UDP period. The degree of their isolation is much more readily appreciated with hindsight than it was at the time. The kidnapping of Siles in June 1984 by elements of his bodyguard and the elite UMOPAR police unit; the 'passive mutiny' by the staff college in Cochabamba against General Sejas for four months in mid 1984; and the abortive rebellion by General Olvis at the end of the year, all underscored the fragility of the constitutionalist entente at a time when military dissidence was breaking cover in Argentina and popular mobilization against the Pinochet regime in Chile had been forced into retreat.

In each instance both the COB and the majority of the left rallied to the defence of the constitution, curbing their offensive against the government. Nonetheless, this desistance from escalating tension in the face of open rightist threats was paralleled by a deep suspicion of reactionary manoeuvres to subvert democratic institutions from within. Denunciations of '*golpes constitucionales*' often reflected reluctance to accept the new rules of governance, but they were not always baseless, especially once the relationship between Siles and Paz Zamora became antagonistic and opened the possibility (March and November 1983) of a 'formal succession', which had in the past been a mechanism for altering governments (1925; 1934; 1949). Eventually, of course, the UDP administration was terminated by an even more overt dispensation with the letter of the 1967 constitution, against which the left was poorly positioned to complain partly because much of it had called for fresh elections in 1982, partly because the November 1984 accord was signed by all the major political forces and arbitrated by the Church, and in part because there now existed widespread support for any resolution of the stalemate. The right certainly helped to contrive such a situation by insisting on the impeachment of Siles's senior official Rafael Otazo over his discussions with the *narcotraficante* Roberto Suárez, by threatening to impeach Siles himself, and by effectively vetoing the president's amnesty for a handful of leftists captured by the army in the village of Luribay in unclear circumstances and given jail sentences the harshness of which contrasted with the absence of any judicial action over scores of well-publicized cases on the right. Indeed, if under the UDP attention remained focused on the relationship between a debilitated executive and an aggressive legislature, the interested immobility of the judiciary was a factor of consequence well before the disorganized efforts to replicate application of the rule of law in the neighbouring republics with the 'trial' of García Mesa from 1986. Siles's eventual recourse to his traditional tactic of hunger strike in October 1984 signalled an incapacity to secure even a minimum degree of co-operation between the powers of the state, where vested interests remained exceptionally strong even if they had been obliged to adhere to institutional protocols and the strategem of non-compliance.

The nature of Siles's response to his embattlement greatly facilitated the intervention of the ecclesiastical hierarchy, which constituted a peculiar amalgam of the first and fourth estates in that its appreciable authority was expressed through the country's leading daily *Presencia*, under the directorship of the conservative (and soon to be disgraced) Monseñor Genaro Prata, and its premier radio station Fides, dominated by the astute anti-communist Jesuit José Gramunt. Both stuck strenuously to the liberal voice that had been developed under the *banzerato* and lay at the core of their legitimacy, but the editorial impetus towards '*concertación*' was vital to sealing Siles's fate in that it provided a non-partisan imprimatur for the less high-minded horse-trading immediately dubbed as the '*golpe eclesiástico*' by the left.

The clergy remained politically divided, but the radical current was poorly represented in an aged hierarchy exhausted by its remonstrations over human rights under Banzer and García Mesa and pre-occupied with administering aid and charity programmes amongst the poor, who continued to concentrate their political activity within the orbit of secular organizations. This general pattern – closer to that of Argentina and Peru than Chile and Brazil at that time – deserves a far fuller analysis than is possible here, but mention should be made of the historically weak position of Christian Democracy, which had suffered an early and decisive division in the 1960s and proved incapable of expanding a small confessional constituency. Although the 1988 papal visit witnessed some of the most robust language ever employed by John Paul II on the social question, this reflected the relatively low level of clerical radicalism, the exceptionally severe impact of the MNR's deflationary policies, and a justified perception that the Church no longer faced a challenge from Marxism. After November 1984 the good offices of the hierarchy were largely limited to the resolution of sectoral conflicts and almost exclusively directed towards obtaining a modicum of moderation from the government – a role to which it was accustomed and which bore little political risk.

The adroit use of congress by the right took the traditional form of obstructionism. Although there were very few precedents of a conservative legislature assailing a more progressive executive – certainly nothing of the order witnessed in Chile under Allende – conflict between these two arms of the state had arisen in the late 1950s through intra-MNR faction-fighting, re-emerging in 1979–80. The MNR and ADN now stole a leaf from the left's book to stage a series of censures, impeachments and procedural obstacles that were sanctioned by law and required the UDP to govern by decree-law and ordinance within months of coming to office. No instance was in itself of critical consequence, but the accumulated effect was to cast the government in an unconciliatory light and strengthen the identification of the right with the strict letter of the law. It may be doubted that a great many electors took this to be more than self-serving *politiquería* of the old school. Still, the campaign increased from mid 1984 when the opposition won a majority in congress and immediately turned it to sharp effect with prosecution of the Otazo scandal, which significantly damaged the moral standing of Siles and the MNRI, if not the UDP as a whole.

The manipulation of this affair combined unremarkable hypocrisy – in 1988 senior members of the ADN were revealed to be in close and friendly contact with Suárez – with a more novel exploitation of the media, particularly television. Here it is worth noting that the parallel existence of widespread popular access to television and competitive politics had only previously existed in 1979–80, when the state possessed an effective monopoly over broadcasting (the few, disorganized, university stations being closed to the right). By 1984 this position had changed sufficiently for the right to launch telling attacks on the regime across the board, from the press, where the UDP possessed no popular journal and was supported by none (even the weekly *Aquí* was critical from the left), to the radio, where the proliferation of independent stations diminished the impact of pro-regime broadcasting, to television, where the poor quality of the state channel and chaotic conditions of the university stations provided a commercial as well as political logic to the emergence of a private sector. Although this only came to flourish with complete – albeit semi-legal – deregulation under the MNR, when La Paz enjoyed the dubious benefits of six channels, during the last year of the UDP it expanded public access to the constitutional process. Moreover, it provided the right with the capacity to address a mass constituency that did not read the press or attend the relatively few rallies held by conservative parties. (The MNR remained a 'closed' and cell-based organization whilst the ADN's more frequent public events were dominated by its youth and tended to be aggressive.) In the process, conservative politicians acquired new rhetorical skills, replacing the customary injunctions to sacrifice with a preparedness to field direct questions and engage in frank interviews. The results were not always impressive – Banzer remained a notably poor speaker – but television coverage undoubtedly assisted the 1985 election victory and laid the ground for much more concerted exploitation of the medium thereafter. The left, attached to the culture of mass meetings and pamphleteering, lagged badly even when it possessed access.

The importance of television as an effective 'journal of record' as well as the primary medium for political exchange was reflected by the attention given to the televised political forum of May 1985 organized by the CEPB. This event, which in the past would have taken place in the university (with the attendant disputes over access for the right), ratified the emergence of the entrepreneurs' corporate association as a major political actor, signalling a 'new right' that subsequently gained considerable influence – but not outright dominance – in the conservative governments of Paz Estenssoro and Paz Zamora.

Prior to 1982 the CEPB had operated principally as a lobby group and had a lower profile than that of the private mineowners' Asociación

Nacional de Mineros Medianos (ANMM), which, along with the *ganaderos* of the Beni and commercial farmers of Santa Cruz, campaigned on a sectoral basis rather than through regional chambers of commerce. The CEPB's rapid rise to prominence under the leadership of Fernando Illanes may be attributed to a number of factors. First, when the UDP entered office it was far from clear that the MNR would consistently support the interests of private capital, and while the ADN was far more reliable in this respect, its political prospects did not look particularly good. Second, the inclusion of the PCB in the government and the high profile taken by the COB engendered a genuine fear of expanded state intervention. Third, the rapid deterioration of the economy damaged many productive businesses. Fourth, low expectations of military intervention prompted local business to 'go public' where previously it would have negotiated with officers behind the scenes. This had the added advantage of demonstrating the CEPB's 'civic responsibility', and it tended to give more prominence to the positive promulgation of capitalist 'common sense' than to simple expressions of anti-communism, although this was certainly not lacking.

Finally, it has been suggested that economic developments over the previous decade had encouraged the emergence of a 'new entrepreneur' – a beneficiary of the expansion of agro-business and cheap credit under Banzer, bolstered by the relative strengthening of private mining (ANMM) and banking (ASOBAN), better educated and less overtly 'political' than the generation that had arisen in the 1950s in the penumbra of the MNR's short-lived but extremely powerful Célula de Importadores. It should be stressed that this interpretation is based on only impressionistic evidence and may easily be qualified on a range of points, but it is far from implausible. Leading figures such as Illanes, the Sánchez de Lozada brothers and Ronald Maclean were by no means 'apolitical' – Gonzalo Sánchez de Lozada (MNR) and Maclean (ADN) were highly active militants of their parties – but they presented themselves first and foremost as entrepreneurs.[22] Relatively young, bilingual and university educated (usually in the US), they eschewed the customary reticence of local businessmen, and possessed strong ties with both foreign capital and professional economists. Moreover, all shared a commitment to neo-liberalism, which by no means enjoyed absolute hegemony within the CEPB but had considerable external academic and political support, particularly from Chile, where these groups had longstanding links. Extreme caution should be exercised in viewing these attributes with relation to interpretative models for the restructuring of other South American political economies in the 1970s, not least because that of Bolivia was qualitatively smaller and more backward as well as being chronically dependent upon revenue from an illegal export. Indeed, it is indicative that the MNR's Nueva Política Económica (NPE) was devised by a Harvard professor (Jeffrey Sachs) and directed by a local businessman who had spent much of his life in the US (Sánchez de Lozada).

As has been noted, neo-liberalism was not rapidly embraced by either the ADN or the MNR, which initially preferred the short-term rewards of berating the UDP for failing to maintain real wages. However, by November 1984 it was clear that the economy would be the most important issue in an election that the right was almost certain to win. Heterodoxy had manifestly failed; true 'shock' had not been attempted since 1956; resumption of relations with the IMF and international creditors had become a priority after March 1984; and the internal opposition to deflation had already exhausted its political resources in combating a less than radical variant. The principal problem was the adoption and propagation of a mercantilist ideology capable of resisting the inevitable backlash under democratic conditions. Neither the (distant) memory of the 1956–57 stabilization nor the more recent experience of stability under Banzer provided sufficient conditions for this, although the former undoubtedly recommended the policy to significant sectors of both parties. In the event, the very scale of the crisis compelled the taking of an option that provoked widespread dissent, could only be realized through the use of force, and depended upon *narcodólares* for its success.

The MNR-ADN Alliance, August 1985-89

Within a fortnight of assuming office in August 1985 the government of Víctor Paz Estenssoro gave Bolivians a new phrase – '*veintiuno zero sesenta*' – that was henceforth to occupy a central place in the lexicon of both daily life and politics. Decree 21060, introduced on 29 August, set a regional precedent for rapid and dramatic stabilization measures adopted by incoming administrations. (The examples of Carlos Andrés Pérez in Venezuela and Menem in Argentina, both in 1989, most clearly follow the pattern.) Nowhere else in Latin America, however, were the results so emphatic and enduring – the very reason why this decree, alone of all republican ordinances (including those for the nationalization of the mines and agrarian reform in October 1952 and August 1953 respectively), is known by its number of issue, which soon acquired a status akin to that of an alchemic formula to celebrants and detractors alike. For the government the decree was but the first – if the most vital – step of a 'New Economic Policy', but this term never achieved popular resonance, perhaps because it inferred a superior modernity for the many whom it prejudiced and who were less impressed by the stabilization it brought to prices than by the acute contraction in jobs and welfare that accompanied it. The results of this were, as the authors of the policy readily admitted, conducive to existential instability and a substantial reduction in the standard of living – neither of which was properly measured or reflected in official statistics.

Although Decree 21060 will undoubtedly dominate both the formal history and popular memory of the 1985–89 government, it was not, of course, the sole issue of consequence – even in the economic sphere, where the collapse of the international tin price in October 1985 and continued *narcotráfico* had a major impact. The axis of political life shifted substantially to the right but despite the relative solidity of the MNR-ADN alliance until the final months of the Paz Estenssoro government, politics was by no means stagnant. The trial of García Mesa; increasing collaboration by the MIR with the administration; the emergence of a 'cholo populism' headed by Carlos Palenque; and the holding in 1987 of the first municipal elections since 1949 all interacted closely with popular discontent over stabilization and its attendant reductions of real wages and public expenditure to make public life both charged and unpredictable. Such conflict was no longer determined by the 'ultimatumist tests' of both policy and institutionalism witnessed under the UDP. Yet it signalled that, however widespread popular resignation and debilitated the mass organizations, activism remained vital and could not be ignored in either the formulation or implementation of official policy.

The Economy

Sánchez de Lozada's prescription for economic recovery was one of orthodox neo-liberalism. Under Decree 21060 he sought to obtain a 'realistic' exchange rate, decrease the public sector wage bill, free almost all prices, and lift most restrictions on financial operations, including those on dollar transactions. Through Decree 21369 (July 1986) he effectively opened up the economy to full external competition by imposing a uniform import tariff of 20 per cent. In March 1986 the government introduced a major tax reform to enhance state revenue. In August of that year (Decree 21377) Comibol was 'decentralized' as a first step towards privatization; in June 1987 the Caja Nacional de Seguro Social (CNSS) was deprived of many of its central welfare functions. In March 1988 the government declared the 'decentraliza-tion' of the Corporación Boliviana de Fomento (CBF) to regional deve-lopment corporations, and also attempted to devolve responsibility for education to local authorities.

Only some of these policies registered success in their own terms, but all were undertaken with the clear objective of maintaining tight control of the money supply and eradicating the fiscal deficit so as to restore finance flows from the IMF and foreign banks. Although these institutions had long urged both monetarist and free-market policies, the Paz Estenssoro government adopted such policies of its own voli-tion, and only later (March 1986) sought external support. The Sánchez de Lozada team was convinced of the merits of 'shock', deter-mined to rectify the fiscal crisis in short order, and entertained few doubts as to the methods for 'restructuring'. Although the Fondo Social de Emergencia (FSE) was established in December 1985, and 'reactivation' of the economy formally begun under Decree 21660 of July 1987, the former was but a minor palliative and the latter remained moribund.[23] Despite protestations to the contrary in the period prior to the 1989 poll, the real thrust of economic management from August 1985 was towards deflationary stabilization. This was affected in contradictory fashion by both the collapse of the tin price – which facilitated the break-up of Comibol but had a profoundly adverse effect on both export and fiscal revenue – and the continuation of *narcotráfico* – which provided an important source of dollars and 'informal' employment, alleviating some of the rigours of contraction, but also bolstering regional inflation and prejudicing US aid. In broad terms it is difficult to deny that the cocaine trade (see below) provided a critical support for stabilization, and many account it a decisive factor, certainly off-setting the recession in mining. Nevertheless, proper weight should be given to the radicalism of government policy and the resolution with which its core elements were implemented.

The heart of Decree 21060 and its immediate impact lay in exchange-rate policy. Here Sánchez de Lozada produced a de facto devaluation of the order of 93 per cent by unifying overnight the official and informal rates for the dollar. The official rate was subsequently allowed to float through the mechanism of daily dollar auctions by the Central Bank (BCB). Between December 1985 and February 1986 internal MNR disputes over the degree of contraction this was causing led to some relaxation in control of money supply with the result that the now legal informal rate began to rise faster. However, this was rapidly curbed, and thereafter the official rate shadowed that on the open market sufficiently closely for the general effect to be one of parity. (Appendix Two gives the monthly figures through to February 1986, when the differential became a matter of minimal consequence. Formal reform of the currency took place in January 1987, when the Boliviano replaced one million pesos.)[24]

The essential corollary to the unification of the exchange rates was a freeze on all public sector wages at pre-devaluation rates. Although the important and complex system of bonuses was consolidated into the basic wage, the impact of this measure was extremely severe. At the same time, indexation and the minimum wage were abolished in both public and private spheres, and legal curbs on redundancy were greatly relaxed. By the first half of 1986 total real wages had fallen to less than two-thirds of their level of the previous year (Appendix V), those in the public sector being significantly lower. Moreover, the state wage bill was further diminished by the 'voluntary retirement' of public sector workers as a result of the massive reduction in real pay. The number of state employees fell by at least 10 per cent within twelve months, the impact being sharpest in rural education, where perhaps 25,000 teachers left their posts.[25]

The liberalization of prices that accompanied the fluctuation of the exchange rate produced an immediate increase in inflation as previously compressed prices rose to their 'real' levels. In September 1985 inflation was still at 57 per cent per month. But in October inflation became negative as demand all but disappeared and the collapse of the COB's resistance made it plain that wage compensation would not be conceded. Notwithstanding the flurry of official nerves (bitterly opposed by Sánchez de Lozada) at the end of the year, the enforced contraction of the economy was secured. In 1986 GDP decreased by nearly 3 per cent, the per capita level by nearly 6 per cent. Overall growth thereafter oscillated between 2 per cent and 3 per cent – that is, barely retrieving the 1984 level – whereas per capita growth continued to be negative in 1987, and barely exceeded zero in 1988. In 1987 formal exports stood at 60 per cent of the 1980 level and were well below those registered under the UDP; reductions in imports proved extremely hard to achieve – narcodollars undoubtedly playing a part – but a trade balance was finally reached in 1988. This did not, however, produce a significant amelioration in the levels of un- and under-employment generated by stabilization. The first rose almost instantaneously to 20 per cent whilst the second – in many respects more indicative of the health of an economy such as Bolivia's – touched 60 per cent.[26] By the end of the government the official level of open unemployment stood at 11.5 per cent, but the real level was undoubtedly several points higher – probably 15 per cent – whilst underemployment had been reduced by a smaller margin.

The central objective of Decree 21060 to eliminate the fiscal deficit was pursued equally vigorously in terms of revenue and expenditure. Aside from the ordained and de facto reduction in the state payroll, a freeze was imposed on all public investment, tight controls placed on financial management, and ceilings on prices either lifted or removed altogether. Here the impact was most marked in the case of the state oil company, YPFB, the price of oil and its derivatives being raised from one day to the next by a factor of seven to slightly above international prices. Whilst this contributed to the immediate post-stabilization inflation rate, it enabled YPFB to meet all its tax liabilities and thereby become the principal source of public revenue under the MNR, its contribution to the treasury rising from 12.7 per cent of the total in 1983 to 56.7 per cent in 1986.[27]

Exchange rate unification depended upon 'redollarization' – either directly or through indexation – of domestic accounts and the lifting of all but basic fiscal controls over the banking sector. A key factor in this regard was the maintenance of an open 'dollar window' permitting the circulation of narcodollars. This legalization of the 'grey market' undoubtedly bolstered the banks, which also benefited from processing tax payments and other state transactions. However, the new financial climate did little to suppress existing illegal or foolhardy customs with respect to loans, resulting in a number of collapses and closures as well as the withdrawal, in September 1987, of the banks' responsibility for administering 'reactivation funds'. On the other hand, the government proved more resolute and successful in removing a particularly powerful 'union mafia' from the BCB, restoring a semblance of sobriety to a nominally independent institution which had effectively been beyond the control of its directorate (and the government) for a number of years.

The introduction of the uniform import tariff at 20 per cent took place nearly a year after Decree 21060, and since to all intents and purposes it opened the borders to foreign commodities, it was predictably criticized by the Cámara de Industrias. However, the Cámara was a weak lobby and could not win support from the CEPB. Moreover, exporters were provided a modicum of help through a 10 per cent rebate on their inputs. In fact, in 1986 manufacturing industry registered its first positive growth for nearly a decade, having experienced a much deeper and earlier contraction than any other sector. After being driven to the wall by inefficiency, contraband, extremely high interest rates, and formidable foreign competition, a very small and backward industrial sector now began to exploit the suppression of wages, open labour market, and the appreciable spare capacity left by the recession.

The dismantling of barriers to external trade was clearly signalled in August 1985, and by March 1986 the government had already secured the basis upon which to reopen relations with the IMF through the first standby loan agreement in the better part of a decade. In June the Club of Paris agreed to terms for renewed repayment of the external debt that, if not exactly as bountiful as the government claimed, were less onerous than some feared. This accord laid the basis for later and much-publicized purchases of debt on the discount market as well as a controversial 'debt for nature' swap. What had initially seemed a strange, even ambitious, step by Sánchez de Lozada and Jeffrey Sachs (who harboured no amity for the banks) – to administer the purge on their own first and then petition for help from the banks – proved viable.

It is notable that agreement with the IMF was secured two days before congress approved the 1986/7 budget – the first time in more than two decades that this process had been undertaken. Both the

Fund and the government were determined that there should be absolute compliance with budgetary limits, particularly by the state corporations, which had a very long history of exceeding their allocations from the treasury and were the principal source of official debt. In 1986 congress agreed to a fiscal deficit of $175 million, or 6 per cent of GDP. In fact, so efficient were the government's constraints that the year ended with a deficit of only 4 per cent of GDP, which must have been the cause of as much shock as gratification in Washington; the pupils were proving more zealous than their masters. Henceforth the government attempted, with partial success, to limit adjustments in public sector wages to the budget, but although this acquired unprecedented importance in terms of policy, it failed to become a dominant feature in broader political life, probably because it ceded very little in exceptionally straitened times.

In 1986 the budget certainly attracted far less popular attention than did the tax reform of May which had already been agreed with the IMF. This measure introduced a property tax and a value-added tax on consumption (initially set at 10 per cent). Although both the MNR and ADN had been quick to scupper the UDP's efforts at fiscal reform, it was evident that Decree 21060 needed substantial administrative and legislative supplementation if government revenue was to regain a measure of reliability. Between 1978 and 1983 the ratio of central government taxes to GDP had declined from 11.5 per cent to 2.8 per cent, not least because of collection time-lags in inflationary times. To oversee the new schemes the government established a separate fiscal ministry, but this was soon reintegrated with that of finance, and collection – but not assessment – was farmed out to the private banks. In 1986 all taxes rose to 13 per cent of GDP, and by 1988 they stood at 17.5 per cent; in the same period internal revenue taxes increased from 3.2 per cent to 6.3 per cent of GDP.[28] However, this rather impressive scenario should be seen in the light of the fact that between 1986 and 1988 the proportion of central government revenue derived from these taxes rose from 24 per cent to 36 per cent whilst the share provided by YPFB remained at over 50 per cent. Indeed, the Paz government's policy of 'liberating' the corporation's prices and enforcing its strict compliance with fiscal obligations meant that at the end of the decade YPFB's share of treasury revenue was roughly four times higher than at its start. (In the same period taxes on mining fell from 16 per cent to 0.4 per cent.)

Fiscal recovery, then, relied more heavily upon the freeing of prices in a single strategic sector than upon reform. In this regard it should be noted that the majority of urban Bolivians use canister gas for cooking and were thus directly hit by YPFB's price hikes – a fact made abundantly clear by the frequent impromptu *bloqueos* of streets by consumers whose empty containers provided most useful impedimenta. Equally, it is of no little consequence that the new property tax was not applied in the countryside, where there were well-supported demonstrations against the reform in June 1986 after the government agreed only to delay implementation for one year. Renewed protests in October 1987 forced a further delay, and in April 1988 (Decree 21923) small rural properties were formally excluded from the new regime. However, the 1989 budget restored the provision despite the fact that no enforcement took place in an election year.

This official nervousness was not misplaced since in both the altiplano and the valleys there were tangible indications that the proposed tax was suspected of heralding an attack on the agrarian reform of 1953. For many this was more of a concern than the direct financial impact, although the contraction of agriculture throughout the MNR government did not bode well in that respect either. Indeed, it may not be fanciful to suggest that core sections of the *campesinado* viewed the proposal as similar to the measures of the tyrant Mariano Melgarejo, whose 'free market' legislation laid the basis for a concerted offensive against communal lands in the last third of the nineteenth century. Here one might also note that, immediately upon coming to office, the MNR tried to levy a forced loan, which was the standard fiscal mechanism of the last century. This measure was opposed – for sound political reasons – by the ADN, and was eventually rejected by congress in January 1986, not to be heard of again.

The MNR was, in fact, planning to alter the structure of highland agriculture in particular, and in September 1988 it tabled before congress an agrarian development law that proposed, albeit in very vague terms, the reduction of the minifundia that had been propagated by the 1953 reform. These were correctly depicted as diminishing the overall efficiency of production. Yet if arguments based on economies of scale were irrefutable within the portals of the ministry and its think-tanks, they stood to cut very little ice indeed with those beneficiaries of the reform for whom title was sacrosanct and economic rationality only partly dependent upon input–output ratios. The legislation was withdrawn in January 1989, presumably because it threatened to jeopardize the MNR campaign for the May election. Whatever the reason, the government could scarcely afford to aggravate the problems it was already experiencing in the coca zones, and since Víctor Paz had relied heavily upon the peasantry in the 1950s and early 1960s as a counterweight to the miners and left, he would have been acutely aware of the importance of retaining at least a neutral constituency in the countryside. (In the event, on the basis of a calculation limited to the results of *provincias* – that is, all votes except those of departmental capitals – the MNR narrowly won the 1989 poll in the countryside from the MIR with 165,800 votes against 156,900, but it did not come first in any highland department and was forced into a poor third position in rural La Paz.) In 1985 the MNR had campaigned under the somewhat strange slogan of '*agropoder*', which appeared to be equally addressed to the subsistence/local market and lowland agro-export sectors. However, little was heard of this catchphrase after 29 August and, following recovery from *El Niño* in 1984 and 1985, the recession in agriculture (most of coca and all of cocaine excepted) remained more consistent than in any other sector of the economy.

The crisis in mining was more acute and widely publicized because of the traditional importance of minerals to exports and central government revenue and the fact that progressive decline in the first part of the decade was rapidly brought to a head by the collapse of the tin price (Appendix IV). Although this affected both public and private sectors, the immediate impact on Comibol was by a wide margin the most severe because of its size, relative inefficiency and simultaneous vulnerability to external pressure and direct state intervention. Between 1985 and 1987 both were applied without quarter, with the result that approximately 23,000 workers of a total labour force of 28,000 were made redundant, the core tin complex of Siglo XX-Catavi all but mothballed, total production scythed to a fifth of the levels of the 1970s, and public sector exports halted altogether for a year.[29] It is here that one encounters the single most important factor in the decline in legal exports that was, in fact, more pronounced than that witnessed under the UDP: from \$827.7 million in 1982 to \$759.6 million in 1984 against a fall from \$665.4 million in 1985 to \$580.6 million in 1988.

Although the government formally 'decentralized' Comibol into regional enterprises (Decree 21377, August 1986), the ministry retained direct control over '*relocalización*', which was too large and conflictive an issue to be managed by small and effectively bankrupt holding companies dedicated to maintaining plant and administering the sale of easily realizable assets to the private sector. (This was also the case with YPFB, where central control was formally stronger and worker resistance to lay-offs more effective.) Throughout the regime the FSTMB and individual plant unions battled over both closures and the terms of redundancy, proffering plans to maintain production and seeking to buy certain camps. However, with the partial exception of the Huanuni mine, the strike was now an impotent weapon and the rank and file divided over whether to defend jobs or fight for the best conditions in surrendering them; this became the central issue dividing the union, the first option generally being supported by the more political currents whilst the second was increasingly favoured by independents whose comrades were often voting with their feet out of resignation.[30] As pits were formally closed, *pulperías* left unsupplied, and funds for Comibol's schools and clinics cut off, the diaspora of miners and their families to the cities – principally El Alto and Cochabamba – and the Chapare marked a watershed in the country's industrial history. Even the gradual recovery of the tin price at the end of the decade did little to reverse this process, most of the upturn in production occurring within the private sector.

Whereas decentralization in Comibol and YPFB amounted to little more than an ideologically convenient fiction, this policy had a sharp impact when applied (March 1988) to the management of the departmental development corporations, education and health. The corporations inherited the regional installations of the CBF with varying degrees of success depending upon existing infrastructure whilst the CNSS was effectively disestablished (June 1987) and sectoral health systems acquired increasing importance as the already impoverished public hospital network was subjected to withering cuts (administered directly through the central budget). As a consequence, the normally cautious medical profession made frequent recourse to strikes and found itself converging with the union movement to an unprecedented degree. (The Colegio Médico, which had been established under Banzer as a strictly professional association, now became the site of rising partisanship.)

This was far more the case with regard to education, where the efforts of the highly unpopular minister Ipiña (who had transferred his allegiance from the MNRI) first to reduce expenditure and then to make the departments responsible for administration and finance, were stalled by both union and regionalist mobilization throughout the government's term. Indeed, it was perhaps this issue that most effectively concentrated popular antipathy to the consequences of Decree 21060 and damaged the regime's image. By 1989 Ipiña had not been able to realize his reforms and yet he had presided over four years of stoppages, demonstrations, growing truancy and radically reduced school rolls as the combination of absent teachers (notable transferees to contraband and the penumbra of *narcotráfico*) and the demands of maintaining family subsistence drove thousands of children into full-time 'informal' work.[31]

It appears that the government was rather taken aback by this development and failed to appreciate that grudging popular acquiescence in the imposition of mercantilist logic with respect to productive industry did not extend to basic services and welfare, where decentralization was soon recognized to be consubstantial with further budgetary decreases and an erosion of entitlement. The fact that education enjoyed a particularly high status and was still an inextricable feature of daily life gave this opposition a notably broad and non-partisan quality. This was channelled through the Comités Cívicos, which gained unprecedented authority and support in their battles with a government that was formally committed to devolution and yet strenuously resisted this in practice with regard to payments of the important departmental royalties from YPFB production (long an issue of contention between the capital and the departments). Facing an unexpectedly strong backlash from bodies it had assumed would be compliant, the government retreated and had to accept the political consequences of itself administering cuts from the centre. As was evident from the municipal elections of 1987, the MNR was unprepared for the revivalism of local politics that its economic policy generated.

Coca and Cocaine

Table 3 presents the principal public developments in the political economy of coca and cocaine under both the UDP and MNR administrations. From this it can be seen that official efforts to suppress *narcotráfico* were hindered by a number of factors: lack of political will;

the strength of the coca lobby; disagreements and inefficiency within the military; and confusion over policy. (It should be noted that the table does not include general, low-scale activity within the police and judiciary.) Such a picture is familiar and, indeed, conforms quite closely to the objections raised by Washington, which in 1986 and 1987 withheld some $17.5 million in economic aid as a result of failure to meet targets for the eradication of coca.[32] (A much smaller quantity of military aid was frozen due to problems with suppression of cocaine.) However, the obstacles to this were truly formidable and encompassed much more substantial issues than the debility of the Bolivian state and questionable practices by elements of its servants. Important though these factors are, they remain symptomatic of a more profound crisis rooted in the collapse of the formal economy, popular desperation, and misconceived North American policy and actions. The debate over these issues is as complex as it is passionate, and it cannot be properly rehearsed here. Yet a few brief observations may serve to provide a broad context within which to approach this major phenomenon.

First, it should be noted that the illegal production of cocaine stems directly from the legal production and consumption of the coca leaf in the same country. As in Peru – but not Colombia – the market in coca has been an integral element of Aymara and Quechua society for centuries, possessing important cultural and religious features that could only be criminalized at the cost of a major breakdown in social order. As a consequence, the insistence of the US that *narcotráfico* be attacked via an offensive on coca was from the start riven with problems. Whilst the claim that the 'free sale in coca is equivalent to legalizing the production of cocaine'[33] may be disputed, it is nevertheless the case that during the 1980s the connection became very strong. Moreover, coca bushes and leaves are more readily detectable than is low-bulk, high-value cocaine paste. Yet in operational as well as political terms concentration upon coca presents sharp difficulties that La Paz tried consistently to avoid and Washington was late and reluctant to recognize.

The sheer scale of coca production presents a major challenge to control. By the mid 1980s Bolivia accounted for perhaps one third of the world supply of leaf, and if estimates vary widely – in 1988 the Bolivian government put production at 155,000 tons from 60,000 hectares whereas the State Department figure was 56,500 tons from 40,300 hectares – they still reflect a significant economic activity that may properly be called an industry.[34] Although this tonnage was less than that produced in Peru (and Bolivia's production of finished cocaine lags well behind that of Colombia – in terms of direct imports into the US it probably stood at 15 per cent against 75 per cent), the industry has a far greater impact within the national economy than does coca/cocaine in the much larger and more diversified economics of the other two countries. In terms of revenue, coca production in 1986 was worth approximately $230 million – or 20 per cent of total receipts from agriculture – whilst income from cocaine was, in all likelihood, in excess of $600 million – barely less than formal export revenue.[35]

Sums of this scale do not simply reflect the high price of an illegal substance; in fact, the US wholesale price fell between 1980 and 1988 from $55,000 to $15,000 per kilo – the ratio between the prices of leaf and derived cocaine on US streets being of the order of 500:1.[36] They also indicate extensive participation in the industry. The estimate of the Bolivian Senate of a total of 80,000 cultivators of leaf in the two core growing zones of Yungas (La Paz) and Chapare (Cochabamba) is not unreasonable.[37] However, to this figure must be added at least 25,000 *pisadores* (treaders of leaf), 20,000 other people employed in semi-skilled or skilled work, and at least 1,000 at the upper end of the trade. If the total of growers – identified as heads of family – is multiplied by three to allow for family and other labour, the resulting figure for those engaged directly in production of coca is 240,000 and those in cocaine at over 45,000.

Yet these figures still do not represent the full human reach of the industry, which not only depends upon protection and allied services (legal, financial, and so on) but has also generated a dynamic sub-economy of inputs – both at local retail level (for example, kerosene and toilet paper in the city of Cochabamba) and at wholesale level (ether; sulphuric acid) – as well as local marketing (for example, through established networks for trading in chicha beer in Cochabamba valley) and probably affects 5 per cent of the population directly. The population of Chapare – the main cocaine-related coca zone – rose from 27,000 in 1967 to 120,000 in 1985, but even by 1981 over 400,000 people (29,000 vehicles) were entering this region.[38] This reflects the importance of seasonal migratory employment, initially undertaken largely through kinship ties but after the mid 1980s increasingly prompted by climatic disruption and economic slump in

Table 3   Coca and Cocaine, 1983–89

1983

April	Visit of US Attorney General William French Smith; US–Bolivian agreement to reduce coca production to 'level of legitimate demand'; CSUTCB national *bloqueo* cuts off major cities, suspended upon government agreement to reconsider accord with US.
June	Rafael Otazo meets with Roberto Suárez.
Aug.	Confidential accord with US to reduce Chapare production by 4,000 hectares by end of 1985 breaks April agreement with growers. Government establishes permanent control of transport and sale of leaf, promises 'substantial police presence' in Chapare; US to channel development aid to region.

1984

Jan.	August 1983 agreement revealed.
Feb.	Cochabamba deputies attack agreement as unconstitutional.
March	2,000 Chapare growers demonstrate in Cochabamba.
May	Congress of Chapare growers demands Supreme Court ruling on constitutionality of agreement with US.
Aug.	Military zone declared in Chapare; UMOPAR deployed. Coca growers' *bloqueo* of Cochabamba; action ends with official agreement not to intervene in coca market; UMOPAR withdrawn from area; military enters for six months. Otazo–Suárez meeting revealed.
Sept.	Sinahota cocaine market halted; trading shifts to Yapacaní region.
Oct.	Government bans shipments of leaf from Chapare and controls movements within it; capture of Suárez ordered.
Nov.	*Bloqueo* of Cochabamba in demand of free sale of leaf and end to military occupation; transport ban and curfew lifted; military withdraw.

1985

Feb.	UMOPAR redeployed in Chapare.
June	Coca price at $800–850 per *carga* (100 lb); *bloqueos* of Cochabamba; three *campesinos* killed by police.
Nov.	Ministry of Interior agreement with representatives of Chimore and Chapare growers' federations to eradicate 1,000 hectares by mid December at $350 compensation per hectare. Pact rejected by rank and file. US Foreign Assistance Act for FY 1986 stipulates that Bolivia eradicate 1,000 hectares by end 1985 to receive full aid.

Dec.   Coca price at $200–400 per *carga*.

1986

Jan.   UMOPAR camp at Ivirgarzama besieged by *campesinos* after rape of local woman.

April   'Fuerzas Unidas' joint military operations with US forces.

May   Coca leaf price at $125–150 per *carga*.

June   Growers halt voluntary eradication due to government failure to release economic aid.

July   'Operation Blast Furnace' with 170 US troops and 6 helicopters. Widespread protests; Chapare leaf price falls to $10–20 per *carga* (production costs at $30–40); resignation of Ñuflo Chávez from MNR in protest at US troop presence.

Aug.   c.100 hectares eradicated under Nov. 1985 agreement; government petitions US for $500 million in aid to fight *narcotráfico*.

Sept.   Assassination of scientist Noel Kempff Mercado by traffickers at Huanchaca, Santa Cruz.

Oct.   UMOPAR attacked by populace of Santa Ana de Yacuma, Beni. Official closure of Huanchaca case; accusations of 'cover-up' of complicity/inefficiency of UMOPAR and DEA.

Nov.   US troops leave; leaf price rises to $40–50 per *carga*. Departamento Nacional de Sustancias Peligrosas (DNSP) purged. *Plan Trienal para la Lucha contra el Narcotráfico* published; calls for eradication of 50,000 hectares of illicit coca by 1990, including half of Yungas production; $320 million 'reactivation funds' promised, 80% to come from foreign donors; compensation for eradication set at $2,000 per hectare.

Dec.   Negotiations with Club of Paris include aid to fight cocaine trade.

1987

Jan.   *Plan Trienal* introduced.

March   COB declares state of emergency in protest at *Plan*; draft drug law published.

May   Growers demand closure of UN agricultural project in Yungas. *Bloqueos* in La Paz and Cochabamba coca zones against *Plan*; four *campesinos* killed by police, many arrested.

June   Leaf price at $100 per *carga*.
Official agreement with COB, CSUTCB and Yungas and Chapare federations for voluntary eradication; specifically excludes eradication by force and use of herbicides; guarantees legal status of cultivation; effectively nullifies *Plan Trienal*.

Aug.   Publication of US–Bolivian agreement to eradicate 1,800 hectares by August 1988.

Sept.	$8.7 million in US aid frozen for failure to meet 1986–87 eradication target.
Nov.	*Campesino* leaders denounce government failure to pay credits and provide services under June 1987 agreement.
Dec.	c.1,000 hectares eradicated since September at compensation of $2,000 per hectare (mostly in Carrasco province).

1988

Jan.	Leaf price at $25–40 per *carga*. National congress of growers (ANAPCOCA) in Cochabamba suspends voluntary eradication because of government's 'bad faith'.
Feb.	COB–ANAPCOCA–government agreement ratifies that of June 1987, provides for growers' participation in *Plan Integral de Desarrollo y Sustitución* (PIDYS) for coca zones.
March	Chapare growers halt eradication due to alleged UMOPAR abuses and lack of aid.
April	Visit of US Attorney General Edwin Meese; COB hunger strike over drugs law and budget. '*Narcovídeo*' scandal implicates leading members of ADN with Suárez.
May	*Campesino* demonstrations in La Paz and Cochabamba in opposition to proposed drug law defining coca as a 'controlled substance'; ANAPCOCA breaks negotiations with government.
June	Leaf price at $50–65 per *carga*. Growers' *bloqueo* of Cochabamba for two days; government offices occupied and 10 Bolivian and US officials held hostage. Suárez dubs Víctor Paz 'the Viceroy of Cocaine'. Ten *campesinos* killed by UMOPAR in Villa Tunari, Chapare. ANAPCOCA–government talks collapse again.
July	Drugs law approved by congress; establishes maximum of 12,000 hectares for legal demand, the rest being subject to eradication (at annual target of 5–8,000 hectares); compensation retained at $2,000. Roberto Suárez arrested, in unclear circumstances, in the Beni.
Aug.	ANAPCOCA congress, Cochabamba, declares non-compliance with law. Leaf price at $120–130 per *carga*.
Sept.	120 hectares eradicated since July.
Oct.	Removal of Commander of army's VII Division for selling arms to traffickers; UMOPAR withdrawn from Guayamerín after clashes with populace.
Nov.	ANAPCOCA congress rejects eradication under new law.
Dec.	Total of 200 hectares eradicated in last 12 months.

1989

Jan.	Drugs law comes into operation.
	Jorge Alderete (as Subsecretario de Desarrollo Alternativo, in charge of coca/cocaine policy) accuses DEA of domination of operations and withholding information.
	Publication of extracts of 'narco-cassettes' in London and Madrid ties ADN leader Arce Carpio and others to Suárez; Arce later resigns.
March	Alderete resigns, accusing US of failure to reduce consumption.
April	ANAPCOCA resumes talks with government.
June	Ministry of Interior announces forcible eradication in Chapare from July but without presence of military.
	DEA criticizes lack of local support in fighting *narcotráfico*. Six killed in Santa Ana de Yacuma in exchange of fire between UMOPAR and navy during operation to detain traffickers. ANAPCOCA–government agreement ratifies growers' participation in PIDYS.
	Cochabamba *campesino* leader Evo Morales arrested and tortured by police for 'protecting' trafficker 'El Cura'.
July	US Ambassador Gelbard declares 'the Bolivian government does not have control over its own territory' with reference to Santa Ana incident.
	Drugs law date for forced eradication in Chapare falls due; no action taken or forces deployed.
	Government postpones forced eradication *sine die* and calls for fresh talks with growers.
Sept.	PIDYS ratified by new government and given statutory basis in DS 22270; no move on forced eradication.

the altiplano (particularly Oruro and Potosí). These factors, together with the overwhelming concentration of coca production on small and modest plots, bestow a resolutely 'popular' character on all but the very highest echelons of the industry.

During the 1980s the price of both coca and cocaine was highly elastic, but even at its lowest level – in mid 1986 – coca yielded a revenue per hectare ($2,600) four times greater than that from citrus fruits or avocadoes, with which the US wished to replace it. (At the time of the highest prices – late 1984; $9,000 per hectare – the ratio was 19:1).[39] Simple crop substitution was therefore, contrary to all economic sense for the growers. Equally, government purchase of leaf – the main UDP strategy – could not match 'real' prices, and official compensation for eradication was, at $2,000 per hectare from early 1987, well below the growers' demands, which, at $6,000 were realistic in terms of 'opportunity cost' if not in terms of the state's capacity to pay. The incentives to abandon an activity that provided a modicum of security against the process of pauperization coursing through the rest of the economy were minimal. (This applied even more within processing, where a *pisador* could earn in a night more than a school-teacher did in a month.)[40]

These major obstacles to both criminalizing and suppressing production were accentuated by the fact that in those areas where the trade was largely in the form of semi-processed or (occasionally) finished paste – principally Santa Cruz and the Beni – the state was unusually weak and the control of wealthy *narcotraficantes* strengthened by longstanding traditions of contraband and landlord patronage. Here conspicuous consumption was complemented by significant expenditure on infrastructure and services, enhancing popular support for the trade and raising the threat of social conflict no less than was the case in the core cultivation areas (e.g. popular resistance in Santa Ana de Yacuma, San Borja and Guayamerín listed in Table 3).

More broadly, the close association of the military regimes of 1980–82 with *narcotráfico* had not, principally for the reasons cited above, generated widespread repudiation of the industry as a whole. On the contrary, as the economic crisis deepened under the civilian administrations it acquired a measure of legitimacy, and the political scope for attacking it diminished significantly except in two respects. First, the pressure from Washington was considerable and required some form of response. (The real impact of moral pressure was negligible until mid 1989, when the scale of killing by the Colombian *narcos* engendered genuine revulsion and sympathy for the plight of that country; as a result North American sermons were treated with rather less disdain.) Second, outside of the Oriente the leading traffickers were popularly viewed as corrupt *arrivistes* as well as major beneficiaries of the dictatorship; beyond their own regions they could not bank on much sympathy, still less stage a political campaign under their own colours. Yet, if suppression in general threatened to close off a critical economic safety-valve, compliance with US demands raised authentic problems with regard to sovereignty and claims on national pride. Equally, the failure to conduct all but the most token purge of the military and civil service after 1982 meant that many who were subsequently charged with directing suppression were simultaneously benefiting directly or, more often, indirectly from the trade. Thus, in addition to the overwhelming economic and logistical problems – never resolved despite appreciable US assistance – the governments were faced with an acute ideological challenge.

One notable feature of this was the convergence of interested parties on the right with the left in objecting to suppression on anti-imperialist grounds, which, it might be noted, were even employed by the García Mesa regime once it had been ostracized by the Reagan White House. The arguments for this opposition were simple. Reduction of the *cocales* directly prejudiced the means of subsistence of hundreds of thousands of poor *campesinos*, whatever its final objective with respect to cocaine. These small farmers produced a legal crop for which there was no substitute that yielded remotely comparable earnings. Destruction of the cocaine factories invariably involved the punishment of lowly workers, not major dealers, very few of whom were ever caught and fewer still brought to trial. These raids were staged selectively – often to settle scores – and simply drove production centres deeper into the backlands; they had no lasting impact on prices or production, and even the catharsis experienced by the gringos was ephemeral. Furthermore, 'interdiction operations' were frequently attended by violence on the part of the police and armed forces, and they depended increasingly upon US intervention. Perhaps most important of all, the entire strategy of attacking production and supply, rather than demand and consumption, stemmed from a North American determination to transfer the blame and cost from its own rich citizens and state to their impoverished counterparts in Bolivia. The opprobium attached to this was further sharpened by the fact that the US was viewed as directly responsible for generating the broader economic crisis that prompted the upsurge of popular involvement in *narcotráfico*, by its strenuous resistance to provision of adequate recompense for the sacrifices incurred on its behalf for adhering to free market (outlaw) forces. Such a position was not only hypocritical; its immorality was decidedly imperialist.

Such an outlook is not, of course, unique to Bolivia; aspects of it are equally evident in both Peru and Colombia, where it had an even sharper impact on national political life. However, the Bolivian experience was distinctive in two important and related respects: the generally low level of social violence associated with *narcotráfico* itself (closer to Peru than Colombia) and the absence of any guerrilla movement or substantial paramilitary forces (different from both the other countries). While not exactly peaceable, production was partly legal and exacted a relatively slight social cost, at least until the late 1980s, when growing use of the debased and dangerous cocaine derivative *bazuko* by youths, particularly in Cochabamba, began to sharpen anxieties.[41] Even then, the violence surrounding the trade was seen as stemming from suppression, the state and the US – not local *traficantes*, and still less the growers, whose principal means of resistance were passive (the *bloqueo* above all else), mass-based and in conformity with the traditions of the popular movement. Furthermore, since involvement in the upper reaches of the trade was less based on clearly defined clans outside the political system than linked to membership of all sections of its civilian and military elite, no amount of official blandishments could overcome popular cynicism.

The passage of events outlined in Table 3 shows that despite its recourse to national and US troops and the introduction of major new legislation, the MNR fared little better than had the UDP. Its more decisive actions were met with greater resistance, obliging resort to negotiations in which the state made strictly limited progress towards eradication. The conduct of UMOPAR remained unreliable, the armed forces persisted in their reluctance to be involved in unpopular operations, dependence upon US support opened up conflict within the party (Alderete; Ñuflo Chávez) as well as outside it, and the threat of scandal was never far off. Judging solely (and thus very conservatively) on the basis of 'errors and omissions' in the national accounts, the formally registered infusion of *narcodólares* was at least $64 million in 1986 (much higher thereafter). It is unlikely, however, that the MNR actively contrived this situation, which might be best viewed as an embarrassing windfall resulting from forces that otherwise transpired to be more intractable than those it faced in stabilizing the formal economy.[42]

Popular disdain for the North American position did not lack some justified foundation. The US was exceptionally reluctant to deal with its unwanted monopsony (the European market remained slight) other than in time-honoured fashion. It held to the policy of crop substitution long after it had been shown to be fruitless; the public pronouncements of its local representatives exhibited an arrogance – sometimes intended, sometimes depressingly ingenuous – that infuriated senior

Bolivian officials; and it could not break from a coercive and conditional approach to development aid for the coca zones where, according to Ambassador Corr (later 'promoted' to El Salvador), electrification would only 'allow narcos to work at night'.[43] (The fact that they already did casts an even more forlorn light on this remark.) The price to be paid for an alternative approach was deemed too high, even after cocaine became a major issue in domestic politics. Like the MNR's drug law, the Bennett report was conspicuous by its failure to introduce real change.

Aware of this, the MNR, which had already invested the great bulk of its ideological capital in stabilization, adopted a distinctly opportunist course. Haunted (if not taunted) by its supposed policy of *agropoder*, it failed to match rhetoric with practice when it came to curbing the most *agropoderosos*. Realistically depending upon a reputation for managerial efficiency rather than outstanding moral probity, it shuffled past the option of launching a popular crusade. Exasperated by the exigencies of ministering to the protests of the victims of its economic policies, it forebore from tarnishing the growers as another group of 'anarcho-syndicalists'. Last, but by no means least, it recognized that voluble inaction was the key to preserving the boon provided to stabilization policy by cocaine revenue. This, quite naturally, was a hostage to fortune, but Víctor Paz had good cause to be unconcerned about it, and despite all the bravura complaint after the 1989 poll, many a *movimientista* had reluctantly accepted that the price of the fearlessness of stabilization was a resounding *voto de castigo*, leaving others to deal with the consequences. In the event, this view was shown to be correct, but it is a reflection of the extraordinary vagaries of politics over the prior four years that it very nearly transpired to be false.

Politics

After the tumult of the UDP, formal political life under the MNR became 'little' in the sense that it was primarily concerned with tactical manoeuvres and administrative issues. There were few 'grand events' to interrupt the institutional calendar, and those that did occur – the visits of the West German president, the King of Spain, and the Pope – had a strictly marginal impact on policy. Víctor Paz's sombre comportment was a significant element in this picture, not least by containing the tensions within the MNR caused by the severity of stabilization.

These rotated predictably about the person of Sánchez de Lozada, who some claimed – incorrectly – had never actually sworn loyalty to the party and others saw – justifiably – as little less than a heretic in his attitude to *movimientista* traditions. His leading critic was Guillermo Bedregal, foreign minister and recent returner to the ranks after splitting with Paz over support for the coup of Colonel Natusch (whose short-lived cabinet Bedregal had effectively led). Since Bedregal had headed the initial effort in the early 1960s to restructure Comibol in the face of bitter union resistance it was somewhat ironic that he should baulk at the social cost of this two decades later; a more plausible cause for his ill-concealed rancour lay with ambitions to succeed Paz as *jefe* or at least to become presidential candidate in 1989. Although Bedregal failed on both counts, this was not before he had succeeded in summoning appreciable support from the party's 'old guard' headed by the eternally unpredictable Ñuflo Chávez, who could still command some authority beyond his stronghold of Santa Cruz. The traditional-ists disliked 'Goni's' refusal to adhere to rhetorical customs, his independent outlook and mercurial disposition, and, perhaps most of all, his bourgeois background – none of which was typical of the party leadership (except Víctor Paz himself). The fact that his policies also threatened to damn the MNR to electoral defeat provided the unstated impetus to this campaign, which emerged in the first months of the government and then receded until the pre-electoral period once it was clear that their success had ensured that Paz would support Sánchez de Lozada's policies and endure his candour in presenting them.

The insistence upon making a virtue out of a necessity in defending stabilization was distinctly novel and won the minister a surprising degree of respect that only began to erode when his abject inability to resist a good joke or telling insult came to be seen in the context of the presidency from late 1988. At that stage it became plain how comple-mentary the characters of Paz and his de facto chief minister had been; the prospect of the troubleshooter operating on his own was far from reassuring. (In this sense the party would possibly have been better advised to by-pass both Sánchez de Lozada and Bedregal, who had a widespread and far from undeserved reputation for mendacity, and present a more 'statesmanlike' candidate, such as Vice-President Julio Garret Ayllón, to preside over the squabbling factions.)

The MNR was historically a party of 'sectors' and internecine intrigue, originally based upon authentic ideological divisions and feudal competition (often localist as well as over the spoils of office and patronage). Subsequently this tendency was sharpened by the high incidence of expulsions, repudiations and prodigal homecomings in exile, opposition or at the service of military governments. By 1985 there were no significant survivors from the left of the party – the initial appointment of the old FSTMB activist Sinforoso Cabrera as minister of mines reflected nothing more than a personal conversion. Nevertheless, both longstanding animosities and the infusion of 'newcomers' to the cabinet – notably Defence Minister Fernando Valle, previously of the ADN and a senior adviser of García Mesa – provided ample potential for schism. That this did not occur may be attributed to a number of factors. First, Paz, as founder and historic leader of the MNR, was personally *intachable* and possessed binding powers of arbitration. Second, there was minimal disagreement over the basic necessity of stabilization, and since this – rather than 'reactivation' – preoccupied the government for most of its term, the authors of Decree 21060 held the initiative. Third, the MNR was only able to govern with the support of the ADN, and the extremely sharp challenge made by Banzer immediately following the 1985 poll on the basis of his superior vote was not forgotten once he had been denied the presidency by congress (with the support of the left) and then became a party to the *Pacto por la Democracia* in October. Unity within the MNR was essential both to the preservation of the pact – and thus the maintenance of office – and to any successful emergence from its demise (which was more widely anticipated within the MNR than was publicly recognized). The support of both Washington and the armed forces, where there were many more or less closet militants, together with the absence of a concerted challenge from the left, provided further, unprecedented incentives to keep the party cohesive and disciplined.

The Pact of October 1985 was undoubtedly the lynchpin of the administration although it should be noted that it did not formally provide for a coalition, merely collaboration at legislative level, thereby largely overcoming the conservative sectarianism so evident in the election campaign. It is significant that the agreement, which lasted until February 1989, was not sealed until after the government had survived the COB's general strike of September and the consequent declaration of a state of siege. Although the ADN fully supported

Decree 21060 – and indeed declared that it had been all but stolen from them and their adviser Juan Cariaga – it studiously awaited the outcome of the inevitable clash with the unions before pledging its strategic support. Moreover, it did not gain a foothold in the cabinet until Sánchez de Lozada had outfaced Bedregal over the necessity of keeping firmly to the government's initial economic policies. Thereafter differences were of a strictly secondary order within an alliance that permitted appreciable latitude in terms of local competition and appeared to rest on the understanding that, in a variant of the Colombian and Venezuelan 'models' after 1958, Banzer would be allowed to reap the benefits of the 1989 poll. (Here the MNR acted no less opportunistically in ending the Pact than had the ADN in entering it.) There was plenty of confident talk of the accord taking Bolivia into the twenty-first century.

As the 'junior partner' the ADN celebrated its 'responsibility' and 'selflessness' rather more quickly than the resulting Pact, especially in the initial stages of the administration when it appeared that the MNR would gain the lion's share of benefit from directing the economic policies the agreement was primarily designed to support. *Adenista* dissidence was relatively slight in extent, but it did lead to the loss of Banzer's running-mate Eudoro Galindo, who left with a section of younger, more 'ideological' cadre and eventually entered the ranks of *movimientismo*. As a result, the party became a more firmly personalist organization. Nonetheless, the high profile of ex-mayor of La Paz Ronald Maclean provided a forceful and modern entreprenurial image that contrasted markedly with that of his successor Raúl Salmón, an independent but traditional machine-politician who had previously served under sundry regimes with no apparent prejudice to his reputation – underlining, perhaps, the dangers of ascribing to 'modernity' the qualities of unambiguous appeal. Security through familiarity was no less a requirement in troubled times.

It was the MIR, which most lacked authority gleaned from experience in office, and most assiduously promoted its 'newness', that attempted to court Salmón. Their short-lived liaison following the 1987 municipal elections was perhaps the most prominent – certainly the most erratic and contentious – feature of the party's strategy of expanding its activity through the development of a loose alliance of sympathizers under the name of Nueva Mayoría, which soon became a permanent suffix to the party's acronym.[44] This initiative yielded significant reward in the elections of 1987 and 1989 in that it offered some shelter for politicians and middle-class activists who wished to remain in mainstream politics and retain their progressive *bona fides*. They could no longer countenance support for the left, and neither could they succumb to the lure of *movimientismo*, which, for all its new-found dynamism, was tacking the most conservative course in its forty-year history. The loss of its left wing deprived the MIR of both organizational strength and ideological coherence. Jaime Paz had already begun to move further rightwards, but within congress the MIR stood as the only significant party of opposition after the Pact of October 1985; the logic of this position was that it attacked the MNR-ADN alliance from the left. Thus, under circumstances very different to those prevailing under the UDP, the MIR was confronted with a number of taxing challenges whereby it had, on the one hand, to divorce itself from a discredited left and yet maintain its progressive pretensions, and, on the other, take a critical position on the NPE that did not evoke a return to the *status quo ante* and enable the government to dismiss it as the shamefaced rump of the UDP.

The MIR's relative success in manoeuvring through these uncharted waters owed much to the MNR's moderation in assailing it. Amongst the reasons for this were the need to be assured of coopera-tion in both houses of congress, particularly the senate, where the balance of forces was more delicate; the (correct) perception that there was little to be lost by celebrating the constitutional opposition of a 'moderate and civilized' left; and, to some degree, the affinity felt by Sánchez de Lozada for the MIR leadership, whom he excoriated with characteristic panache but whom he also treated seriously. (This was a prescient attitude in view of the 1989 election results and could have laid the basis for the much vaunted 'second phase' of stabilization in 'reactivation' under an MNR–MIR alliance were it not for 'Goni's' tardy shift from campaign invective, at which he excelled, to overture, for which his skills were indifferent.) The MIR's own trajectory may plausibly be viewed as a combination of Jaime Paz's single-minded presidential vocation (no doubt sharpened by his experience as vice president yet extraordinary in that he so ardently coveted the office without any corresponding explanation as to why); the 'hegemonic' status of stabilization; and a broader transition within international social democracy away from Keynesianism – and its modern corollary in equitable association with organized labour – towards managerialism, wherein neither pragmatism nor the discourse of moderate welfarism were greatly altered. In this latter respect, the increasingly desperate gyrations of Alan García's APRA government across the border in Peru certainly exercised a sobering influence.[45]

The combination of the Pact, the MIR's dedication to compliant opposition, and the weakness of the parliamentary left accounts for the relatively subdued conduct of affairs within cabinet and congress. At government level more attention was paid to disorderly conduct – the unprovoked assault on a traffic policeman by the industry minister (December 1986) and Defence Minister Valle's drunken speech to congress (April 1987, when the high command protested that he had revealed 'matters of national security') – than to the residual animus displayed by Bedregal and Sánchez de Lozada. Within congress matters such as the MIR's barter of support for tax reform in return for the new electoral law (April 1986) raised minimal public interest – the statute is inordinately complex, possibly purposefully so – compared with the legislators' concern to award themselves munificent pay rises (October 1986; July 1988). This provoked sufficient ire within the public that an acutely embarrassed government was obliged to take rapid action in order to avoid a critical loss in that institutional legitimacy which constituted a major prop for its own programme.

This also came under challenge in a more novel fashion from the referendum – *Consulta Popular* – organized by the COB in July 1986 on the tax reform, payment of the external debt, and the deployment of US troops. The threat posed by this poll lay less in its result – an overwhelming repudiation of government policies by a surprisingly large 'electorate' (1,428,000, of whom 898,000 voted against the policies) – than in its restitution of the impulses of 'popular democracy'. The level of participation indicates at the very least that these were not dormant since the government waged a strong campaign against the referendum and came close to banning it altogether. Held less than a year after the introduction of Decree 21060, the *Consulta Popular* may simply be viewed as a predictable expression of discontent in much the same light as the result of the 1987 municipal elections. However, it also indicated a significant shift on the part of the COB, which had perforce to move beyond reliance on strikes and the diminishing membership of its constituent unions. In this sense the referendum marked the first step in a process whereby the COB acquired a more reactive role in relation to popular discontent, coordinating rather than leading protest. Increased resort to hunger strikes similarly indicated a defensive position in which appeal to popular sentiment replaced industrial strength as a means of bargaining. This approach was most closely determined by the position of the *relocalizados* from Comibol, whose wretched fate was the subject of incessant disputes throughout the government and reached its apogee in the mock 'crucifixion' of redundant miners in La Paz in April 1989. Following the visit of the Pope, and after three years' experience of penniless miners and their families camped in El Alto, the populace of the capital responded to such acts of desperation with a sympathy that stood in sharp contrast to its hostile reaction to the March 1985 occupation. There was an increase in talk of the country's historic debt to the miners, public recognition of their sacrifice, and some qualification of earlier emphatic epitaphs for the industry.

Of course, such matters neither cost the government very much nor offered the miners more than ephemeral consolation in what was an indisputable defeat. Only at the Huanuni mine was the FSTMB able to sustain any substantive resistance (tellingly, on health and safety grounds), and after the government's use of troops in September 1986 to halt the union's 'March for Peace and Life' from Oruro to La Paz – which accumulated great popular support and threatened a major political crisis – the FSTMB was thrown into confusion over how to react. Conflict over the form and degree of response produced three major shifts in its leadership in 1986 and ended in an uneasy compromise whereby the balance between the radicals of the DRU/Eje de Convergencia and the PCB was publicly sustained by Víctor López – associated with Lechín but also autonomous from him – and practically determined by Filemón Escobar, erstwhile *porista* and now the most ardent advocate of *autogestionismo*. This pattern was broadly reproduced within the COB itself at the seventh congress of July 1987, when Lechín's fiat was finally eliminated, first López and then Simón Reyes presiding over a tense truce between two weakened blocs, neither of which possessed the capacity to realize their antagonistic stratagems outside the debating hall.[46]

Such a scenario evoked the experience of the dictatorial era and reflected a loss of authority and direction more profound than that witnessed after the 1957 stabilization, when the mines were not greatly affected by redundancies. It raised the pertinent question of whether the traditional leadership of the COB by the FSTMB could be maintained. However, the reiterated claims to this role by the CSUTCB were undermined by its own deep divisions, which the COB itself had to arbitrate and which emphasized the continued preponderance of *caudillismo* and dubious practices of patronage over ideology in a sector that was poorly suited to operate according to the norms of industrial syndicalism. Yet if this presented a major organizational challenge to the COB, it did not, as has been seen, marginalize the *campesinado* from wider political life, even if the succession of *bloqueos* and the emergent influence of the federations of the coca zones were – like the protests over health, education and local administration – only loosely associated with the orthodox political opposition.

In one sense, the fact that the left had strictly limited influence over these movements complicated life for the government, which found little relief in stock anti-communist and anti-syndicalist invective and had to contend with a variety of organizations that lacked firm control over their supporters. The price of victory in the realm of formal politics was an uncontainable fluidity in regional and sectoral disputes, none of which posed a threat to the government's national authority but which, in sum, severely constrained its writ. Whilst this corresponded in part to a 'natural' retreat by the effectively disenfranchised constituency of the left that redeployed its political energies in a more quotidian and tactical fashion, it also raised the spectre of a dangerous anomie conducive to the emergence of forces similar to Sendero Luminoso. Fears of this grew from mid 1988 as it became evident that some elements associated with *katarismo* were abandoning faith in either constitutionalist or quasi-syndicalist/collectivist methods of struggle and seeking more direct and violent means. At the same time, occasional scares about Senderista intromissions gained some substance when, in December 1988, the Peruvian naval attaché was assassinated in the middle of La Paz. The subsequent killing of three Mormon missionaries by the hitherto unknown Fuerzas Armadas de Liberación Nacional-Zárate Willka (FAL-ZW) sharpened apprehension in this quarter although the little available evidence – far exceeded by rumour – suggested both that the group was tiny and isolated and that the government was determined at all cost to avoiding provoking Sendero, which probably did make use of Bolivian territory around Lake Titicaca but continued to experience greater problems with the Aymara communities of the border region than it had with the Quechua majority around Cusco. Although the progression from participation in legal politics to those of subversion is rarely linear, and the two are seldom as mutually exclusive as theorists and proponents of counter-insurgency claim, this space had evidently been crossed by very few. Perhaps because of a flexibility endowed by the very weakness of the state, the system neither generated such despair nor unlocked enough residual millenarian convictions to promote a movement comparable to that in Peru.

As in Peru, the continued existence and very modest recovery of the orthodox left played little part in this. The reconstruction of electoral unity around the MBL and PCB as Alianza Patriótica (1987 municipal elections) and then Izquierda Unida (1989 poll) and the spirited but strictly limited activity of the PS-1 and MRTKL had minimal impact on the national balance of forces. But, in contrast to the Peruvian case, the retention of some systematic equilibrium may be attributed to the rise of a new form of populism that succeeded far better than the left in voicing the preoccupations of the poor. This movement may be characterized as reactionary in that its principal protagonist – Carlos Palenque – had good right-wing credentials (part *movimientista*, part *barrientista*), a considerable fortune, and manifest talent for constructing alliances with a status quo that he simultaneously berated for its callow indifference to the commonwealth. Moreover, whilst Palenque's exploitation of radio and television was overwhelmingly dedicated to the expression of individual complaints and tales of misfortune (the hourly '*Tribuna Libre del Pueblo*'), its concentration on CONDEPA's distribution of free spectacles, food and other hand-outs was understandably more insistent than was the promulgation of indecipherable 'autochthonous' economic policies by which the fledgling party proposed to resolve the wider crisis that made this old-style clientelism so necessary and popular.

On the other hand, the synthesis of an unmediated *vox populi*, attacks on a 'dictatorial' and 'uncaring' government, effusions of sympathy for the miners and coca growers, and celebration of popular culture – from Cantinflas to *el Gran Poder* – unnerved the established parties and rapidly dislocated customary political allegiances in the capital and surrounding provinces. If '*Compadre*' Palenque himself was too 'white' and accomplished a media personality – he had previously played in a popular folk group – to pass himself off as an authentic member of the newly urbanized Aymara underclass, he was exceptionally adept at projecting its travails. Moreover, his co-presenter on television, '*Comadre*' Remedios Loza, operated as a perfect foil in that as an articulate, bilingual and attractive *chola* she generated considerable appeal amongst women – very poorly represented in other parties – across the class and ethnic divide whilst inviting but failing to provoke a macho backlash. Both Palenque and the instinctively more radical Loza concentrated their attention on the domestic sphere, which was either ignored or dismissed with pious platitudes by the orthodox politicians. They thereby largely circumvented the greatest potential obstacle to CONDEPA in the widening economic chasm between impoverished recent migrants and the enriched market traders and rentiers of similar social and ethnic background whose operations appeared petty but who had, for some, become a veritable bourgeoisie.[47]

It is telling that the emergence and rapid rise to prominence of CONDEPA in La Paz followed the 1987 municipal elections, which in the capital witnessed a quite extraordinary decomposition of both protocol and mores amongst the established forces. The real casualty of this was Salmón, who was supported for his first election for the post of mayor by the MIR and a loose grouping known as the 'Friends of Don Raúl' against the candidacy of Ronald Maclean, backed by the ADN and MNR. The poll resulted in the election of six *concejales* (aldermen) for each bloc, opening up a tortuous process of negotiation that soon collapsed into an *opéra bouffe* when one of Salmón's supporters changed sides upon the alleged – and never fully denied – payment of $100,000 by the government parties. However, just as the partners of the Pact were set to ratify and celebrate their 7–5 victory on television, the Machiavellian qualities of Don Raúl Salmón surpassed even their literary depiction by Mario Vargas Llosa in the offer by his camp to Walter Mur, a prominent *movimientista*, to back him as mayor. This utterly unexpected proposal so enticed Mur that he cast aside party loyalty and voted against Maclean, thus returning the contest to a stalemate from which neither side emerged with a modicum of credit although one was a great deal worse off financially and the other had inherited the services of a mathematical dunce.

This unedifying spectacle continued for a full three months after which the office was given to each of the original candidates for half the term, beginning a race for popularity through expenditure on grandiose projects, particularly by Salmón, whose remodelling of Laikacota hill for a new 'central park' was but a transient triumph of civic imagination over geological realities. Subsequently Salmón threw in his depleted lot with the MNR as the best means by which to exact revenge on the bourgeois upstart Maclean, but he was soundly defeated in the 1989 senatorial race. The MIR, for its part, perhaps reconciled to the loss of the city under the twin pressures of Palenque's media appeal and Maclean's cash, set its sights on the rural vote through alliance – under the auspices of the Nueva Mayoría – with the dissident *movimientismo* of Carlos Serrate Reich, whose close supporter Zenón Barrientos Mamani could still command a sizeable proportion of the votes he had delivered to the MNR from the northern altiplano in the 1950s and early 1960s.

Such manoeuvres produced results, but it is clear that these were obtained at a rising cost in terms of legitimacy, the myriad paths for tactical *votos de castigo* amongst contestants of comparable ideological hue threatening to lead all into a cul-de-sac. Disenchantment was not lessened by the much-publicized failure to bring the García Mesa trial to a conclusion, even in the absence of the defendant, who absconded from military supervision with an ease that only fortified popular disdain for claims to resolute impartiality on the part of the authorities. This sentiment was further enhanced by the fact that when Suárez and Palenque attacked Víctor Paz they were either apprehended or punished with unusual celerity and efficiency. However questionable their past or motives, they had at least stood up to the system and therefore deserved sympathy. This distinguishes them from another aggressive *arriviste*, Max Fernández, who had bought La Paz's highly profitable brewery with funds of uncertain origin and now tried to contest the 1989 poll by distributing largesse, particularly in the Oriente. However, Fernández soon discovered that overnight purchase of a political party is a problematic undertaking when his bargain-basement apparatchiks – mostly from the moribund FSB – simply took the money and ran. His later response to the '*triple empate*' in calling for a military coup endeared him to very few, but the fact that he could make such a bold entrance into the political arena suggested that Palenque was not a singular phenomenon and that the rules of politics were undergoing a disturbing transformation.

The results and immediate consequences of the 1989 poll, however, indicated that these new political figures posed a more limited challenge to the status quo. CONDEPA won the vote in the capital by a very clear margin (121,024 against second-placed ADN with 82,524), but it lost to the MIR in the departmental provinces and trailed very poorly elsewhere in the country, amassing just 11 per cent of the total vote. This score was roughly equal to the combined vote of the left (IU – 7.2 per cent; PS-1 – 2.5 per cent; MRTKL – 1.5 per cent). Equally, it should be recalled that the MIR polled only 19.6 per cent of the vote – enough to give Jaime Paz the presidency, albeit under tight ADN control in cabinet. In these circumstances it can be appreciated that any percentage of the vote in double figures had to be treated seriously, and CONDEPA had concentrated its support most effectively for the purposes of winning congressional seats and thus negotiating terms. Its opposition to the MNR was immovable and based almost exclusively on the closure of Palenque's television station in 1988. However, the '*compadre*' was quick to join in talks with Jaime Paz and Banzer, and although no formal agreement was signed, CONDEPA's voting record in the new parliament proved consistently supportive of the governing alliance. The cost to the ADN and MIR would be loss of the city council and the departmental development corporation, taken over to much fanfare shortly after Jaime Paz's inauguration with immediate promises – conditional upon treasury support – to start construction of a road from La Paz to Pando. CONDEPA thus set down a marker for its ambitions and the direction of blame should they not be fulfilled. Nonetheless, the limits of co-optation had not been stretched very far to incorporate the party.

A similarly sober interpretation of the fragility of the political system may be derived from the process of negotiation between the country's three leading forces. Here the MNR's decision early in 1989 to abandon the Pact of October 1985 and make an independent 'dash for power' constituted a calculated risk that came close to success in simple electoral terms. However, it also helped to sharpen the incidence of malpractice before, during and after the poll, pushing the party extremely close to repudiating an election held under its government but effectively controlled by the ADN and MIR, which dominated the electoral courts and now felt little need to curb manipulation by their supporters. Yet despite extensive partisan intervention in the results, these stood and a new government was elected according to the constitutional timetable. The fact that it began as a coalition suggested that the division of the dominant political bloc into three was not as debilitating or dangerous as many feared. Indeed, some held that the '*triple empate*' provided the best electoral foundation for '*concertación*'. Moreover, following Jaime Paz's inauguration, all parties accepted the need for electoral reform, and Sánchez de Lozada adopted the role of leader of a responsible opposition without undue difficulty.

Amongst the chief features identified as underpinning this outcome were the flexibility and skill of Banzer and the erosion of *movimientismo*. The former may be accepted only with the caveat that Banzer was no longer in any position to pose an authoritarian alternative and had, alone of the three leading candidates, already served as president; his ambitions for office were not as sharp and had been further reduced by physical frailty and the death of his sons. Under the circumstances his actions were unremarkable, providing the ADN with a dominant voice in policy-making whilst Jaime Paz attended football matches and signed agrarian reform titles. Equally, notice of the death of the MNR was somewhat exaggerated, even if the generation and many of the traditions of 1952 were in advanced decline. Between 1985 and 1989 the party's exploitation of the revolutionary legacy was slight and indirect, revolving principally around the figure of Víctor Paz. It will not, of course, be entirely jettisoned since it lends some gravitas and resolution to the image of the MNR. Yet a further diminution of 'historical' *movimientismo* would little affect the substance of the party's conduct.

Certainties with respect to the weakness of the left were no less well founded in mid 1989 than in mid 1985, at least in terms of established party organizations. However, a degree of caution is in order here in terms of the wider potential for a renewal of a radical movement. In the first place, the electorate will by 1994 have experienced government by all components of what might be termed the 'triple conservative alliance'. From a purely electoral viewpoint this may simply enhance the degree of tactical voting on the basis of a more informed logic of the '*mal menor*'. (It should be noticed that the MNR-MIR option remains untested.) On the other hand, the prospect of 'more of the same' is likely to be upheld by all these parties and, after a prolonged period of recession in the poorest country in mainland America, this may well exasperate the evidently large number of uncommitted voters as well as supporters of CONDEPA. In order to evade this scenario the right will have to achieve not only the economic growth that has persistently eluded it but also a qualitative expansion of welfare and an authentic resolution to the dilemmas posed by *narcotráfico*.

The prospects on all three fronts are less than bright, as is that of a thorough reform of state institutions, where the customs of malpractice and partisanship persist to growing popular discontent. If these issues have long been the left's stock-in-trade and offer fertile ground for recovery, a less familiar challenge lies in adjusting to the decline of the COB and the emergence of forces such as CONDEPA. Failure to address these critical developments could well result in more than the left being reduced from the status of a minority to that of an entirely peripheral entity; it might also encourage the incidence of social violence, drawing Bolivia much closer to the Peruvian experience. The desiderata in this regard are peculiarly taxing since they include a simultaneous move away from surpassed traditions and defence of those that take a similar form but remain vital – as demonstrated by Palenque for La Paz – in affirming ethnic and social identity. As yet the full gamut of distinctions is unclear, even within the discourse of 'Western' ideologies and practice. Yet failure to address both the 'American' and 'European' features of this dilemma is likely to produce a far nastier future than that of Bolivia quietly queuing up to take its modest place in 'the end of history'.

Notes

1. The most contemporary English language study of Bolivia is James Malloy and Eduardo Gamarra, *Revolution and Reaction: Bolivia 1964–1984*, New Brunswick 1988. Although Malloy and Gamarra employ the terms 'populism' and 'authoritarianism' quite extensively, their study seeks to discover inflections within these very broad categories, and I would not wish to attribute to them a single-minded commitment to model-building, just as I reject their characterization of my narrative survey, *Rebellion in the Veins: Political Struggle in Bolivia, 1952–82*, London 1984, as reductionist and class determinist. Salvador Romero reviews both texts in *Estado y Sociedad*, año 4, no. 2 (1988). Perhaps the widest disseminated caricature of Bolivian personality is the scriptwriter in Mario Vargas Llosa's novel, *Aunt Julia and the Scriptwriter*, London 1983, an individual based closely on Raúl Salmón, mayor of La Paz in the 1980s and a personalist political figure of some consequence although distinctly vulnerable to his own grandiose ideas. If Bolivians felt ambivalent about Vargas Llosa's lampooning of Salmón, there was a far wider and deeper sense of outrage at the publication in the *Atlantic Quarterly* of an article 'A Cowboy High in the Altiplano', by the former press attaché to the US embassy, Mark Jacobs, who referred to Bolivians as primitive 'gnomes'. The piece – in fact, a very mediocre ramble – was reproduced in two Sunday papers and generated sufficient indignation to prompt the embassy to issue a disclaimer.

2. See Dunkerley, *Rebellion in the Veins*; Malloy and Gamarra, *Revolution and*

Reaction; Laurence Whitehead, 'Bolivia's Failed Democratization, 1977–80', in G. O'Donnell, P. Schmitter and L. Whitehead (eds), *Transitions from Authoritarian Rule. Latin America*, Baltimore 1986.

3. See, in particular, Juan Antonio Morales, 'Inflation Stabilization in Bolivia', in M. Bruno, G. Di Tella, R. Dornbusch and S. Fischer (eds), *Inflation Stabilization. The Experience of Argentina, Brazil, Bolivia, Israel and Mexico*, Cambridge, Mass. 1988, for an assessment of the 1985 stabilization plan by one of its principal overseers (but not one of its architects). A less detailed survey may be found in J. Morales and J. Sachs, 'Bolivia's Economic Crisis', Working Paper no. 2620, National Bureau of Economic Research, Boston (1988). The original document behind the plan is República de Bolivia, *Decreto Supremo 21060* (29 August 1985), whilst the principal agreements and documents supporting it are collected in Muller and Machicado (eds), *Acuerdos y Documentos de la Nueva Política Económica 1986*, La Paz 1987. Excellent assessments of the economy are given in *Coyuntura Económica Andina*, La Paz, annual 1985–, and a radical critique is provided in Pablo Ramos, *¿Hacia dónde Va el Neoliberalismo?*, La Paz 1987. Full statistics are provided in Muller y Machicado Asociados, *Estadísticas Económicas*, La Paz, annual 1985–. A full background to the tin industry is given in Mahmood Ali Ayub and Hideo Hashimoto, *The Economics of Tin Mining in Bolivia*, Washington 1985, and its collapse is surveyed in Latin America Bureau, *The Great Tin Crash, Bolivia and the World Tin Market*, London 1987. The important 'informal' economy is outlined in Samuel Doria Medina, *La Economía Informal en Bolivia*, La Paz 1987.

4. See, in particular, Kevin Healy, 'The Boom within the Crisis. Some Recent Effects of Foreign Cocaine Markets on Bolivian Rural Society and Economy', in Deborah Pacini and Christine Fraquemont (eds), *Coca and Cocaine. Effects on People and Policy in Latin America*, Cambridge, Mass. 1987; Kevin Healy, 'Coca, the State and the Peasantry in Bolivia, 1982–1988, in the special issue of *Journal of Interamerican Studies*, vol. 30, nos. 2 and 3 (September 1989). For background material see G. Flores and J. Blanes, *¿Dónde va el Chapare?*, Cochabamba 1984; R. Bascopé, *La Veta Blanca. Coca y Cocaína en Bolivia*, La Paz 1987; O. and J. Canelas, *Bolivia. Coca y Cocaína*, La Paz 1983; IEPALA, *Narcotráfico y Política*, Madrid 1982. Rensselaer W. Lee III, *The White Labyrinth. Cocaine and Political Power*, New Brunswick 1989, provides a very useful synthesis of the main policy issues but some of its considerable factual information should be treated with caution.

5. There is, as yet, little consolidated literature on this important issue, which relates closely both to the political failures of the UDP regime and the collapse of the mining proletariat. See, inter alia, FLACSO, *El Sector Minero Crisis y Perspectivas*, La Paz 1986; Jorge Lazarte, 'Movimiento Sindical y Transformaciones del Sistema Socio-político Boliviano', *Estado y Sociedad*, año 4, no. 2 (1988); MIR-Bolivia Libre, *Repensando el País*, La Paz 1987. *Autodeterminación*, nos 6 and 7 (December 1988), reproduces an interesting debate between leaders of various radical currents.

6. My comments here are, of course, highly contentious and are developed later in the chapter. For an alternative view that proclaims the unambiguous victory of conservatism, see Javier Hurtado in *Presencia*, 2 August 1989.

7. Kenneth P. Jameson, 'Dollarization and Dedollarization in Bolivia', mimeo, University of Notre Dame 1985; Ramiro Carrasco, in Facultad de Ciencias Económicas, Universidad Mayor de San Andrés, *Dinámica Económica*, no. 8 (December 1982), p. 97.

8. For details see Jameson. The MIR disowned the policy as fast as possible, but for an appreciation of its intended aims and the context in which it was understood to operate, see Rolando Morales, 'La Crisis Económica', *Informe R*, May 1985.

9. Morales and Sachs, 'Bolivia's Economic Crisis', p. 25; Arthur J. Mann, 'The Political Economy of Tax Reform in Bolivia', mimeo 1986, p. 6.

10. Morales and Sachs, 'Bolivia's Economic Crisis', p. 21.

11. *El Mundo*, Santa Cruz, 9 November 1982.

12. *Presencia*, La Paz, 10 November 1982.

13. See the comments of Gail E. Makinen in Bruno et al., *Inflation Stabilization*, pp. 347–51.

14. At the *Foro Político* of 25 May 1985 Victor Paz indicated that an agreement with the IMF would be necessary and that he would grant favourable conditions to private capital. Significantly, it was at this meeting that Hugo Banzer declared, 'No me voy a sentir incómodo si el Doctor Paz gana las elecciones', despite the fact that the MNR presented itself to the voters as 'inserta en la izquierda nacional, anti-imperialista y democrática'.

15. It should be recalled that the coup of Colonel Natusch in November 1979 received support from leading figures in the MNRI as well as the MNR.

16. Whilst Siles declared the FSTMB occupation of Comibol illegal and ultra-leftist, Paz Zamora welcomed the move fulsomely. *Presencia*, 21 April 1983.

17. For example, 'Durante el gobierno del general Vildoso se dio una clara situación revolucionaria y el POR fue el único partido político que así lo dijo'. G. Lora, *La Insurrección*, La Paz 1983, p. 7. For a rather more sober analysis, still couched in boisterous rhetoric, see the opening two pages to G. Lora, *Lo que será y hará la dictadura del proletariado*, La Paz 1985, drafted in the immediate aftermath of the March general strike.

18. For the internal polemic over strategy, see *Unidad*, no. 639, 19 July 1985 (for the official line) and *Unidad*, no. 641, 20–26 July 1985 (for the dissident line). Both factions issued their own versions of this paper until September.

19. For an outline of this and other congresses, see Jorge Lazarte, *Movimiento Obrero y Procesos Políticos en Bolivia*, La Paz 1989. A fuller picture is given in Hisbol, *VI Congreso de la COB. Protocolos y Tesis de la Discusión Política*, La Paz 1985. It is noteworthy that at this congress a leading *cobista*, Filemón Escobar, effectively sided with the PCB against the DRU although he argued for the development of the COB itself as a focus of political struggle. The DRU's position was that 'there are only two alternatives: either to advance the objective of social and national liberation through transforming the process into a revolutionary one, or to perish under imperialism and fascism'.

20. Renzo Abruzzese, 'Formas democráticas en los procesos de transición: el caso de Bolivia', *Estudios Sociológicos*, Mexico, vol. 4, no. ii (May–August 1986).

21. Kevin Healy, 'The Rural Development Role of the Bolivian Peasant *Sindicatos* in the New Democratic Order', Paper to the XII Congress of LASA, Albuquerque, April 1985.

22. For a full and suggestive discussion of the emergence of the 'new right', see Carlos F. Toranzo Roca and Mario Arrieta Abdalla, *Nueva Derecha y Desproletarización en Bolivia*, La Paz 1989.

23. *Coyuntura Económica Andina*, June 1989; Pablo Ramos, *¿Hacia Dónde?*

24. Juan Antonio Morales in Bruno et al., *Inflation Stabilization*, pp 337–41.

25. Ibid., p. 319.

26. Ibid., p. 329.

27. Mann, 'Political Economy of Tax Reform'.

28. Ibid.

29. Ibid.

30. Ricardo Calla, *La Derrota de Lechín. Luchas Políticas en el XXI Congreso Minero*,

Mayo 1986, La Paz 1986; Lazarte, *Movimiento Obrero*.

31. Rolando Morales and Fernando Rocabado, *Los Grupos Vulnerables en las Economías de Desarrollo. El Caso Boliviano*, La Paz 1988.

32. Lee, *White Labyrinth*, p. 1.

33. Ibid., p. 60.

34. Ibid., p. 23.

35. República de Bolivia, *Plan Trienal para la Lucha contra el Narcotráfico*, La Paz November 1986, p. 6.

36. Lee, *White Labyrinth*, pp. 8 and 30.

37. Hon. Senado Nacional, 'Informe Preliminar sobre el Narcotráfico', La Paz 1986, pp. 23–4.

38. J. Blanes, *De los Valles al Chapare*, La Paz 1983; Healy, 'Boom within Crisis', pp. 102; 115; Temas de Política Social, *Efectos del Narcotráfico*, La Paz 1988, pp. 53–73.

39. Lee, *White Labyrinth*, p. 27.

40. Ibid., p. 46.

41. *Efectos del Narcotráfico*, pp. 13–51.

42. *Coyuntura Económica Andina*, 1986, p. 19. This is the IMF figure and thus conservative.

43. *Narcotráfico y Política*, p. 152.

44. A full account of the 1987 local elections is given in José Baldivia, *Balance y Perspectivas: Elecciones Municipales*, La Paz 1989.

45. The platform of the MIR and other parties for the 1989 elections is reproduced in Asociación de Periodistas de La Paz, *Foro Debate. Elecciones Nacionales 1989*, La Paz 1989. For a humorous but telling view of the campaign, see Paulovich, *Elecciones a la boliviana*, La Paz 1989.

46. Lazarte, *Movimiento Obrero*.

47. Toranzo and Arrieta, *Nueva Derecha*.

APPENDIX I
Basic Economic Indicators

	1980	1981	1982	1983	1984	1985	1986	1987	1988
GDP growth (%)	−1.37	0.92	−4.36	−6.51	−0.30	−0.15	−2.93	2.12	2.81
GDP per cap. growth (%)	−4.51	−2.61	−4.94	−8.58	−2.94	−2.68	−5.86	−0.76	0.17
GDP sectoral growth (%)									
agriculture	1.35	−0.93	6.92	−16.40	22.88	9.11	−4.68	−0.20	−1.09
mining	−2.88	3.06	−7.78	−2.27	−19.62	−20.35	−25.90	1.73	32.96
manufactures	−3.25	−7.75	−12.36	−4.60	−13.98	−9.31	2.06	3.49	6.29
oil/gas	4.75	5.11	5.71	−8.53	0.45	−1.95	−3.96	1.48	4.83
services	1.63	2.23	−1.91	−1.65	−1.40	0.89	−0.67	2.73	−0.33
Exports (US$m)	942.2	912.4	827.7	755.1	759.6	655.4	620.4	553.1	580.6
Imports (US$m)	665.4	917.1	554.1	567.7	488.5	690.9	674.0	766.3	578.6
External debt (US$bn)	2.53	2.65	2.80	3.18	3.21	3.30	3.53	4.16	3.99
Debt service (% GDP)	8.2	7.3	7.4	7.6	8.4	6.6	4.5		
Debt service (% exports)	28.4	28.1	31.7	33.3	39.5	34.8	26.2		
Inflation (%)	23.9	25.2	296.5	328.5	2,177.2	11,850.0	66.0	10.7	21.5
Public sector deficit (% GDP)	9.0	7.8	14.7	19.1	27.4	9.1	4.0		
Open unemployment (% EAP)	5.8	9.7	10.9	13.0	15.5	18.2	20.0	21.15	11.5

Sources: Muller y Machicado, *Estadísticas Económicas, 1989*, La Paz 1989; Juan Antonio Morales, 'Inflation Stabilization in Brazil', in Bruno et al., *Inflation Stabilization*, Cambridge, Mass. 1988.

APPENDIX II
Exchange Rates, 1980–86 (Bs/US$)

		Official Rate	*Parallel Rate*
1980		25	25
1981		25	25
1982	November	196	250
1983	January	196	341
	March	196	475
	June	196	432
	September	196	761
	December	500	1,244
1984	January	500	2,300
	February	500	2,100
	March	500	2,800
	April	2,000	3,000
	May	2,000	3,400
	June	2,000	3,250
	July	2,000	4,350
	August	5,000	6,500
	September	5,000	14,600
	October	5,000	15,000
	November	8,571	17,090
	December	8,571	22,124
1985	January	8,571	63,240
	February	45,000	113,090
	March	45,000	120,204
	April	45,000	159,816
	May	67,000	272,375
	June	67,000	481,756
	July	67,000	885,476
	August	75,000	1,182,303
	September	1,077,887	1,087,441
	October	1,102,065	1,120,206
	November	1,197,367	1,336,719
	December	1,588,613	1,715,869
1986	January	2,057,645	2,240,216
	February	1,840,118	1,916,881

Sources: Instituto Nacional de Estadísticas; Banco Central de Bolivia.

APPENDIX III
Monthly Inflation Rate, October 1982–December 1986

1982	Oct.	14.63		Dec.	60.85
	Nov.	16.76	1985	Jan.	68.76
	Dec.	7.76		Feb.	182.77
1983	Jan.	0.60		Mar.	24.94
	Feb.	10.25		Apr.	11.78
	Mar.	11.82		May	35.66
	Apr.	8.37		June	78.46
	May	9.25		July	66.30
	June	3.20		Aug.	66.46
	July	10.07		Sept.	56.51
	Aug.	25.94		Oct.	−1.87
	Sept.	16.41		Nov.	3.20
	Oct.	11.57		Dec.	16.80
	Nov.	24.78	1986	Jan.	32.96
	Dec.	25.92		Feb.	7.95
1984	Jan.	9.56		Mar.	0.07
	Feb.	23.00		Apr.	3.59
	Mar.	21.13		May	0.97
	Apr.	62.97		June	4.26
	May	47.01		July	1.78
	June	4.06		Aug.	0.66
	July	5.17		Sept.	2.28
	Aug.	14.99		Oct.	0.59
	Sept.	37.32		Nov.	−0.11
	Oct.	59.12		Dec.	0.65
	Nov.	31.55			

Source: Instituto Nacional de Estadísticas.

APPENDIX IV
Tin Production and Exports

(i)

	Production (tonnes)	Exports (US$000)	Average Price (US$ per tonne)
1980	28,000	378,149	16,784
1981	29,781	343,096	14,148
1982	24,660	278,344	12,712
1983	26,660	207,906	12,961
1984	17,000	247,748	12,218
1985	16,136	186,747	11,570
1986	11,500	89,810	4,832
1987	5,800	47,638	6,771

(ii) *Exports by Sector (US$000)*

	Comibol	Minería Mediana	Minería Chica
1980	83,699	15,216	38,344
1981	32,097	11,816	32,612
1982	19,713	8,869	11,911
1983	13,282	6,578	11,872
1984	33,129	5,240	17,628
1985	4,773	24,741	23,186
1986	1,695	13,273	18,388
1987	—	16,278	11,052

(iii) *Comibol Mines Production (tonnes)*

	1980	1981	1982	1983	1984	1985	1986	1987
Catavi	3,950	3,438	2,578	2,630	2,168	1,318	751	
Huanuni	4,694	4,730	3,460	3,017	2,754	2,643	1,626	91
Quechisla	1,919	2,184	1,500	1,458	1,122	736	372	12
Unificada	1,756	1,499	455	255	178	351	171	
Colquiri	1,730	1,883	1,750	1,864	1,141	799	534	71
Others	4,572	7,144	8,158	6,807	5,642	4,191	795	210

Source: Asociación Nacional de Minería Mediana.

APPENDIX V
Real Wages

(i) *Index, 1982–6 (Quarterly; November 1982 = 100)*

1983	1st	103.4
	2nd	88.2
	3rd	80.9
	4th	91.9
1984	1st	65.5
	2nd	69.5
	3rd	65.5
	4th	150.5
1985	1st	122.0
	2nd	100.5
	3rd	34.0
	4th	67.8
1986	1st	71.1
	2nd	70.1
	3rd	73.6

Source: Juan Antonio Morales, 'Inflation Stabilization in Brazil', in Bruno et al., *Inflation Stabilization*, Cambridge, Mass. 1988.

(ii) *Structure of Waged Income by Sector, July 1988 (%)*

Bolivianos	Total	Workers	Employees	Self-Employed	Professionals	Owners
0 – 100	25.7	25.0	22.8	30.7	4.9	10.7
101 – 200	19.5	26.2	21.6	15.5	8.6	11.9
201 – 300	13.9	19.0	16.4	10.6	9.4	10.7
301 – 400	10.0	12.4	11.9	7.8	9.2	9.3
400+	30.9	17.3	27.3	35.4	67.9	57.3
Average (Bs)	358.8	240.7	307.0	470.1	815.1	720.1

Source: *Coyuntura Económica Andina*, La Paz, 1989.

APPENDIX VI
Central Government Revenue

	1980	1981	1982	1983	1984	1985	1986	1987
Internal revenue (% total)	32.6	32.0	39.9	52.5	24.4	12.8	24.0	35.8
External revenue (% total)	21.7	22.9	20.0	15.2	18.0	15.4	14.1	15.1
Mining taxes (% total)	16.1	6.2	9.1	4.0	27.6	2.7	0.2	0.4
Hydrocarbon taxes (% total)	15.7	30.2	24.3	12.7	12.2	64.8	56.7	49.7
Total tax revenue as % GDP	9.6	9.2	4.8	2.8	3.3	10.1	13.2	17.4

Source: Arthur Mann, 'The Political Economy of Tax Reform in Bolivia', mimeo 1986.

APPENDIX VII
Synoptic Election Results, 1980–89*

	% votes	seats
1980: General		
Hernán Siles Zuazo (UDP)	38.74	53
Víctor Paz Estenssoro (MNR)	20.15	40
Hugo Banzer Suárez (ADN)	16.83	25

(Siles elected by congress, October 1982, with 113 votes)

	% votes	seats
1985: General		
Hugo Banzer Suárez (ADN)	28.56	51
Víctor Paz Estenssoro (MNR)	26.47	59
Jaime Paz Zamora (MIR)	8.84	16

(Paz Estenssoro elected by congress, by 94
votes against 51 for Banzer)

	% votes
1987: Municipal	
ADN	24.94
MIR–Nueva Mayoría	22.88
MNR	11.78

	% votes	seats
1989 General		
Gonzalo Sánchez de Lozada (MNR)	23.07	49
Hugo Banzer Suárez (ADN)	22.07	46
Jaime Paz Zamora (MIR-NM)	19.64	41

(Paz Zamora elected by congress, by 97
votes against 50 for Sánchez de Lozada)

*Note: Leading parties only; congress has 157 seats (deputies – 130; senators – 27).